Apache Tomcat 7

■ ■ ■

Aleksa Vukotic
James Goodwill

Apress®

Apache Tomcat 7

ISBN-13 (pbk): 978-1-4302-3723-5

ISBN-13 (electronic): 978-1-4302-3724-2

President and Publisher: Paul Manning
Lead Editor: Chris Nelson
Technical Reviewer: Chád Darby
Editorial Board: Steve Anglin, Mark Beckner, Ewan Buckingham, Gary Cornell, Jonathan Gennick, Jonathan Hassell, Michelle Lowman, James Markham, Matthew Moodie, Jeff Olson, Jeffrey Pepper, Frank Pohlmann, Douglas Pundick, Ben Renow-Clarke, Dominic Shakeshaft, Matt Wade, Tom Welsh
Coordinating Editor: Corbin Collins
Copy Editor: Tracy Brown
Compositor: Bytheway Publishing Services
Indexer: SPI Global
Artist: SPI Global
Cover Designer: Anna Ishchenko

Distributed to the book trade worldwide by Springer Science+Business Media, LLC., 233 Spring Street, 6th Floor, New York, NY 10013. Phone 1-800-SPRINGER, fax (201) 348-4505, e-mail orders-ny@springer-sbm.com, or visit www.springeronline.com.

For information on translations, please e-mail rights@apress.com, or visit www.apress.com.

Apress and friends of ED books may be purchased in bulk for academic, corporate, or promotional use. eBook versions and licenses are also available for most titles. For more information, reference our Special Bulk Sales–eBook Licensing web page at www.apress.com/bulk-sales.

The source code shown in this book is available to readers at apress.com. You will need to answer questions pertaining to this book in order to successfully download the code.

To Jelica

—Aleksa Vukotic

Contents at a Glance

Contents

About the Authors

 **Aleksa Vukotic** is a keen agile advocate, author, trainer, software architect, and developer, and has years of experience leading successful deliveries of business critical software projects.

He has a track record of success with the agile transformation of large companies, helping senior management lead the way in turning business requirements into effective software products. Aleksa has vast experience with Java technologies, and has been involved with the Spring Framework since the early days, becoming an expert in enterprise Java development with Spring, along with other open-source technologies. In addition to his Java EE expertise, Aleksa often utilizes his problem-solving skills to tackle the most complex issues that arise with projects. This combination of high-level management skills and technical knowledge has made Aleksa invaluable in motivating software teams to bring out the best in themselves and make rapid progress toward successful project delivery. His experience includes working with large and small teams on all levels—from high-level management, planning, and architecture to low-level technical implementation of critical software components. Aleksa co-authored *Pro Spring 2.5*, published by Apress, and has had several articles published in respected open-source publications. Aleksa is currently working at Open Credo, a London-based company of technical experts specializing in maximizing software development value for its clients. Outside of the working environment, Aleksa enjoys following football and exploring the latest technology gadgets.

 **James Goodwill** James Goodwill is an eight-time published author on leading technologies such as Java Servlets, JavaServer Pages (JSPs), Tomcat, and Struts. He is a senior enterprise iOS and Java consultant in the Denver metro area and a frequent speaker and article writer. You can follow James on Twitter at jamesgoodwill.

About the Technical Reviewer

 **Chád Darby** is an author, instructor, and speaker in the Java development world. As a recognized authority on Java applications and architectures, he has presented technical sessions at software development conferences worldwide. In his 15 years as a professional software architect, he's had the opportunity to work for Blue Cross/Blue Shield, Merck, Boeing, Northrop Grumman, and other IT companies.

Chád is a contributing author to several Java books, including *Professional Java E-Commerce* (Wrox Press), *Beginning Java Networking* (Wrox Press), and *XML and Web Services Unleashed* (Sams, 2002). He is also the author of numerous magazine articles for the *Java Developer's Journal* (Sys-Con Publishing).

Chád has Java certifications from Sun Microsystems and IBM. He holds a B.S. in Computer Science from Carnegie Mellon University. In his free time, Chád enjoys running half-marathons.

Acknowledgments

I would like to thank Jelica, for standing beside me during the writing of this book. Without her support and encouragement, completing this book would have been a much more difficult task.

I'd also like to thank my parents for providing me with the life guidance that enabled me to be where I am.

I would like to express my gratitude to all the people helping me to make this book better: Chád Darby, who helped to achieve a higher technical standard for this book; Chris Nelson, who patiently helped me improve my writing style and make the book read better with his excellent editorial skills; Corbin Collins, Steve Anglin, and everyone else at Apress for all the hard work they did to get this book published.

Big thanks to all who contribute to the Apache Tomcat project and other open-source software for being part of a community that creates such great products.

And finally, I'd like to thank all my colleagues and friends with whom I've worked throughout my career, for contributing to my professional development, which prepared me to be co-author of this book.

—Aleksa Vukotic

Preface

The first edition of this book covered the then-new Jakarta Tomcat 4. Tomcat has come a long way from there, becoming Apache Tomcat in the process, with version 7 released in January 2011. During this time, Tomcat has become the most popular and used Java servlet container on the market. Other open source application servers also have started using Tomcat as their embedded servlet engine. With the shift of focus in enterprise Java development toward more lightweight architecture and tools, Tomcat has grown to become the deployment platform of choice for business-critical enterprise Java applications.

This edition has been revised to cover the latest features of Apache Tomcat 7 and Servlet API 3.0. In the world of technology, changes are introduced quickly, and yesterday's new ideas are the legacy systems of tomorrow. Although Tomcat is still a leading open source servlet container, a lot has changed in Java web technologies since version 4. The biggest change was Java Servlet specification, which advanced to version 3.0, bringing a lot of new features along the way.

This book is based on the original text by James Goodwill, and the concepts and structure of the original book have been kept where possible. However, where the changes to Tomcat architecture and Java Servlet specification have been too great, the text was changed significantly, and some chapters have been entirely rewritten. In addition, some of the chapters from the original book have been removed, because they are now outdated. Instead, new chapters, covering up-to-date Tomcat concepts and Java web technologies, have been included. All code and configuration examples have been either updated to use up-to-date Tomcat 7 and Servlet API 3 syntax and structure, or have been entirely replaced to match the architectural changes to the underlying technology.

This book will be useful to the reader who is familiar with Java, but new to servlet development with Tomcat. That's why it contains an introduction to the development of Java web applications using servlets and JSPs. Server administrators new to Tomcat 7 also will find a lot of useful information in this book related to Tomcat management and configuration tasks.

It was not the aim of the authors to provide a detailed Tomcat reference covering all aspects of Tomcat configuration. The authors did try to write a book that introduces Tomcat in the context of web application development, so that readers can implement, deploy, and manage their Java web applications using Apache Tomcat 7 server. This is a practical guide to Apache Tomcat, with a lot of real-world examples and solutions to common problems in web application development and deployment. We hope you will find this book useful in your day-to-day experience with Tomcat—that would mean it has served its purpose.

CHAPTER 1

Introduction to Apache Tomcat 7

In this chapter, we introduce the world of Apache Tomcat server.
Throughout this chapter, we

- Describe the Apache Tomcat architecture

- Discuss the requirements for installing and configuring Tomcat

- Describe the steps of installing and configuring Tomcat

- Test your Tomcat installation

At the end of this chapter, you will understand the Tomcat architecture, have an instance of Tomcat server installed and running on your computer, and have a sample web application displayed in your browser.

The Apache Tomcat Server

The Apache Tomcat server is an open source, Java-based web application container that was created to run servlet and JavaServer Pages (JSP) web applications. It was created under the Apache-Jakarta subproject; however, due to its popularity, it is now hosted as a separate Apache project, where it is supported and enhanced by a group of volunteers from the open source Java community.

Apache Tomcat is very stable and has all of the features of a commercial web application container – yet comes under Open Source Apache License. Tomcat also provides additional functionality that makes it a great choice for developing a complete web application solution. Some of the additional features provided by Tomcat—other than being open source and free—include the Tomcat Manager application, specialized realm implementations, and Tomcat valves.

Currently supported versions on Apache Tomcat are 5.5X, 6.0X, and 7.0X. Versions earlier than 5.5 are still available for download, but they are archived and no support is available for them, so users are encouraged to use the latest possible version of Tomcat where available.

Major versions on Apache Tomcat coincide with versions of the Java Servlet specification, or Java Servlet API, released. So, Tomcat 5.5X supports Servlet API 2.3, Tomcat 6.0X supports Servlet API 2.4, and the latest Tomcat 7.0 is a reference implementation of current Servlet API 3.0. In addition to Servlet API versions, Tomcat versions support corresponding JSP API versions.

The JVM compatibility also depends on the version chosen. Table 1-1 provides a cross-reference of Tomcat versions, supported JVM versions, and Servlet API and JSP API releases.

Table 1-1. Tomcat Versions and Supported API and JDK Versions

Apache Tomcat	Servlet API	JSP API	JDK
7.0	3.0	2.2	1.6
6.0	2.5	2.1	1.5
5.5	2.4	2.0	1.4
4.1	2.3	1.2	1.3
3.0	2.2	1.1	1.1

This book will cover version 7 of the Apache Tomcat Server. However, most of the content can be applied to versions 5.5 and 6—where that is not possible, it will be clearly stated.

The Tomcat Manager Web Application

The Tomcat Manager web application is packaged with the Tomcat server. It is installed in the context path of /manager and provides the basic functionality to manage web applications running in the Tomcat server from any web browser. Some of the provided functionality includes the ability to install, start, stop, remove, and report on web applications. Chapter 4 covers the details of the Tomcat Manager web application.

Specialized Realm Implementations

Tomcat provides container-managed security methods for protecting resources within the container. These "databases" of users that can be authenticated by the container are called *realms*.

We will cover two types of realms supported by Tomcat in more detail: MemoryRealm, where user information is simply read from a file and stored in memory, and JDBCRealm, which uses relational database to store users. You can read more about realms with examples in Chapter 6.

Tomcat Valves

Tomcat valves are a technology introduced with Tomcat 4, and available in all later versions. Valves allow you to associate an instance of a Java class with a particular Catalina container. The configured valve class is then acting as a preprocessor for all requests coming to the container. Valves are proprietary to Tomcat and cannot, at this time, be used in a different servlet/JSP container.

Servlet API defines similar functionality in form of Filters. We will also discuss the differences between valves and servlet filter implementation in Chapter 8.

Further Information

Throughout this book, we will discuss all of these Tomcat-specific features, and a lot of other features that are common to all web application containers. More information about Tomcat can be found on its homepage at http://tomcat.apache.org, which is shown in Figure 1-1.

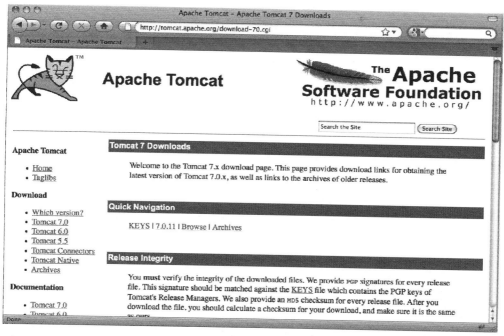

Figure 1-1. The Tomcat project homepage

You can also subscribe to the Tomcat mailing lists, which can be found at
`http://tomcat.apache.org/lists.html`.

This page contains all of the mailing lists controlled by the Apache Tomcat project. Once you are on the mailing lists page, you can choose the list that you're interested in.

In addition to the official documentation and mailing lists from the Apache Tomcat Project web site, you can find useful information on a number of web sites and forums online. We'd like to recommend `www.tomcatexpert.com`, a relatively new web site promoting adoption of Tomcat in enterprise environments.

The Architecture of Tomcat

A Tomcat instance, or server, is the top-level component in Tomcat's container hierarchy. Only one Tomcat instance can live in a single Java Virtual Machine (JVM). This approach makes all other Java applications, running on the same physical machine as Tomcat server, safe in case Tomcat and/or its JVM crashes.

■ **Note** You can still run multiple instances on same physical box, but as separate Java processes running on separate network ports.

Tomcat instance consists of grouping of the application containers, which exist in the well-defined hierarchy. The key component in that hierarchy is the Catalina servlet engine. Catalina is the actual Java servlet container implementation as specified in Java Servlet API. Tomcat 7 implements Servlet API 3.0, the latest specification from Sun.

Listing 1-1 provides an XML representation of the relationships between the different Tomcat containers.

Listing 1-1. *XML Outline of the Tomcat Architecture Components*

```
<Server>
        <Service>
                <Connector />
                <Engine>
                        <Host>
                                <Context> </Context>
                        </Host>
                </Engine>
        </Service>
</Server>
```

Figure 1-2 shows the relationship of the main components of Tomcat architecture that correspond with the described XML code snippet.

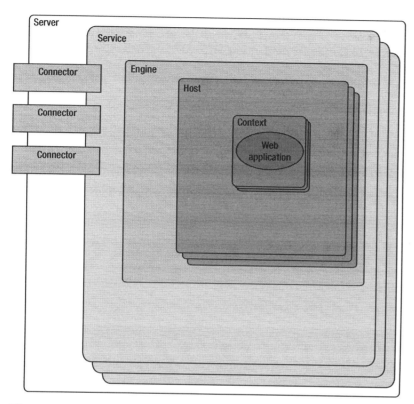

Figure 1-2. *Tomcat architecture with main components*

This instance can be broken down into a set of containers including a server, a service, a connector, an engine, a host, and a context. By default, each of these containers is configured using the server.xml file, which we describe later in more detail.

The Server

The first container element referenced in this snippet is the <Server> element. It represents the entire Catalina servlet engine and is used as a top-level element for a single Tomcat instance. The <Server> element may contain one or more <Service> containers.

The Service

The next container element is the <Service> element, which holds a collection of one or more <Connector> elements that share a single <Engine> element. N-number of <Service> elements may be nested inside a single <Server> element.

The Connector

The next type of element is the `<Connector>` element, which defines the class that does the actual handling requests and responses to and from a calling client application.

The Engine

The third container element is the `<Engine>` element. Each defined `<Service>` can have only one `<Engine>` element, and this single `<Engine>` component handles all requests received by all of the defined `<Connector>` components defined by a parent service.

The Host

The `<Host>` element defines the virtual hosts that are contained in each instance of a Catalina `<Engine>`. Each `<Host>` can be a parent to one or more web applications, with each being represented by a `<Context>` component.

The Context

The `<Context>` element is the most commonly used container in a Tomcat instance. Each `<Context>` element represents an individual web application that is running within a defined `<Host>`. There is no limit to the number of contexts that can be defined within a `<Host>`.

Installing and Configuring Tomcat

In this section, we install Tomcat as a standalone server, which means that Tomcat will service all requests, including static content, JSPs, and servlets. Before continuing with the installation steps, let's take a look at the prerequisites for Tomcat installation.

Requirements for Installing and Configuring Tomcat

Before we get started performing the tasks outlined by this chapter, you need to download the items listed in Table 1-2.

Table 1-2. Tomcat Requirements

NAME	LOCATION
Tomcat 7	http://tomcat.apache.org
JDK 1.6 Standard Edition	www.java.com/en/download/index.jsp

To install and configure Tomcat, first download the packages from the previously listed locations. You should choose the appropriate downloads based on your operating system. (We cover the steps involved in installing to both Windows and Linux.)

Installing Tomcat Using Windows Service Installer

The first installation we will be performing is for Windows. The first thing you need to do is install the Java Development Kit (JDK). Since we're using Tomcat 7, we will need JDK 1.6 or later. To download Java, just type **download Java** in your favorite web search engine, and follow the top result link.

■ **Note** Make sure you follow the instructions included with your OS-appropriate JDK.

Tomcat 7 comes with easy-to-use executable Windows installer, which will do all tasks explained in previous section automatically.

First step to do is to download the Apache Tomcat Windows service installer from the Tomcat download page (http://tomcat.apache.org/download-70.cgi). Tomcat Windows installer interface is very similar to any other Windows installer. Follow the steps, choose the installation location, and the installer will take care of extracting and copying files to correct directory, and configuring Environment variables and service properties. Figure 1-3 shows the running Tomcat installer for Windows.

Figure 1-3. Tomcat Windows Service installer

After the installation is completed, you can check that the environment variable CATALINA_HOME has been set, from the System Properties application.

The Windows installer will install Tomcat 7 as a Windows Service automatically, so the Tomcat can be started automatically on Windows start-up, and run in the background as a Windows Service.

If you are not going to perform a Linux installation, you should skip the section "Installing to Linux" later in this chapter and move on to the section "Testing Your Tomcat Installation."

Manually Installing on Windows

If you want to control all aspects of Tomcat installation, manage the environment variables required for Tomcat to run and configure your system so you have easy command line access to your Tomcat server, you will need to install Tomcat manually.

For a manual Tomcat installation, you will need to have installed and configured Java Runtime Environment. For this example, we will install the JDK to drive D:, so therefore JAVA_HOME directory is D:\jdk1.6.

To check whether Java is configured correctly, run your version of Java from the Windows command prompt. You should get the full version of the installed JDK.

After you have extracted Tomcat, you need to add two environment variables to the Windows system: JAVA_HOME, which is the root directory of your JDK installation, and CATALINA_HOME, which is the root directory of your Tomcat installation. To do this in Windows, perform the following steps:

1. Open the Windows Control Panel, select System and Security, and then click on System in the list of available options. You should see an image similar to that shown in Figure 1-4.

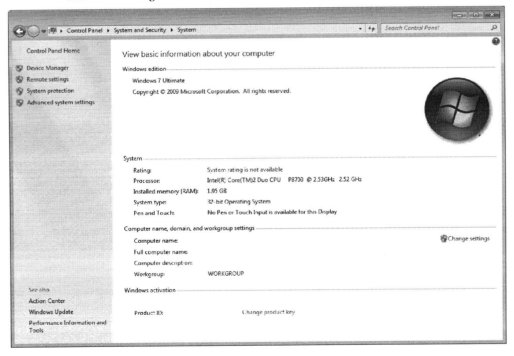

Figure 1-4. Windows System Control Panel

2. Now select Advanced system settings from the list in the left-hand side menu. You should see a dialog box similar to that shown in Figure 1-5.

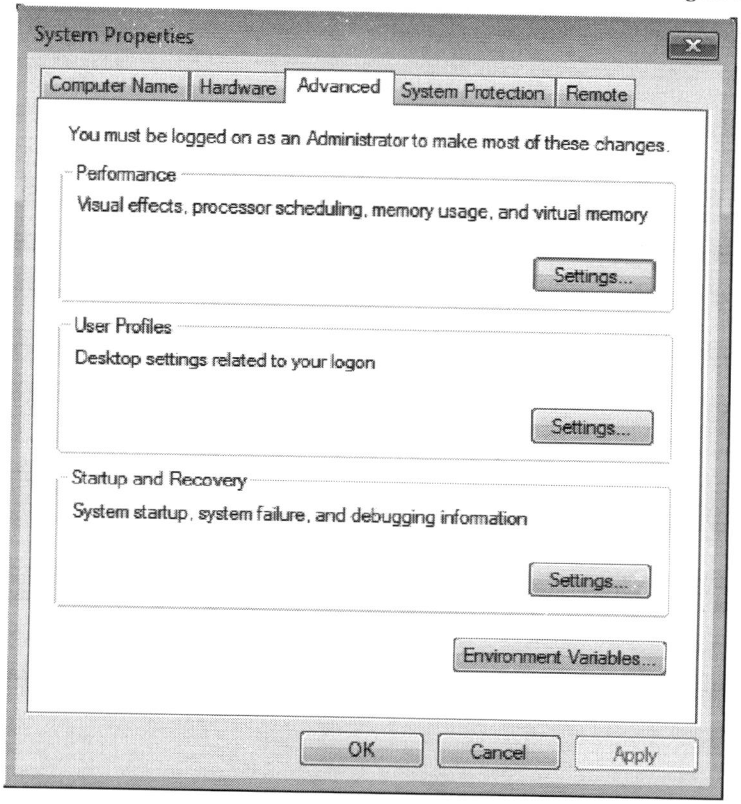

Figure 1-5. Windows System Properties dialog box – Advanced tab

3. Next, click on the Environment Variables button. You will see a dialog box similar to that shown in Figure 1-6.

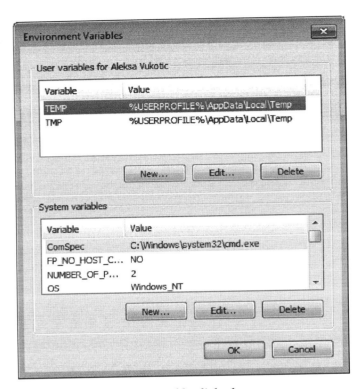

Figure 1-6. Environment Variables dialog box

4. Now, click on the New button on the System Variables section of the Environment Variables dialog box. Add a variable named JAVA_HOME, set its value to the location of your JDK installation, and click OK to complete the step.

5. Your final step is to repeat Step 4, but this time using CATALINA_HOME for the variable name and the location of your Tomcat installation as the value. For our installation, we are setting the value to C:\opt\Tomcat7. Figure 1-7 shows the settings associated with our installation.

Figure 1-7. CATALINA_HOME environment settings

6. Make sure you click OK to accept the new variable, and then click OK in the Environment Variables and System Properties dialog boxes to accept all your changes.

That is all there is to it; Tomcat is installed and configure on your Windows system. Before we test the installation, let's take a look at the automated process of installing Tomcat on Windows, using Tomcat Windows Service Installer.

Installing to Linux

A Linux installation is a much simpler process compared to a Windows installation. The first thing you need to do is install the downloaded JDK.

You can either download the correct Java version from www.java.com, or use built-in application management tool for Linux to download and install Java automatically. On Debian/Ubuntu Linux for example you can install Java by running following command:

```
sudo apt-get install sun-java6-jdk
```

We will assume at this point that the JDK is installed to /usr/local/java/jdk1.6.0_02.

To check whether Java is configured correctly, run your version of Java from the command line. You should get the full version of the installed JDK.

After the JDK has been installed, you need to set the JAVA_HOME environment variable. To do this in Linux, find the shell that you are using in Table 1-3 and type the matching command. You need to replace /usr/local/java/jdk1.6.0_02 with the root location of your JDK installation.

Table 1-3. JAVA_HOME Environment Commands

SHELL	JAVA_HOME
Bash	JAVA_HOME=/user/java/jdk1.3.0_02 export JAVA_HOME
Tsh	setenv JAVA_HOME /user/java/jdk1.6.0_02

▓ **Note** You should also add the location of the Java runtime to your PATH environment variable.

You now need to extract the Tomcat server to a directory of your choosing. This directory will become the CATALINA_HOME directory. For this installation, we assume that Tomcat is installed to /opt/tomcat7.

The last step is to set the CATALINA_HOME environment variable. Find the shell that you are using in Table 1-4 and type the matching command. You need to replace /var/tomcat with the directory of your Tomcat installation.

Table 1-4. CATALINA_HOME Environment Commands

SHELL	CATALINA_HOME
Bash	CATALINA_HOME=/var/tomcat export CATALINA_HOME
Tsh	setenv TOMCAT _HOME /var/tomcat

And that is all there is to the Linux installation. You should now be able to move on to the next section, "Testing Your Tomcat Installation."

Testing Your Tomcat Installation

To test the Tomcat installation, you need to first start the Tomcat server. Table 1-5 contains the startup and shutdown commands for both operating systems.

Table 1-5. Tomcat Startup/Shutdown Commands

OS	STARTUP	SHUTDOWN
Windows	CATALINA_HOME\bin\startup.bat	CATALINA_HOME\bin\shutdown.bat
Linux	CATALINA_HOME/bin/startup.sh	CATALINA_HOME/bin/shutdown.sh

---

▓ **Note** If you have installed Tomcat on Windows, a folder was placed in your Windows Start menu with shortcuts that allow you to start and stop your Tomcat server from there.

Once Tomcat has started, open your browser to the following URL:

http://localhost:8080/

You should see a page similar to that shown in Figure 1-8.

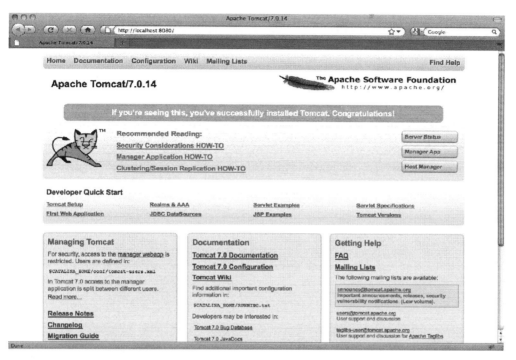

Figure 1-8. *The Tomcat default homepage*

Tomcat is by default accepting all requests on port 8080. This is set on purpose, to clearly differentiate Java servlet container from the standard HTTP servlets that are accepting incoming requests on port 80 (for example MS IIS or Apache Http Server). If you would like to have all requests serviced on the default HTTP port of 80 instead of port 8080, you need to make the following change to the CATALINA_HOME/conf/server.xml file and restart Tomcat.

Find the following line in the server.xml file:

```
<!-- Define a non-SSL HTTP/1.1 Connector on port 8080 -->
<Connector className="org.apache.catalina.connector.http.HttpConnector" port="8080"↵
 minProcessors="5" maxProcessors="75" acceptCount="10" debug="0"/>
```

and change the port property to value "80," as shown in the following code snippet:

```
<!-- Define a non-SSL HTTP/1.1 Connector on port 80 -->
<Connector className="org.apache.catalina.connector.http.HttpConnector" port="80"↵
 minProcessors="5" maxProcessors="75" acceptCount="10" debug="0"/>
```

Now you have to restart Tomcat. In order to restart Tomcat instance, first stop the server using the shutdown command for your operating system. When the command finishes, start the server again using the startup command. Table 1-5 shows startup and shutdown commands for Windows and Linux, respectively.

After Tomcat is restarted, you will be able to open your browser to the following URL and see results similar to those shown previously in Figure 1-8:

```
http://localhost
```

■ **Note** This URL does not have the port number specified. The URL convention for browsers is that if the port is omitted from the URL, value 80 is assumed. Therefore, URL `http://localhost:80/` would have the same effect.

The next step is to verify if the JSP pages are handled correctly from the Tomcat. You do this by executing one of the JSP examples provided with the Tomcat server. To execute an example JSP, start from the page shown in Figure 1-8 and choose JSP Examples. You should see a page similar to that shown in Figure 1-9.

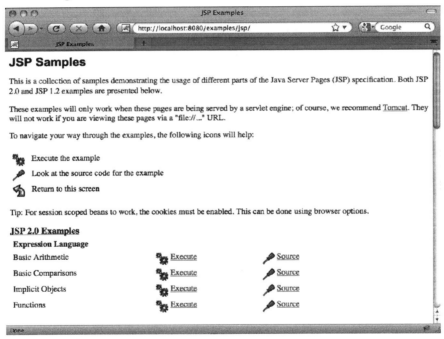

Figure 1-9. The JSP examples page

Now choose the JSP example Date and select the Execute link. If everything was installed properly, you should see a page similar to Figure 1-10 (with a different date, of course).

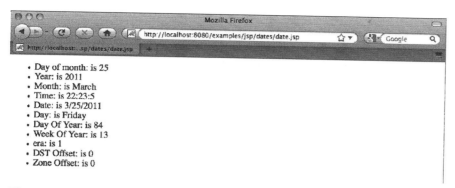

Figure 1-10. The JSP date page

If you do not see the previous page, make sure that the location of your JAVA_HOME environment variable matches the location of your JDK installation.

Summary

In this chapter, we introduced the Apache Tomcat server and discussed its main components and architecture. We went on to install and configure Tomcat on both Windows and Linux. We also discussed some simple steps to test your new installation and run Tomcat-provided JSP examples.

In the next chapter, "Deploying Web Applications to Tomcat," we begin our discussions on how to create and deploy real Web applications using the Tomcat server.

Deploying Web Applications to Tomcat

Now that Tomcat is installed and running, let's look at the steps necessary to deploy a web application. To do this, we need to first examine the directory structure of Tomcat, and then move on to actually deploying a web application.

In this chapter, we:

- Describe the Tomcat directory structure

- Introduce the structure of Java web applications that can be deployed to Tomcat

- Manually deploy web applications to Tomcat

- Configure Tomcat's hosts and contexts components

Use Eclipse IDE to deploy sample web application to Tomcat

The Tomcat Directory Structure

Before you can start creating your own web applications, you need to be familiar with the Tomcat directory structure.

The Tomcat installation directory is referred to as CATALINA_HOME. Table 2-1 describes the directories that compose a Tomcat installation. It is assumed that each of these directories is contained within the CATALINA_HOME directory.

Table 2-1. The Tomcat Directory Structure

Directory	Contents
/bin	Contains the startup and shutdown scripts for both Windows and Linux. Jar files with classes required for tomcat to start are also stored here.
/conf	Contains the main configuration files for Tomcat. The two most important are server.xml and the global web.xml.
/lib	Contains the Tomcat Java Archive (jar) files, shared across all Tomcat components. All web applications deployed to Tomcat can access the libraries stored here. This includes the Servlet API and JSP API libraries.
/logs	Contains Tomcat's log files.
/temp	Temporary file system storage.
/webapps	The directory where all web applications are deployed, and where you place your WAR file when it is ready for deployment.
/work	Tomcat's working directory where Tomcat places all servlets that are generated from JSPs. If you want to see exactly how a particular JSP is interpreted, look in this directory.

Executing Tomcat scripts

All Tomcat executable files are located in the CATALINA_HOME/bin directory. Tomcat distributes executables for both Windows and Linux-based systems in this directory, so you will see that it contains pairs of scripts with the same name and different extensions (*.bat for Windows executables and *.sh for Linux executables).

The most important executable located in this directory is Catalina script (catalina.sh on Linux or catalina.bat for Windows). This script is responsible for starting and stopping Tomcat, and it accepts different command line arguments for different operations. For example, to start Tomcat, you can simply invoke the command catalina start from your command line, and catalina stop to stop Tomcat.

■ **Note** Catalina script is only available if you download the zip distribution of Tomcat. If you install Tomcat using the Windows service installer, you won't have access to Catalina script. In that case, you can use the tomcat7w.exe GUI application to manage the Tomcat service.

Table 2-2 shows all the command arguments you can use when executing Catalina script.

Table 2-2. The Catalina script command line argument options

Command Line Argument	Description
catalina start	Starts Tomcat server as a new detached process. On Windows, Tomcat will be started in the new command prompt window. On Linux, the Tomcat will be started in the background, so you can continue using the command line.
catalina stop	Stops the Tomcat server.
catalina run	Starts the Tomcat server in the current window/terminal. On Windows, the output of the Tomcat startup will be added to the current command prompt window, while on Linux the Tomcat process will run in the current terminal session. It's useful for diagnostics when Tomcat fails to start.
catalina debug	Starts Tomcat in debug mode.
catalina version	Displays the Tomcat version.
catalina configtest	Checks if the current Tomcat configuration is correct. The script will try to start Tomcat and load all configuration files, and then exit gracefully in case the configuration is correct. If any of the configuration files are incorrect, it will report the problem.
catalina jpda start	Starts Tomcat in Java Platform Debugging Architecture (JPDA) debug mode.

In addition, you can append option -security to any of the start commands, so that Tomcat starts with the security manager enabled. The security manager is the Java mechanism for protecting the Java-managed resources from unauthorized access. For example, if your Java code has a line of code like System.exit(1), and that code is executed in Tomcat, the Tomcat server will exit. Security manager can, using security policies configured, forbid explicit calls to specific classes or methods, so the Tomcat server is protected. In cases where the Tomcat server runs only the known code, running Tomcat with security manager is not required. However, if you're administering Tomcat with third-party web applications deployed, it's recommended to run with security manager enabled.

Tomcat's bin directory also contains two convenient scripts for starting and stopping Tomcat: startup.sh (and the corresponding startup.bat) and shutdown.sh (and shutdown.bat). These scripts are just thin wrappers around the catalina script, and are commonly used instead of catalina script to start and stop Tomcat without any command line arguments.

Passing Runtime Options to Catalina Script

When running Java applications, it is often required to pass different options to the Java Virtual Machine (JVM), such as memory settings, file encoding setting, hostnames, addresses, and ports. These options are passed to Tomcat's catalina script using the standard Java and Tomcat environment variables.

The JAVA_OPTS environment variable contains options available to all Java processes running on the machine, including Tomcat. For example, to make sure JVM reads all files using UTF-8 encoding, you can add standard file.encoding Java parameter to JAVA_OPTS environment variable:

```
export JAVA_OPTS="-Dfile.encoding=utf-8"
```

If you start Tomcat after exporting JAVA_OPTS, it will make sure to use UTF-8 encoding for all file reads, but this behavior will not be restricted to Tomcat's Java process only, but to all JVM processes running on the same machine.

To pass specific JVM arguments to Tomcat only, you can use the CATALINA_OPTS environment variable. A typical scenario is adding more heap memory to the Tomcat process, without affecting the memory settings of other Java applications. The following snippet exports the memory settings to CATALINA_OPTS variable:

```
export CATALINA_OPTS=" -Xms256m -Xmx1g -XX:MaxPermSize=256m"
```

If you start Tomcat after these setting are exported to the environment variable, catalina start script sets the JVM memory settings as configured, with a maximum heap size of 1GB.

▪ **Note** You have to restart Tomcat to apply any changes to the JAVA_OPTS or CATALINA_OPTS environment variables.

Tomcat Configuration Files

This directory contains all the configuration files for the Tomcat server. We will be discussing the configuration files in the chapters that cover their specific options; however, we will mention the most important ones here.

The main Tomcat configuration file is server.xml, located in conf directory. The main Tomcat elements like engines, hosts, and contexts are configured here. You can read more about host and context configuration in server.xml file later this chapter. Appendix A contains a reference of all configuration options in server.xml file.

The context.xml configuration contains the default context settings that will be shared across all Tomcat contexts. You can read more about default context configuration in the section "Configuring Web Application Contexts" later in this chapter.

In addition to global context configuration in the server.xml and context.xml files, each context can have its own configuration file within the conf directory. The location of the context configuration file depends on the engine name and the host name in which the context is defined. The convention is that the context with name CONTEXT_NAME, configured within the host with name HOST_NAME, which is configured in engine with name ENGINE_NAME, will have its configuration file located in following file location:

```
CATALINA_HOME/conf/ENGINE_NAME/HOST_NAME/CONTEXT_NAME.xml
```

For example, if you're deploying a web application to context apress, using the default host with name localhost in the Tomcat's standard Catalina engine, the configuration file location will be:

```
CATALINA_HOME/conf/Catalina/localhost/apress.xml
```

We will cover the host and context configuration in more detail later in this chapter, in the section "Configuring Hosts and Contexts."

Java Web Applications

The main function of the Tomcat server is to act as a container for Java web applications. Therefore, before we can begin our Tomcat-specific discussion, a brief introduction as to exactly what web applications are is in order. The concept of a web application was introduced with the release of the Java servlet specification 2.2. According to this specification, "a web application is a collection of servlets, html pages, classes, and other resources that can be bundled and run on multiple containers from multiple vendors." What this really means is that a web application is a container that can hold any combination of the following list of objects:

- Servlets

- Java Server Pages (JSPs)

- Utility classes

- Static documents, including HTML, images, JavaScript libraries, cascading stylesheets, and so on

- Client-side classes

- Meta-information describing the web application

One of the main characteristics of a web application is its relationship to the ServletContext. Each web application has one and only one ServletContext. This relationship is controlled by the servlet container and guarantees that no two web applications will clash when accessing objects in the ServletContext. We discuss this relationship in much more detail in Chapter 3.

The Directory Structure

The container that holds the components of a web application is the directory structure in which it exists. The first step in creating a web application is creating this directory structure. Table 2-3 contains a sample web application, named /apress, and a description of what each of its directories should contain. Each of these directories should be created from the application base directory of the web application container, the root directory where web applications are stored and accessed from the servlet container. The default application base directory for Tomcat is CATALINA_HOME/webapps directory.

Table 2-3. The Directories of a Web Application

Directory	Description
/apress	The root directory of the web application. All JSP and HTML files should be stored here. Usually each type of static content is stored in a separate subdirectory (images/, styles/, js/).
/apress/WEB-INF	Contains all resources related to the application that are not in the document root of the application. This is where your web application deployment descriptor is located (defined in the next section). Note that the WEB-INF directory is not part of the public document. No files contained in this directory can be requested directly by a client.
/apress/WEB-INF/classes	Where servlet and utility classes are located.
/apress/WEB-INF/lib	Contains Java archive files (jar libraries) that the web application is dependent upon. For example, this is where you would place a jar file that contained a JDBC driver or JSP tag library.

As you look over the contents of the web application's directory structure, notice that web applications allow for compiled objects to be stored in both the /WEB-INF/classes and /WEB-INF/lib directories. Of these two, the class loader loads classes from the /classes directory first, followed by the jar files that are stored in the /lib directory. If duplicate objects in both the /classes and /lib directories exist, the objects in the /classes directory take precedence.

The Deployment Descriptor

At the heart of all web applications is a deployment descriptor that is an XML file named web.xml. The deployment descriptor is located in the WEB-INF/ directory within the main application directory. It contains configuration information for the entire web application. For our application, the web.xml file is in the CATALINA_HOME/webapps/apress/WEB-INF/ directory. The information that is contained in the deployment descriptor includes the following elements:

- Servlet definitions

- Servlet initialization parameters

- Session configuration parameters

- Servlet/JSP mappings

- MIME type mappings

- Security configuration parameters

- Welcome file list

- List of error pages

- Resource and environment variable definitions

Listing 2-1 is a limited example of a web application deployment descriptor. As we move through this book, we will be looking at the web.xml file and its elements in much more detail.

Listing 2-1. XML Outline of the Web Deployment Descriptor File (web.xml)

```
<web-app>
      <display-name>
            Apress Demo
      </display-name>

      <servlet>
            <servlet-name>TestServlet</servlet-name>
            <servlet-class>
                  com.apress.TestServlet
            </servlet-class>
            <load-on-startup>1</load-on-startup>
            <init-param>
                  <param-name>name</param-name>
                  <param-value>value</param-value>
            </init-param>
      </servlet>

      <session-timeout>30</session-timeout>

</web-app>
```

In this example, we are setting three application-level elements, the first of which is the <display-name>. This element simply describes the name of the web application, and doesn't initiate any actions.

The second web application-level element that we have defined is the <servlet> element, which defines a servlet and its properties.

The last web application-level element is the <session-timeout> element, which controls the lifetime of the application's HttpSession object. The <session-timeout> value that we have just used tells the JSP/servlet container that the HttpSession object will become invalid after 30 minutes of inactivity. This means that, if you have been logged to the web application using a username and password, after 30 minutes of inactivity, your session will be lost and you will need to log in again. Session handling in Tomcat will be discussed in more detail in Chapter 5.

Manually Deploying Web Applications to Tomcat

In this section, we cover the manual deployment of Web applications using Tomcat, and we perform a manual deployment to fully explain the steps involved when deploying a web application.

The best way to describe the deployment process is to create a sample web application that includes the major components found in most Java web applications, and then package it for deployment. The following sections walk you through all of the steps involved in manually deploying a web application. The name of our web application is /apress.

Creating the Web Application Directory Structure

The first thing you need to create when building a new web application is the directory structure that will contain the application. The following list contains the directories that you must create to contain the /apress web application. Each these directories must be appended to the CATALINA_HOME/webapps/ directory:

- /apress
- /apress/WEB-INF
- /apress/WEB-INF/classes
- /apress/WEB-INF/lib

■ **Note** The name of our web application, /apress, is the root of our directory structure.

As the purpose of this example is to show how applications are deployed to Tomcat, we will simply create the web application directory structure within the Tomcat's /webapps directory. For the day-to-day development and production deployment to Tomcat, you should build a WAR file that will be deployed to Tomcat. We will cover the deployment of WAR-packaged web applications later in this chapter.

The last step in creating the web application directory structure is adding a deployment descriptor. At this point, you will be creating a default web.xml file that contains only the DTD, describing the web.xml file, and an empty <webapp/> element. Listing 2-2 contains the source code for a default web.xml file.

Listing 2-2. The Source Code for a Default web.xml File

```
<?xml version="1.0" encoding="ISO-8859-1"?>
<web-app xmlns="http://java.sun.com/xml/ns/javaee"
  xmlns:xsi="http://www.w3.org/2001/XMLSchema-instance"
  xsi:schemaLocation="http://java.sun.com/xml/ns/javaee
                      http://java.sun.com/xml/ns/javaee/web-app_3_0.xsd"
  version="3.0">
</web-app>
```

The most important part in this web.xml file is the XML schema definition. The schema definition will verify that the correct syntax is used for the selected Servlet API version. Because Apache Tomcat 7 supports version 3.0 of Servlet API, we reference its schema (http://java.sun.com/xml/ns/javaee/web-app_3_0.xsd) in the web.xml header.

Adding Static Content

In addition to being a servlet container, Tomcat is also a capable web server, so it can serve static files like images, JavaScript files, Flash movies, and cascading stylesheets (CSS).

In order to add static resources for our sample web application, all we have to do is copy the files that we would like to add to the server to the web application root directory (/apress), on the same level as the WEB-INF directory. It is common practice to split the static resources to subdirectories based on their purpose, so we will create subdirectories for images, JavaScript files, and CSS in the /apress directory. The directory structure of our web applications will now look as follows:

- /apress
- /apress/WEB-INF/
- /apress/images/
- /apress/scripts/
- /apress/styles/

Let's copy the logo image, logo.jpg, to the /apress/images/ subdirectory. If you restart Tomcat (the web application will be redeployed), you can now access the image in the browser, by entering the following URL:

http://localhost:8080/apress/images/logo.jpg.

The logo image will be rendered directly in the browser. You can access all other images in the /apress/images directory in the same way. Similarly, if you copy a stylesheet file main.css to the /apress/styles/ directory, you can open the file in the browser by navigating to http://localhost:8080/apress/styles/main.css.

As you can see, the directories with static content can be accessed from your browser directly by entering the directory structure of your web application. Because all static resources are publicly available to anyone who types the correct URL in the browser, they are sometimes called public directories.

Note that the WEB-INF directory cannot be used to serve static content. Only the servlet container (Tomcat and servlets deployed to it) can access resources stored in the WEB-INF directory. You can test that by copying the same image logo.jpg to the /apress/WEB-INF/ directory, and trying to access it on the URL http://localhost:8080/apress/WEB-INF/logo.jpg. The image will not be displayed; all you will see is the "404 page not found" error in the browser.

Adding JSPs

Java Server Pages (JSPs) are a simple but powerful technology used most often to generate dynamic HTML on the server side. They are a direct extension of Java servlets with the purpose of allowing the developer to embed Java logic directly into a requested page. JSP documents typically have the .jsp extension.

Apache Tomcat comes with JSP configuration out of the box, so all you have to do is create JSP files and deploy them with your web application. Listing 2-3 shows a sample JSP file that simply displays the current date and time, and the greeting to the user based on the time of the day.

Listing 2-3. Displaying Current Date and Time in JSP

```
<%@ page import="java.util.Calendar" %>                          #1

<html>
<head>
    <title>Apress Demo</title>
    <meta http-equiv="Content-Type" content="text/html; charset=UTF-8">
</head>
```

```
<body>
    <div class="content">
        <b>Welcome to Apress</b>

        <p>Today is <%=Calendar.getInstance().getTime()%>          #2
        </p>
        <%                                                          #3
            String greeting;
            int hourOfDay =
                Calendar.getInstance().get(Calendar.HOUR_OF_DAY);
            if (hourOfDay < 12) {
                greeting = "Good Morning";
            } else if (hourOfDay >= 12 && hourOfDay < 19) {
                greeting = "Good Afternoon";
            } else {
                greeting = "Good Evening";
            }

        %>
        <p><%=greeting%></p>                                        #4
    </div>
</body>
</html>
```

JSP file contains the HTML markup that will be rendered in the browser. As you can see in Listing 2-3, the entire JSP file is formatted using HTML markup (with <HTML>, <HEAD>, <BODY>, and other enclosed HTML tags). However, it contains some Java code as well.

In the first line (#1), we have something that looks like a Java import statement. It does the same job as an import statement in standard Java files, referencing classes and interfaces required for compilation. In JSP, the import statement is implemented using a JSP page directive, which you can recognize because it starts with <%@ characters, and ends with %>.

Next, we invoke the Java method to get current date, and render the result of the method directly to the HTML (#2). The Java code is enclosed between <%= and %>, and the <%= JSP construct takes the return value of the Java method invoked and renders in to the HTML, using Object.toString () Java method. This example of JSP syntax is called JSP expression, and is an easy way to render values that are easily retrieved in Java to the HTML.

Finally, we demonstrate the standard Java code snippet (or JSP scriptlet), enclosed within <% and %> (#3). You can consider code snippet like this as a Java code that will be inserted to the _jspService() method. However, all local variables you define in such code snippet have global visibility, so you can reference them anywhere else on the JSP page, after it has been introduced. We decide what message to use to greet the user in our code snippet, and store it in the variable greeting (#3). We render the stored greeting to the HTML using the JSP expression (<%= syntax) outside the original code where we introduced the greeting variable (#4).

■ **Note** All JSP syntax constructs end with the characters %>. The start of the construct depends on the type, so it can be <%@ for directive, <% for standard Java JSP scriptlet, and <%= for JSP expression rendering the result of the Java code to the HTML.

All we need to do now is save the JSP resource from Listing 2-3 in the new directory called jsps under root web application directory. The file location will be /apress/jsps/index.jsps.

░ **Note** Tomcat by default recognizes JSP files with either .jsp or jspx extension.

Now you can start Tomcat again. If the Tomcat server has been running all the time, there is no need for the restart, as the new file will be loaded automatically. If you can navigate to http://localhost:8080/apress/jsps/index.jsp, the page will be rendered in the browser. Figure 2-1 shows the resulting page in Firefox browser.

Figure 2-1. JSP page that renders current date and time deployed in Tomcat

Because the JSP page is rendered dynamically, you will see a different result whenever you reload the page, including a different greeting message in the morning, afternoon, or evening. We have our first dynamic page deployed to Tomcat, using Tomcat's built-in support for JSP resources. We will discuss more JSP capabilities in the next chapter. Let's now see how we can add a servlet to the Tomcat server.

Adding Servlets

A servlet is a Java program that runs in the servlet container, with the responsibility of accepting requests from the clients and sending back the responses, all over the HTTP protocol. In Java Servlet API, servlets are defined using the Java interface javax.servlet.Servlet, which any concrete servlet class must implement.

To make the developer's life easier, Java Servlet API ships with javax.servlet.http.HttpServlet class, which is commonly used as a convenient superclass that concrete servlet implementations extend.

Listing 2-4 illustrates the HelloWorldServlet implementation, a simple servlet that renders Hello World message in the browser.

Listing 2-4. Rendering HTML to the Browser Using HelloWorldServlet

```
package com.apress.apachetomcat7.chapter2;

import java.io.*;
import javax.servlet.*;
import javax.servlet.http.*;
```

```
public class HelloWorldServlet extends HttpServlet {

    public void doGet(HttpServletRequest request, HttpServletResponse response)   #1
    throws IOException, ServletException
    {
        response.setContentType("text/html");                                      #2
        PrintWriter out = response.getWriter();                                    #3
        out.println("<html>");
        out.println("<head>");
        out.println("<title>Hello World!</title>");
        out.println("</head>");
        out.println("<body>");
        out.println("<h1>Hello World!</h1>");
        out.println("</body>");
        out.println("</html>");
    }
}
```

In this example, we extend the doGet() method from the HttpServlet class, which is responsible for handling HTTP GET operations (#1). We are going to render HTML content to the browser, so we set the content type of the HttpServletResponse to "text/html" (#2). Finally, to render text to the browser, we're obtaining the PrintWriter instance from the HttpServletResponse (#3), and then just write the HTML markup to it.

The next step is to compile our servlet class, so it can be deployed to Tomcat. In addition to standard Java libraries, we will need servlet API classes and interfaces on our classpath to compile HelloWorldServlet successfully. All required servlet API classes and interfaces are already included with Tomcat (in CATALINA_HOME/lib directory), so we can just add it to the classpath for java compiler. To compile the HelloWorldServlet class run the following command:

```
javac HelloWorldServlet.java -cp CATALINA_HOME/lib/servlet-api.jar
```

The result of the compilation will be HelloWorldServlet.class file, located in the same directory.

■ **Note** JSP files are actually complied into Java servlet classes by the servlet container, and each JSP file is running as a small servlet in Tomcat, invisible to the user.

The next step is to copy the compiled class to the /apress/WEB-INF/classes directory of our web application, so it can be picked up by Tomcat and deployed successfully (compiled Java classes in this directory will be loaded by Tomcat's class loader). Make sure to copy entire compiled class directory structure, as per Java standard; each Java package must have its own directory, with classes stored in directories matching their packages. The code in Listing 2-4 has package com.apress.apachetomcat7.chaper2, so the directory structure will be as follows:

/apress/WEB-INF/classes/com/apress/apachetomcat7/chapter2/HelloWorldServlet.class.

> ■ **Note** As we mentioned before, Tomcat will automatically load compiled Java classes from the `/WEB-INF/classes` and `/WEB-INF/lib` directory, in that particular order. You should keep your application classes in the `/WEB-INF/classes` directory, and all third-party jar dependencies in the `/WEB-INF/lib` directory.

The final step is to configure our servlet in the web deployment descriptor (`web.xml` file). We left web.xml empty when we started (see Listing 2-2), so now it's time to add servlet configuration to it. Listing 2-5 shows the servlet configuration added to web.xml file.

Listing 2-5. HelloWorldServlet Configuration in the web.xml File

```xml
<?xml version="1.0" encoding="ISO-8859-1"?>
<web-app xmlns="http://java.sun.com/xml/ns/javaee"
         xmlns:xsi="http://www.w3.org/2001/XMLSchema-instance"
         xsi:schemaLocation="http://java.sun.com/xml/ns/javaee↵
 http://java.sun.com/xml/ns/javaee/web-app_3_0.xsd" version="3.0">

    <display-name>Chapter 2</display-name>
    <description>Apress demo</description>

    <servlet>                                                    #1
        <servlet-name>helloworld</servlet-name>
        <servlet-class>
            com.apress.apachetomcat7.chapter2.HelloWorldServlet
```

```
        </servlet-class>
    </servlet>

    <servlet-mapping>                                          #2
        <servlet-name>helloworld</servlet-name>
        <url-pattern>/hello.html</url-pattern>
    </servlet-mapping>

</web-app>
```

The servlet is configured using the <servlet> XML element (#1), with two sub-elements: <servlet-name>, the unique name for this servlet, and <servlet-class>, the fully qualified servlet class name.

Finally, we need to map the servlet to the URL, so that the web application knows which URL should invoke the configured servlet. This is achieved using the <servlet-mapping> XML element (#2). Its nested element <servlet-name> references the name of the configured servlet (it must be the same as <servlet-name> in the servlet class configuration #1). The nested element <url-pattern> specifies the pattern of URLs that will be mapped to this servlet. All URL patterns are relative to the context of the web application. Based on the configuration in Listing 2-5, HelloWorldServlet will be mapped to the URL http://localhost:8080/apress/hello.html.

And this completes the servlet configuration. We will need to restart Tomcat in order to reload the servlet class. After Tomcat starts up, you can navigate to the URL http://localhost:8080/apress/hello.html in your browser, and you will see the page with the "Hello World!" message rendered. Figure 2-2 shows the page displayed in the browser.

Hello World!

Figure 2-2. Page rendered HelloWorldServlet in the browser

So far, we have covered how to deploy static resources, JSP files, and now servlets to Tomcat server. We deployed a web application in a subdirectory under CATALINA_HOME/webapps directory. The deployment of the Java web application as the directory with structure defined like in our example is called *exploded directory*. Exploded directory web application deployment is not part of Java servlet specification, and therefore may not work on servlet containers other than Tomcat. In the next section, we will cover the deployment of Java web applications as WAR archives, the deployment method supported by Java Servlet specification.

Deploying WAR Archive

The WAR (Web ARchive) file is a single file that contains all web application resources, and can be deployed directly to Tomcat. The WAR file is actually a zip-compatible archived file that, when unpacked, contains the same directory structure as the exploded directory described in the previous section.

A WAR file is the standard method for packaging Java web applications, and you can create one using Java's archiving tool, jar. You can create a WAR file from the exploded directory by changing into it and running the following command from the exploded directory (/apress in our example):

```
jar cvf apress.war.
```

■ **Note** The period (.) at the end of the jar cvf apress.war. command references the active directory; make sure to include it when running the command, otherwise the jar packaging won't work.

This command produces an archive file named apress.war that contains your entire web application. Figure 2-3 shows the contents of the apress.war file.

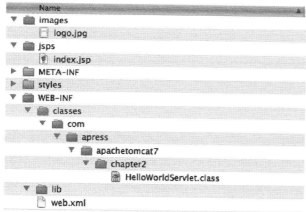

Figure 2-3. Contents of the WAR-packaged web applications, in the same structure as the exploded directory

■ **Note** The *.war file is nothing more than the *.jar file with a different extension. The Java archive standard is the zip file format, so you can read or create jar and war files using any zip-compatible archiving tool.

To deploy a WAR-packaged web application, all you have to do is copy it to the CATALINA_HOME/webapps directory. Make sure you remove the previously deployed application's exploded directory. Upon server startup, Tomcat will pick up the apress.war file and deploy it automatically. When Tomcat is up and running again, you can access the web application from the browser in the same way as before.

While deploying the WAR archive, Tomcat will unpack it in the CATALINA_HOME/webapps directory, in the subdirectory name matching the name of the WAR file, without extension. For example, our apress.war web application will be unpacked to directory CATALINA_HOME/webapps/apress. You can confirm this by inspecting the CATALINA_HOME/webapps directory after deployment, and you will see that it contains both the apress.war file that we copied there, and the apress/ directory, created by Tomcat. The unpacked directory will contain all web application resources that were packaged into WAR archive.

Tomcat unpacks the WAR file for performance reasons, as it's much quicker to load files from file system directly, than to unpack them from the archive file every time they are requested. If you're running Tomcat on a machine where you have limited write permissions, this may not be desired behavior, and you would prefer to serve web resources directory from the WAR archive, without unpacking. You can configure whether WAR files should be unpacked automatically by setting unpackWAR attribute on the <Context> element of your web application. The following code snippet illustrates configuration where the WAR archive won't be unpacked, and all resources will be served from the archive directly:

```
<Context path="/apress" docBase="apress" unpackWar="true">
```

You can add this context configuration directly to the CATALINA_HOM/conf/server.xml file, or you can use other available methods to configure web application context described later in the chapter (see the section "Configuring Web Application Contexts").

Other Methods of Deployment

So far we have seen how to deploy web applications to Tomcat manually, by copying files to an exploded directory, or by creating the WAR archive and copying it to Tomcat's deployment directory.

Copying the files to remote servers for production deployment can become cumbersome, or simply impossible if you don't have access to the remote server's file system. That's why Tomcat distributes with the Manager web application, a built-in front end for management of web applications, which can be used for deployment. You can navigate to Manager web application's home page on a remote server from the browser, fill the web form with your web application details, select the WAR archive to deploy, and press submit. The web application will be deployed automatically.

To learn more about Manager web application, see Chapter 4.

In addition to web interface, Tomcat ships with the set of Ant tasks, which can be used for application deployment (and for other web application maintenance tasks) from the command line. This approach is very useful in development and for automated deployment for testing. Ant tasks available with Tomcat will be covered in Chapter 4 as well.

Configuring Hosts and Contexts

In the Tomcat architecture, each deployed web application is representing a Context within a particular <Host> element. Even without specific configuration, Tomcat ships with sensible defaults out of the box, which is why we could deploy web applications in earlier examples without worrying about hosts and contexts. For simple web applications, the default configuration works well. However, if you need to configure advanced Tomcat options for your web application, you will need to configure these elements manually. In the following sections, we will describe the default Tomcat configuration of hosts and contexts elements, and take a look how we can configure these elements manually.

Configuring Hosts

The hosts are configured in the CATALINA_HOME/conf/server.xml file. If you take a look at this file, you will see that one host is already configured when you install Tomcat. The name of that host is localhost, and it will be sufficient for most Tomcat installations. Listing 2-6 shows the default host configuration.

Listing 2-6. *Tomcat Ships with Default Host Configuration Out of the Box*

```
<Host                               #1
      name="localhost"              #2
      appBase="webapps"             #3
      unpackWARs="true"             #4
      autoDeploy="true"             #5
>
```

The host is configured using the <Host> XML element (#1). Every host must have a name, configured using name attribute (#2). The name of the host is usually set to the network name of the machine the Tomcat is running on, for example www.mycompany.com. The default host preconfigured on Tomcat has the name localhost, which matches the standard loopback network interface; it always resolves to the machine itself.

The attribute appBase configures the *applications base* directory, which is the base directory where the web applications deployed to Tomcat exist (#3). It can have absolute path of the directory (for example, /var/deployments on Linux or c:\deployedapps on Windows), or it can be relative (without starting slash or drive name), when the actual directory will be located relative to the CATALINA_HOME directory. The default configuration, illustrated in Listing 2-6, has the appBase attribute set to value webapps, meaning that application base is located at the CATALINA_HOME/webapps directory. We described this directory as a base directory for web applications when we discussed Tomcat's directory structure, but you can easily change it to the path of your choice.

The next attribute configured by default is unpackWARs, which is set to true (#4). This means that all web applications deployed as WAR archives to this host will be unpacked to the exploded directory in the application base. If this is not your desired behavior, change it to false, and all web applications deployed to this host will be served from the WAR archive directly. When we were discussing the WAR deployment, we disabled this behavior on the single <Context> element. If you want to disable WAR unpacking for all web applications deployed, configuring unpackWARs on <Host> element is more efficient way to do it.

The final attribute on the default host configured by Tomcat is the autoDeploy attribute, set to true (#5). This attribute tells Tomcat to periodically check for the updates of the WAR files and exploded directories (not its contents) within the application base directory, and deploy/redeploy then automatically if any changes are detected.

Single host configuration is usually sufficient for common production configuration. If, however, you need multiple hosts to separate web applications in your setup, you should add another configuration similar to the one in Listing 2-6 to the server.xml file.

The configuration options described should be enough to get you started. For more details about all available host configuration options and attributes, see Appendix A.

Configuring Web Application Contexts

Each web application deployed to Tomcat represents a context in Tomcat's internal architecture. Contexts belong to a configured host, and they are configured using the <Context> XML element. Listing 2-7 illustrates a typical <Context> element configuration.

Listing 2-7. *Typical Context Configuration in Tomcat*

```
<Context                            #1
    path="/apress"                  #2
    docBase="apress"                #3
```

```
reloadable="true"                              #4
/>
```

As mentioned previously, the web application context is configured using the <Context> XML element (#1).

The path attribute specifies the context path for the web application (#2). Every HTTP request to the Tomcat instance that has a Uniform Resource Identifier (URI) starting with the configured context path (after server and port) will be served by this context. This value should only be set if the context is configured in the server.xml file; in all other cases, the context path is inferred from the file and directory names used, as we will demonstrate later. If specified, the context path must be unique within the host.

▓ **Note** A URI is a set of characters that identify a resource on the Internet. Some examples include www.mycompany.com:80/apress or http://localhost:8080/chapter2/index.html?page=2. The part of the URI after the server name and port is used to determine the context path on Tomcat.

The docBase attribute defines the *context root*, which is the path to the contents of the web application deployed under this context (#3). It can contain an absolute path to the WAR file or exploded directory, or a path relative to the application base directory of the host for which it's configured.

The final attribute configured in this example is reloadable (#4). If set to true, Tomcat will monitor WEB-INF/classes and WEB-INF/lib directories of the context root, and redeploy the application if any changes are detected. This feature is very useful for development and testing, as you don't have to restart Tomcat with every change you make to the code, but it does add performance overhead, so it's not recommended in production environments. The default value is false.

Web application context can be configured in the following four ways:

- In `server.xml` file

- In the host configuration directory
  `CATALINA_HOME/conf/ENGINE_NAME/HOST_NAME/CONTEXT_PATH.xml`

- As part of the web application code, in the `/META-INF/context.xml` file in the web
  application WAR or exploded directory

- Implicitly, where Tomcat creates context for a web application for which none of
  the above applies

When configuring a web application context in the `server.xml` file, you should specify all
configuration attributes illustrated in Listing 2-7. However, because the content of the `server.xml` file is
not reloaded until Tomcat restarts, any changes you make will not be visible until Tomcat is restarted.

The second option is to configure context in the separate XML file, and store it in the specific host
configuration directory under `CATALINA_HOME/conf`. The name of the XML file will represent the context
path, so the path attribute must not be set. In addition, the `docBase` attribute should only be set if it
points to the directory outside of the host's application base.

For our sample web application, the configuration file should be located on
`CATALINA_HOME/conf/Catalina/localhost/apress.xml`, and the content of the apress.xml file will look like
the following snippet:

```
<Context reloadable="false"/>
```

Note that we didn't specify a path attribute, as it will be inferred from the name of the xml file (in
this example context path will be set to apress). In addition, we didn't set the `docBase` directory, and it
will be inferred from the xml file name as well, relative to the `webapps` directory.

The third option for context configuration is to configure it in the `/META-INF/context.xml` file in the
actual web application WAR archive or exploded directory. This configuration will only be applied if
none of the first two configurations is detected. The `context.xml` file content will look exactly like the last
code snippet.

The fourth option is to omit the context configuration altogether. It applies to the web applications
auto deployed from the application base directory (`CATALINA_HOME/webapps` directory in the default
Tomcat setup). All exploded directories deployed under the application base are deployed with an
implicit context name that matches the exploded directory name, and the context root is set to the
exploded directory itself. All WAR archives deployed under the application base directory will have a
context created with the name matching the WAR file name without the extension. The context root for
WAR files will be either the unpacked WAR archive directory (in `unpackWARs` is set to true), or the path to
the WAR file itself (if `unpackWARs` is set to false).

In the previous deployment examples in this chapter, we did not configure any context, and we were
still able to deploy and access a sample web application using Tomcat implicit context creation.

Deploying to Root Context

It's common for a production web application not to have a context name at all, so that their URLs look
simpler. For example, we would like our sample web application to be accessible via
`http://localhost:8080/hello.html` instead of `http//localhost:8080/apress/hello.html`, especially
when deployed to a production server (`www.apress.com/apress/hello.html` contains unwanted word
duplication, which is what we would like to avoid).

In the example URL `http://localhost:8080/hello.html`, the content name is empty (""), and it's
known as root context.

You have several options to deploy web applications in Tomcat's root context. But before proceeding, you will have to remove Tomcat's root web application, which is already deployed in root context by default and is responsible for the Tomcat's home page. You can remove the default root web application by simply deleting the directory where it's deployed, CATALINA_HOME/webapps/ROOT, and restarting Tomcat.

■ **Note** Remember that the context name has to be unique for every host, so only one web application can be deployed in every single context; otherwise, the deployment will fail.

The first option is to rename your WAR file to ROOT.war (uppercase), and copy it to the CATALINA_HOME/webapps directory. By Tomcat's convention, WAR with the name ROOT.war will be deployed to the root context. If you're using exploded directory deployment, you should rename the exploded directory to ROOT.

Using another approach, you can keep the WAR file name, but copy it to a separate location, outside of the CATALINA_HOME/webapps directory. For example, let's say we copy the file to the /var/deployments/apress.war path. Then we will create a context configuration file in the host's configuration directory, at following location: CATALINA_HOME/conf/Catalina/localhost/ROOT.xml. The name of the XML file will define the context name, so we have to call it ROOT.xml, to match the Tomcat's convention name for root context. The xml file contents will match the following code snippet:

```
<Context docBase="/var/deployments/apress.war" reloadable="false"/>
```

You could do the same by simply adding the <Context> element to the server.xml file within host element; this, however, isn't a recommended approach for context configuration, so it should be avoided.

After Tomcat restarts, you can access the same apress web application by typing the URL without the context name in the browser's address bar: http://localhost:8080/hello.html.

Context.xml Configuration File

Tomcat's conf directory contains another configuration file that you can use to configure web applications contexts: context.xml. This file contains only one <Context> element without any path or docBase attributes set.

Any settings in this file will apply to all contexts for every web application deployed on the Tomcat instance. You can set the general attributes you want to apply to entire server. For example, if you set the reloadable attribute to true in context.xml, all contexts will have the same attribute set, without the need to configure it explicitly again on every <Context> element. This configuration is particularly useful in development and testing environments. As we mentioned before, you should consider your requirements before setting the reloadable attribute to true in production environments, as it comes with the performance overhead of monitoring filesystem changes by Tomcat.

However, you can override any settings made in the context.xml simply by adding the same attribute to the specific context configuration.

Deploying a Web Application from Eclipse IDE

For all the development and deployment work we've done in the chapter, all we needed was a text editor and a command line terminal window. While we managed to get everything to work, for any non-trivial project this approach can be rather slow and error prone. That's why developers use Integrated Development Environments (IDEs) to code, test, and deploy their projects on their development machines. IDEs have been of great help to developers, with integrated code editor, compilation, debugging, packaging, and deployment tools, and have become the standard tool for any kind of development.

Java ecosystems have a few popular IDEs, from open source and free Eclipse and NetBeans to commercial Intellij IDEA. While each of the IDEs mentioned has its pros and cons, it's probably Eclipse that is used by most of the developers around the world. In this section, we're going to explore Eclipse's tooling capabilities for development and deployment of a Java web application on Apache Tomcat.

Before continuing, you will have to download and install the latest version Eclipse IDE from the Eclipse project's web site: www.eclipse.org/downloads/.

Updating Eclipse for Java Web Development

The basic Eclipse distribution does not contain all the development tools for Java web development, and we need to install them before proceeding. To do so, follow these steps:

1. From Eclipse's Help menu, select the Install New Software option.

2. From the list of available update sites, select the entry "All available sites."

3. Find and select the group called "Web, Xml, Java EE and OSGi enterprise development;" it should be located at the bottom of the alphabetically ordered list. Figure 2-4 shows the Eclipse screen at this stage.

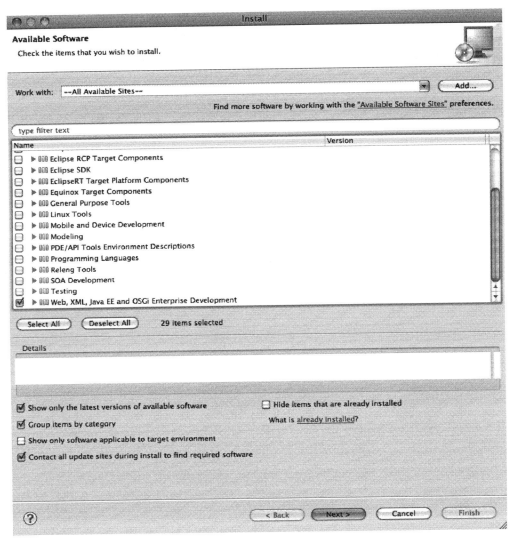

Figure 2-4. Select the Web, Java Web, and Java EE tools packages from the list of available software updates for Eclipse.

4. Select this software (by clicking on the checkbox in front of it) and press Next button.

5. After confirming the selected software and accepting the terms and conditions, press the Finish button and wait for the packages to download.

6. After successful download, you will have to restart the Eclipse IDE for the
    updates to load.

Now that we have all required Eclipse plug-ins installed, we can create Eclipse project for our web
application.

Creating a Dynamic Web Project

Now we'll create a Java web project in Eclipse. Follow these steps:

1. From the File menu, select New   Project. You will be presented with the New
    Project dialog to select project wizard.

2. In the Wizards text box, start typing **web**, and you will be presented with the
    filtered selection of web project wizards.

3. Select Dynamic Web Project (Eclipse's name for the Java Web Project) and
    press the button. Figure 2-5 shows the filtered dialog for project selection.

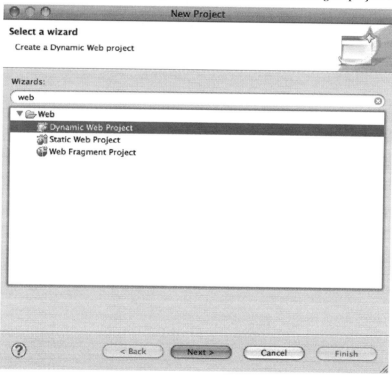

Figure 2-5. From the New Project wizard, select Dynamic Web Project.

4. You will be presented with the Dynamic Web Project details screen, where you should fill in the project name and press Finish. Figure 2-6 shows the details screen.

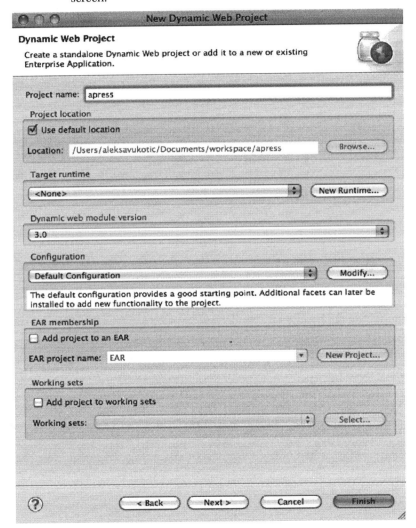

Figure 2-6. Dynamic Web Project details screen

You have now created an empty Java web project. The next step is to create the classes and files within this project to match our sample project. Java classes should be created under the Java

Resources/src directory, and the other web resources—XML configuration files, JSPs, and images—in the correct directories in the WebContent directory.

Figure 2-7 shows the Eclipse project structure matching the apress project introduced in this chapter.

Figure 2-7. Eclipse Project Explorer view with all apress sample project files

Now we have an entire project in Eclipse IDE, and we can avail of all the IDE goodness, such as quick and easy navigation, code auto completion, automatic compilation and packaging, refactoring, and so on.

One thing we still need is to be able to deploy our project to the Tomcat server from the Eclipse. To use Eclipse Tomcat tooling, we first need to add Tomcat runtime environment to Eclipse.

Adding Tomcat Runtime Environment

To configure Server Runtime Environments in Eclipse, go to Tools Settings, and, under Servers, select Runtime Environments. Figure 2-8 shows the Runtime Environments configuration screen.

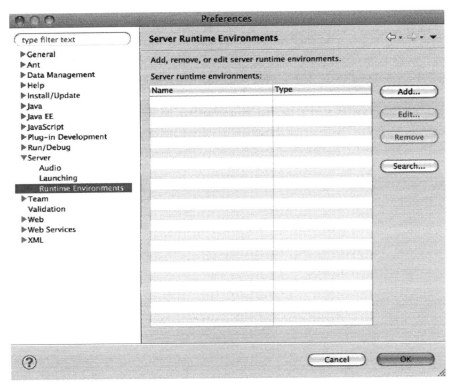

Figure 2-8. *The empty Server Runtime Environments configuration screen from Eclipse preferences*

Click the Add button on the right-hand side to add a new server. You will be presented with the list of available servers for Eclipse. Figure 2-9 shows this screen.

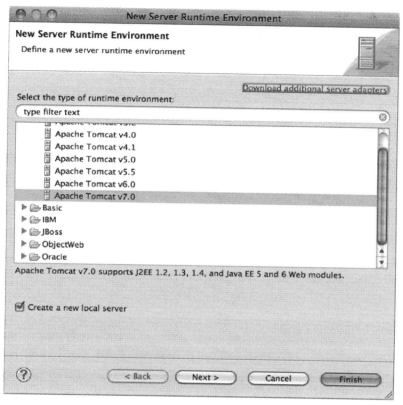

Figure 2-9. Select Apache Tomcat 7 from the list of of available servers.

Select Apache Tomcat 7 from the list of available servers, making sure to check the "Create a new local server" checkbox, and then press Next. On the next screen, select the Tomcat's installation directory and press Finish.

And that's it. You now have Tomcat 7 Runtime Environment configured in Eclipse. The next step is to deploy the Java web project to the configured Tomcat instance.

Deploying a Java Web Project to Tomcat from Eclipse

In order to add the Eclipse project to Tomcat server and deploy it, follow these steps:

1. Locate the configured server by opening Eclipse's Servers view. You can open the Servers view like any other view in Eclipse. From the Window menu, select Show View Other.

2. Start typing **servers** in the filter text box.

3. Select the Servers view and press OK. You will see new view in your workspace, as shown in Figure 2-10.

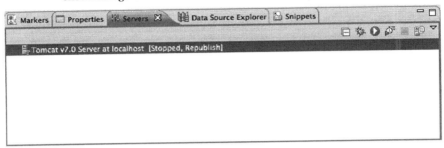

Figure 2-10. Eclipse Servers view displayed in Eclipse perspective

4. To add an Eclipse project to be deployed to a selected Tomcat server, open the server's context menu (by right-clicking on the server instance in the Servers view), and click on the Add and Remove menu entry. See Figure 2-11.

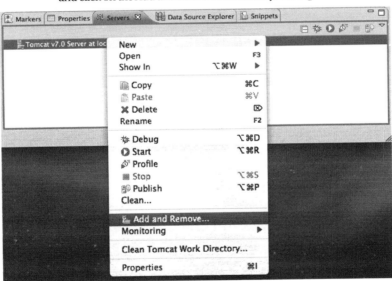

Figure 2-11. Open Tomcat server's context menu from Eclipse's Servers view

On the next screen, on the left-hand side, you see a list of all projects in the Eclipse workspace that are available for deployment to the selected server, and on the right-hand side you see all projects that are already configured for deployment to the server. The right-hand side will be empty when you do this the first time.

5. Select the apress project on the left-hand side of the screen, and press Add. Figure 2-12 shows the project selection screen.

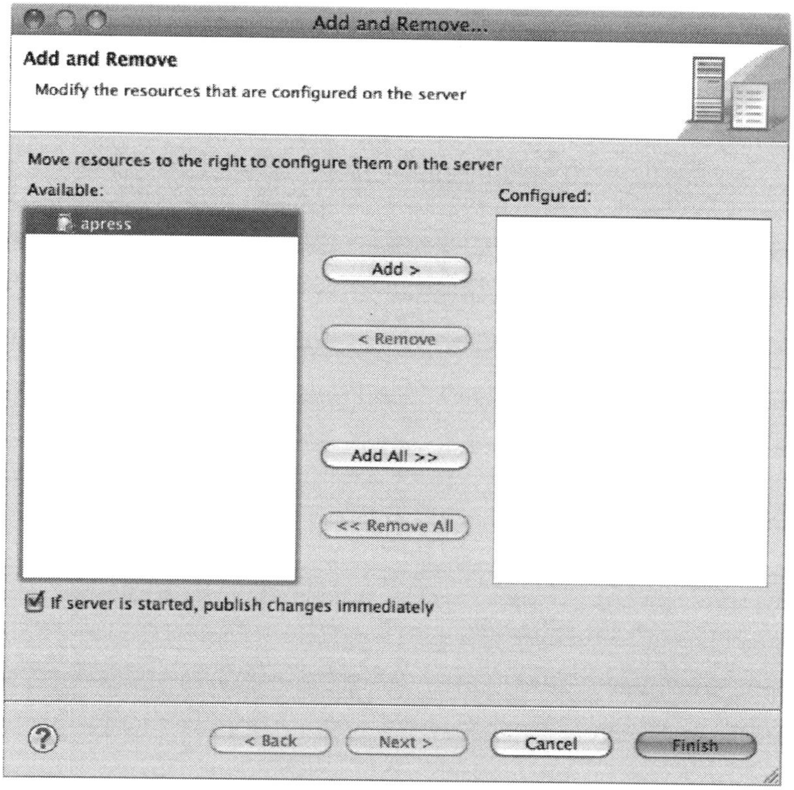

Figure 2-12. *The Add and Remove screen, where you can select projects to be deployed to Tomcat*

6. Press Finish.

7. Start Tomcat from Eclipse by clicking on the Start button, which you can see in the top right part of Figure 2-11 (a green circle with a white "play" sign). You will see Tomcat's log output in the Eclipse console view.

If you navigate your browser to the familiar URL http://localhost:8080/apress/hello.html, you will see familiar Hello World message, like the one in Figure 2-2.

Summary

In this chapter, we discussed Tomcat's directory structure and the role of the main configuration files. We also explained the basics of Java web applications and their packaging structure. We continued with building and deploying a sample web application to Tomcat, demonstrating the deployment of static resources, JSP pages, and servlets, both as exploded directories and WAR archives. Finally, we demonstrated how you can leverage the power of the Eclipse IDE to make Java web application development and deployment to Tomcat easier.

In the next chapter, will cover the details Java Servlets API and its relationship to JSP technology and ServletContext.

CHAPTER 3

Servlets, JSPs and ServletContext

So far, we learned how to install Apache Tomcat server and how to deploy Java web application to it. We briefly discussed the concept of Java web applications components, including servlets and JSPs.

Before we go into more depth explaining Tomcat features, we need to introduce the concepts, components, and syntax of main Java web application components—servlets, JSPs, and their relationship to ServletContext. We won't cover all the details about these broad subjects, but you should gain enough understanding to follow the examples in the chapters that follow, in which we explore the Tomcat server specific functionalities.

If you would like to read more about these technologies, visit the Java web site (www.oracle.com/technetwork/java/index.html).

In this chapter we:

- Describe the Java servlet architecture and its core components

- Describe the JSP architecture with syntax introduction

- Define the ServletContext and its relationship to web applications

Servlets

A Java servlet is a platform-independent web application component that is hosted in a servlet container. Servlets communicate with web clients using a request/response model managed by a servlet container, such as Apache Tomcat. When the user submits a request to the server (i.e., clicks on the link in the browser), the servlet container will accept the request. The servlet container then checks the servlets deployed on it, locates the one that should handle the incoming request (based on the request URL and servlet mapping), and sends the request to it, wrapped as an instance of the ServletRequest class. After processing the request, the servlet produces a response in the form of a ServletResponse instance, and sends it back to the servlet container. Finally, the servlet container sends the response to the calling client, resulting in the web page rendered in the client browser. Figure 3-1 depicts the execution of a Java servlet.

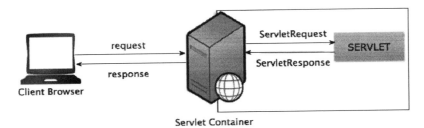

Figure 3-1.The execution of a Java servlet

The servlet architecture comprises two Java packages: javax.servlet and javax.servlet.http. The javax.servlet package contains the generic interfaces and classes that are implemented and extended by all servlets. The second package is the javax.servlet.http package, which contains all the servlet classes that are specific to HTTP, such as a simple servlet that responds using HTML.

At the heart of this architecture is the interface javax.servlet.Servlet. The base class for all servlets, the Servlet interface, defines five methods. The three most important of these methods and their functions are

- the init(..) method, which initializes the servlet;

- the service() method, which services client requests; and

- the destroy() method, which performs cleanup.

These methods make up the servlet lifecycle methods. (We describe these lifecycle methods in the next section.) All servlets must implement this interface, either directly or through inheritance.

The Lifecycle of a Servlet

The lifecycle of a Java servlet follows a very logical sequence. The interface that declares the lifecycle methods is the javax.servlet.Servlet interface. These methods are the init(), the service(), and the destroy() methods. This sequence can be described in a simple three-step process:

1. A servlet is loaded and initialized using the init() method. This method is called when the servlet is reloaded or upon the first request to this servlet.

2. The servlet then services zero or more requests. The servlet services the request using the service() method.

3. The servlet is then destroyed and garbage-collected when the web application containing the servlet shuts down. The method that is called upon shutdown is the destroy() method.

Now, let's look at each of these methods.

init

The init() method is where the servlet begins its life. This method is called immediately after the servlet is instantiated, and it is called only once. The init() method should be used to create and initialize the resources that it will be using while handling requests. The init() method's signature is defined as follows:

```
public void init(ServletConfig config) throws ServletException;
```

The init() method takes a ServletConfig object as a parameter. This reference should be stored in a member variable so that it can be used later. A common way of doing this is to have the init() method call super.init() and passing it the ServletConfig object.

The init() method also declares that it can throw a ServletException. If, for some reason, the servlet cannot initialize the resources necessary to handle requests, it should throw a ServletException with an error message that signifies the problem.

service

The service() method services all requests received from a client using a simple request/response pattern. The service() method's signature is:

```
public void service(ServletRequest req, ServletResponse res) throws ServletException, ↵
  IOException;
```

The service() method takes two parameters, the first of which is a ServletRequest object that contains information about the service request, encapsulating information provided by the client. The ServletResponse object contains the information returned to the client.

You will not usually implement this method directly, unless you extend the GenericServlet abstract class. The most common implementation of the service() method is in the HttpServlet class. The HttpServlet class implements the servlet interface by extending GenericServlet. Its service() method supports standard HTTP/1.1 requests by determining the request type and calling the appropriate method.

destroy

This method signifies the end of servlet's life. When a web application is shut down, the servlet's destroy() method is called. This is where all resources that were created in the init() method should be cleaned up. The signature of the destroy() can be found in the following code snippet:

```
public void destroy();
```

ServletRequest and ServletResponse

Interfaces ServletRequest and ServletResponse are two key abstractions of the client request to the server, and a server response to the calling client in Servlet API. For every request that comes to the server, servlet container will create instance of ServletRequest and ServletResponse and pass them on as arguments to the Servlet.service(..) method.

ServletRequest and HttpServletRequest

ServletRequest object will contain all information collected from the client request so they are accessible to the servlet that processes it, such as a protocol used to receive a request, remote clients IP address and port, content type, language, and the like. Collection of request parameters passed on from the client is stored in ServletRequest object as well. Each parameter consists of the key-value pair, where the key is the name of the parameter, and the value is the parameter value. Similarly, ServletRequest has the collection of request attributes as key-value pairs of attribute names and values. While ServletRequest parameters are passed on from the client initiating the request, ServletRequest attributes are objects stored explicitly by the servlet container component itself, so they are available for inspection in the later stages of servlet lifecycle. In addition, request parameters values are always Strings, while request attributes can be objects of any Java type.

Servlets are designed to be protocol independent, so the ServletRequest abstraction can be applied for request-response communication using any protocol. HTTP is the most widely used protocol for client-server communication over the Internet. For HTTP protocol-based request-response communication, the Servlet API defines interface javax.servlet.http.HttpServletRequest, which extends the ServletRequest interface.

The HttpServletRequest interfaces allows access to the HTTP-specific content of the request, like request HTTP method, HTTP headers, cookies, session information, and so on. Because it extends ServletRequest, all methods defined in ServletRequest are also available in HttpServletRequest objects.

The concrete implementation and instantiation of the ServletRequest and HttpServletRequest interfaces are the responsibility of the servlet container. Tomcat, for example, implements HttpServletRequest interface in the org.apache.catalina.connector.Request class, and Tomcat supplies instances of that class internally to all servlets to conform to Servlet API.

■ **Note** While developing servlets, developers will only have to deal with the ServletRequest and HttpServletRequest interfaces as defined by Servlet API. The concrete implementations of these interfaces will be used by underlying servlet container (e.g., Tomcat), but will not be exposed in any servlet code.

ServletResponse and HttpServletResponse

The ServletResponse interface defines the methods to access the data that will be sent back to the client by the servlet container. Two main methods defined on the ServletResponse interface are getOutputStream() and getWriter().

Method getOutputStream() returns the instance of ServletOutputStream, which servlet developers can use to write binary content to, which is sent back to server. Using this method, you can implement servlets that trigger downloads of binary files like music, video, or documents

Method getWriter() returns the instance of PrintWriter, which developers can write text-content to, which the servlet container will send back to the client to be rendered. Using this method, you can write the HTML content to the returned PrintWriter in the servlet class.

Just like ServletRequest, this interface is protocol independent, and it's the responsibility of concrete implementations to use the required protocol details. Because HTTP is the main target protocol for servlets, Servlet API defines HttpServletResponse interface that in turn defines the methods to access information that will be sent to the client over HTTP protocol, including methods to add headers, cookies, status codes, and other HTTP-specific data to the response that will be sent to the client.

The GenericServlet and HttpServlet Classes

The two main classes that extend the servlet architecture are the GenericServlet and HttpServlet classes. The HttpServlet class is extended from GenericServlet, which in turn implements the Servlet interface. When developing your own servlets, you'll most likely extend one of these two classes.

When extending the GenericServlet class, you must implement the service() method. The GenericServlet.service() method has been defined as an abstract method to force you to follow this framework. The service() method prototype is defined as follows:

```
public abstract void service(ServletRequest request, ServletResponse response) throws↵
  ServletException, IOException;
```

The two parameters that are passed to the service() method are ServletRequest and ServletResponse objects. The ServletRequest object holds the information that is being sent to the servlet, and the ServletResponse object is where you place the data you want to send back to the client.

In contrast to the GenericServlet, when you extend HttpServlet, you don't usually implement the service() method. The HttpServlet class has already implemented the service() method for you. The following prototype contains the HttpServlet.service() method signature:

```
protected void service(HttpServletRequest request, HttpServletResponse response) throws↵
  ServletException, IOException;
```

When the HttpServlet.service() method is invoked, it reads the method type stored in the request and uses this value to determine which HTTP-specific methods to invoke. These are the methods that you want to override. If the method type is GET, it calls doGet(). If the method type is POST, it calls doPost(). Although the service() method has five other method types associated with it, we are focusing on the doGet() and doPost() methods. Table 3-1 shows all HTTP methods and the corresponding methods of HttpServlet class that you need to override.

Table 3-1. HttpServlet Class Methods That Correspond to the HTTP Request Methods

HTTP Method	HttpServlet class Method	Recommended Usage
GET	doGet(HttpServletRequest, HttpServletResponse)	Used to read resources; should never change data.
POST	doPost(HttpServletRequest, HttpServletResponse)	Creates new resources; for example, submitting form to create new user.
PUT	doPut(HttpServletRequest, HttpServletResponse)	Updates the resources; for example, submitting the form to update user details.
DELETE	doDelete(HttpServletRequest, HttpServletResponse)	Deletes the resource; should be used for data removal if available.
HEAD	doHead(HttpServletRequest, HttpServletResponse)	Similarly to GET, it's used to load the resource, but the response contains only meta data, *never* the body of the resource.

HTTP Method	HttpServlet class Method	Recommended Usage
OPTIONS	doOptions(HttpServletRequest, HttpServletResponse)	Returns the communications options to the client.
TRACE	doTrace(HttpServletRequest, HttpServletResponse)	Used for diagnostics where server response contains the same body as the request; enriched with headers for diagnostics.

■ **Note** HTML forms and links that generate requests from the browsers support only GET and POST methods consistently, so you will most likely override doGet(…) and doPost(…) methods in most cases.

You may have noticed the different request/response types in the service() method signature of the HttpServlet as opposed to the GenericServlet class. The HttpServletRequest and HttpServletResponse classes are just extensions of ServletRequest and ServletResponse with HTTP-specific information stored in them.

The HttpServlet.service() method implementation is a convenient way to control access to your servlets in the code. For example, servlets that delete data from the database should always be accessed using the DELETE method, but because browsers only support GET and POST operations, the POST method should be used instead. If the DELETE operation is exposed using the doGet() and GET method, search engine crawlers, which follow all links on a web page using GET method, would be able to delete the data by simply visiting the link. But if you extend HttpServlet to implement your data-deleting servlet, you can leave doGet() method unimplemented, and search engine crawlers will not be able to access it.

Let's take a look again at the HelloWorldServlet example from Chapter 2, and improve it by configuring the text displayed as a servlet init parameter, paying attention to the details we covered in this chapter. Listing 3-1 shows the HelloWorldServlet code.

Listing 3-1. Improved HelloWorldServlet, with Configurable Text Displayed on the Web Page

```
package com.apress.apachetomcat7.chapter2;

import javax.servlet.*;
import javax.servlet.http.*;
import java.io.*;

public class HelloWorldServlet extends HttpServlet {          #1
    private String message;
    public void init(ServletConfig config) throws ServletException {     #2
        super.init(config);
        this.message = config.getInitParameter("message");     #3
    }

    public void doGet(HttpServletRequest request, HttpServletResponse response) #4
    throws IOException, ServletException
```

```
    {
        response.setContentType("text/html");
        PrintWriter out = response.getWriter();                          #5
        out.println("<html>");
        out.println("<head>");
        out.println("<title>" + this.message + "</title>");              #6
        out.println("</head>");
        out.println("<body>");
        out.println("<h1>Hello World!</h1>");
        out.println("</body>");
        out.println("</html>");
    }
}
```

We implemented HelloWorldServlet by extending HttpServlet class (#1), and our code does not implement any of the service() or destroy() methods defined in javax.servlet.Servlet interface. That's because these methods are conveniently implemented in the HttpServlet class (and its super class GenericServlet), so we don't have to worry about them.

We did, however, override Servlet.init(ServletConfig) method (#2), which gives us access to ServletConfig argument and all initialization parameters out of the box. We simply store the initialization parameter with name "message" to private String field message (#3).

However, in case we needed to write destruction code for our servlet, we can easily override Servlet.destroy() method and implement it as required. That will most likely be the case when you're using heavy resources in your servlet (such are database connections for example), so you want to make sure that they are properly released after use. You can read more about database resources used in Tomcat in Chapter 13.

You can do the same with Servlet.service(..) method, override and implement it as per your requirements. However, you will rarely require doing that, because HttpServlet provides very useful and convenient implementation of the Servlet.service(..) method, which invokes the separate Java method based on the HTTP method used to instantiate request. By default, Java methods for each HTTP method are implemented to simply send the HTTP status code 405 (Method not allowed) to the client for every HTTP method. Based on the functionality of the servlet, you can extend one or more of these methods in your servlet code.

In our example, we overrode the doGet(..) method, which means that all GET HTTP request will be processed by this method (#4). Because doGet(..) is the only method we extended, requests using any other HTTP method to this servlet will result in the HTTP status code 405, informing the client that the HTTP method is not allowed.

To send the text message back to the client, we are using the HttpServletResponse.getPrintWriter() method to get hold of the PrintWriter instance (#5), which we used to write HTML string content. The content sent back and rendered in the browser includes the message field stored from the initialization parameter (#6).

Configuring a Servlet in a Servlet Container

In order to register our servlet with the servlet container, we need to supply the web deployment descriptor: an XML configuration file named web.xml. This file must be stored in the WEB-INF/ directory of your web application.

Listing 3-2 shows the web deployment descriptor for our HelloWorldServlet example.

Listing 3-2. HelloWorldServlet Configuration in the web.xml File

```xml
<?xml version="1.0" encoding="ISO-8859-1"?>
<web-app xmlns="http://java.sun.com/xml/ns/javaee"
         xmlns:xsi="http://www.w3.org/2001/XMLSchema-instance"
         xsi:schemaLocation="http://java.sun.com/xml/ns/javaee
http://java.sun.com/xml/ns/javaee/web-app_3_0.xsd" version="3.0">      #1

    <display-name>Chapter 2</display-name>                             #2
    <description>Apress demo</description>                             #3

    <servlet>                                                          #4
        <servlet-name>helloworld</servlet-name>                       #5
        <servlet-class>                                               #6
            com.apress.apachetomcat7.chapter2.HelloWorldServlet
        </servlet-class>
        <init-param>                                                  #7
            <param-name>message</param-name>                          #8
            <param-value>Hello Universe!</param-value>                #9
        </init-param>
    </servlet>

    <servlet-mapping>                                                  #10
        <servlet-name>helloworld</servlet-name>                       #11
        <url-pattern>/hello.html</url-pattern>                        #12
    </servlet-mapping>

</web-app>
```

The root element of the web.xml file is the <webapp> XML element (#1), which contains the schema and namespace definition for the configuration, as well as the version of the Java servlet specification to which our servlet conforms. For this example, and all examples throughout this book, we will be using the latest Servlet API version 3.0.

The sub-element <display-name> specifies the name the web application (#2). Similarly, we define the description of the application using the <description> sub element (#3).

The servlet itself is configured using <servlet> XML element (#4). This element requires two sub-elements configured: <servlet-name> and <servlet-class>. The element <servlet-name> defines the name of the servlet, and it must be unique within the web application (#5). <servlet-class> is the fully qualified name of the servlet implementation class (#6). The class specified must implement javax.servlet.Servlet interface.

Additionally, in case your servlet expects any initialization parameters, you will specify them as sub-elements of <servlet> element. Our improved HelloWorldServlet requires one init parameter, and we have to specify it here. Each init parameter has to be configured using <init-param> element (#7), with two sub-elements. The name of the parameter is specified using <param-name> XML element (#8) and its value using <param-value> element (#9). The parameter name must match the name expected by the servlet class, in our case init parameter name should be "message."

Finally, we need to configure the URLs that will be mapped to this servlet, using the <servlet-mapping> element (#10). Its sub-element <servlet-name> must reference existing servlet name, as defined previously (#11).

The URL pattern to match the servlet to is configured using <url-pattern> element (#12). URL pattern configuration can use wildcard characters—for example /admin/* or *.html.

> ▪ **Note** You can configure multiple servlets in a single web.xml file, mapped to different URLs. In such a case, multiple servlets would make a web application deployed in a single context in Tomcat.

And that's all: you can now package your servlet with its web.xml configuration and deploy it to Tomcat.

> ▪ **Note** You can find more details about web.xml configuration options in the Appendix B of this book.

Servlet API 3.0

Version 3 of the Java Servlet specification was released in December 2009. In addition to the evolution and enhancement of existing features, Servlet API 3.0 brought a few revolutionary changes to the servlet development, namely annotation support for easier configuration, plug-ability using web fragments, and asynchronous servlets support.

Annotation Configuration Support

Servlet API 3.0 allows us to configure the servlet details using annotations, instead of the using XML in web deployment descriptor.

Let's take a look how we can add configuration annotations to our HelloWorldServlet example. Listing 3-3 shows the changes made to the HelloWorldServlet.

Listing 3-3. Using Servlet API 3.0 Annotations to Configure Servlet Class

```
import java.io.*;
import javax.servlet.*;
import javax.servlet.annotation.*;
import javax.servlet.http.*;

@WebServlet(                                                        #1
        name = "helloWorldServlet",                                #2
        urlPatterns = {"/hello.html"},                             #3
        initParams = {                                             #4
                @WebInitParam(name="message", value="Hello Universe!")  #5
        }
)
```

```
public class HelloWorldServlet extends HttpServlet {
        //same as in previous listing, omitted for clarity
}
```

The servlet code in Listing 3-3 stayed exactly the same; no changes to any of the methods have been made. We did, however, add @WebServlet annotation on the class level (#1). This annotation is a new addition to the Servlet API 3.0, and it represents the servlet class.

■ **Note** In order to use the Servlet API 3.0 annotations in your code, you will need to import the javax.servlet.annotation.* package in the Java file header.

Parameters of @WebServlet annotation closely match the parameters we configured in web.xml previously:

- Parameter name specifies the servlet name (#2), the same configuration we defined using the <servlet-name> XML element in web.xml.

- Parameter urlPattern matches the <url-mapping> XML element in web.xml, and contains an array of URL patterns that this servlet maps to (#3).

- Finally, initParams parameter defines the initialization parameters for the servlet, which we previously configured using <init-param> XML element (#4). The value of initParams parameter is the array of @WebInitParam annotations (#5), each of which has name and value parameters, corresponding to the <param-name> and <param-value> elements. For our example, we need to configure one init parameter with name message, as before.

So, we managed to configure our servlet in the servlet class, using Servlet API annotations. But what happened to web.xml file? Because the servlet name, init parameters, and servlet mapping are all configured in code already, we can remove all XML elements that are already configured using annotations. Listing 3-4 shows the new web.xml file.

Listing 3-4. *Web.xml File Without Servlet Configuration Now Configured Using Annotations*

```
<web-app xmlns="http://java.sun.com/xml/ns/javaee"
         xmlns:xsi="http://www.w3.org/2001/XMLSchema-instance"
         xsi:schemaLocation="http://java.sun.com/xml/ns/javaee↵
 http://java.sun.com/xml/ns/javaee/web-app_3_0.xsd" version="3.0">

    <display-name>Chapter 2</display-name>
    <description>Apress demo</description>

    <metadata-complete>false</metadata-complete>                    #1

</web-app>
```

The only configuration left in the web.xml file from before are application name and description, which apply to the entire web application context. All servlet-specific configurations have disappeared.

There is one additional XML element we added to web.xml, <metadata-complete> (#1). This element tells the servlet container that the servlet configuration in this web.xml file is not complete, and that there is one or more servlets that are configured using Servlet API 3.0 annotations. The servlet container will then scan the classpath of the web application (including /WEB-INF/classes and /WEB-INF/lib directories) for any classes annotated with @WebServlet annotation, and load and configure every such class as servlet.

■ **Note** Make sure you include the <metadata-complete> element with the value false to your web.xml configuration when using Servlet API 3.0 annotations, as that will tell Tomcat to scan the classpath for the annotated classes. If you omit this element, the annotated classes will not be discovered, and the servlet configuration will not work.

You can now package the web application and deploy it in the usual manner, and it will be working just as before.

Using annotations to configure your servlets will always have its followers and enemies. While it makes development and configuration easier and more efficient, one could argue that it makes code harder to maintain and upgrade, due to the configuration being scattered across multiple classes and libraries, instead of a centralized configuration web.xml file.

We tried to use the annotation configuration in few examples throughout the book, so you can get an idea how is this new feature used in practice. At the same time, we used the old-style web.xml configuration for some examples, when it was easier to illustrate the learning point of the example with one centralized configuration file.

■ **Note** Servlet API 3.0 contains more annotation options for configuration—for example, for servlet filters or servlet listeners. You can find examples of such configuration in the relevant chapters of this book.

Both XML and annotation-based configurations are here to stay in servlet development, and you should embrace the one that feels more natural to you. The annotation-based approach is perhaps more convenient for Java developers, as you will be writing more Java code, and less XML configuration. It's also good for the early stages of project development and prototyping. For large projects, with large numbers of servlets, XML configuration gives the benefit of central configuration file, so it's easy to understand the bigger picture of the application servlet's organization and mapping. You would have to check many servlet classes in case annotation-based configuration. Finally, if your applications contain a lot of Java classes (large code base or a lot of dependent libraries in /WEB-INF/lib directory), the classpath scanning for servlet annotations may become slow, affecting the start-up time of your application. In such cases, you should consider XML configuration as well.

Web Fragments

We have seen that web.xml is no longer required for most of the servlet configuration. However, sometimes it can be beneficial to use parts of XML configuration, when managing multiple extensions from different vendors, or control versions of different servlet components deployed in production. In servlets using earlier Servlet API, you had to put configuration for all such components in a web.xml. As a result, web.xml would usually grow too big, and become hard to maintain and read.

With Servlet API 3.0, you don't have to put all such configuration in single web.xml file anymore— you can use web fragments.

Web fragments are partial XML servlet configurations saved in a file /META-INF/web-fragment.xml on a web applications classpath (in /WEB-INF/classes/META-INF directory or in a META-INF directory of any jar library located in a WEB-INF/lib directory). Web fragments can contain any part of the standard web.xml configuration, including any components usually configured in web.xml file, including servlets, filters, and listeners.

Asynchronous Servlet Support

Asynchronous request processing is beyond the scope of this book, so we won't go into much detail about this new feature of Servlet API. The key point of asynchronous request processing is the javax.servlet.AsyncContext interface, which defines the execution context for the asynchronous request execution. To start asynchronous request processing, you have to call a new method defined in ServletRequest interface:

```
public AsyncContext startAsync(ServletRequest req, ServletResponse res)
```

You can then invoke operations in the new thread, by invoking AsyncContext.start(Runnable), and use that to keep the HTTP connection open and push the results to the browser once processing is completed, without blocking the original request.

For more details about asynchronous support in Servlet API 3.0, you can read Oracle's tutorial at http://blogs.oracle.com/enterprisetechtips/entry/asynchronous_support_in_servlet_3.

We covered a lot about servlets, the main components of Java web applications deployed on Tomcat. In the next section, we'll take a look at the other key technology used with Java web applications: JSP.

Java Server Pages

Java Server Pages (JSPs) are a simple but powerful technology used most often to generate dynamic HTML on the server side. They are a direct extension of Java servlets with the purpose of allowing the developer to embed Java logic directly into a requested document. Using JSP Expression Language, you can develop powerful dynamic web pages powered by Java servlets without any Java code. A JSP document must end with a .jsp extension.

The following code snippet contains a simple example of a JSP file:

```
<HTML>
<BODY>
<% out.println("HELLO JSP READER"); %>
</BODY>
</HTML>
```

You can see that this document looks like any other HTML document, with a non-HTML block containing Java code. The source code is stored in a file called hello.jsp and copied to the document directory of the web application that this JSP will be deployed to. When a request is made for this document, the server recognizes the `.jsp` extension and realizes that special handling is required. The JSP is then passed off to the JSP engine, which is just another servlet that is mapped to the extension `.jsp`, for processing.

■ **Note** The default servlet for handling JSP pages is located in the class `org.apache.jasper.servlet.JspServlet`, and configured in the `CATALINA_HOME/conf/web.xml` file.

Lifecycle of Java Server Pages

JSP page is processed in several phases during its lifecycle. Table 3-2 describes all the phases of the JSP lifecycle.

Table 3-2. Lifecycles of JSP lifecycle

JSP Phase	Description
Translation	The JSP file is translated to the Java servlet source. The generated servlet implements additional interface javax.servlet.jsp.HttpJspPage, which defines the JSP-generated servlet lifecycle.
Compilation	Generated Servlet class is compiled using a Java compiler.
Loading	Compiled servlet class is loaded in memory.
Instantiation	The JSP servlet is instantiated by the servlet container.
Initialization	The JSP servlet is initialized, using the JSP API standard HttpJspPage.jspInit(..) method.
Servicing Request	Service is servicing requests by executing the HttpJspPage._jspService() method.
Destruction	The JSP-generated servlet is destroyed, using the HttpJspPage.jspDestroy(..) method.

The first time the file is requested, it is translated into a servlet and then compiled into a servlet class that is loaded into resident memory. The JSP page then becomes a standard Java servlet, and it goes through the same lifecycle steps as we described in the previous section: the servlet is instantiated, initialized, and it finally starts to service the client requests until it's destroyed. After the loaded JSP servlet services each request, the output is sent back to the requesting client.

The servlet generated from the JSP file implements `javax.servlet.jsp.HttpJspPage` interface, which is responsible for its lifecycle. This interface is very similar to the servlet lifecycle, but with JSP-specific features. The lifecycle methods of the `HttpJspPage` interface correspond with the `Servlet` interface methods: `HttpJspPage.jspInit(..)` for jsp servlet initialization, `HttpJspPage.jspService(..)` for request servicing, and `HttpJspPage.jspDestroy(..)` for jsp servlet destruction.

On all subsequent requests, the server checks to see whether the original .jsp source file has changed. If it has not changed, the server invokes the previously compiled servlet object, skipping the translation and compilation phases. If the source has changed, however, the JSP engine re-parses the JSP source, going to all phases of the JSP lifecycle. Figure 3-2 illustrates these steps.

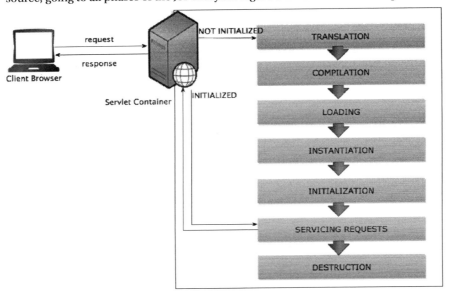

Figure 3-2. The steps of a JSP request

■ **Note** An essential point to remember about JSPs is that they are just servlets that are created from a combination of HTML and Java source. Therefore, they have the same resources and functionality of a servlet.

The Components of a Java Server Pages

In this section, we are going to talk about the components of JSP, including directives, JSP scripting, implicit objects, and JSP standard actions. We are going to use most of the JSP components described here in the examples throughout the book. If you are unsure about any JSP component used later in the book, you can use the following sections as a reference and a reminder.

If you need a more in-depth reference about JSP features, I suggest you pick up *Pro JSP 2* by Simon Brown, Sam Dalton, Sing Li, and Daniel Jepp (Apress, 2005)

JSP Directives

JSP directives are JSP elements that provide global information about a JSP page. An example would be a directive that included a list of Java classes to be imported into a JSP. The syntax of a JSP directive is as follows:

```
<%@ directive {attribute="value"} %>
```

Three possible directives are currently defined by the JSP specification: page, include, and taglib. Each of these directives is defined in the following sections.

The page Directive

The page directive defines information that globally affects the JSP containing the directive. The syntax of a JSP directive is

```
<%@ page {attribute="value"} %>
```

Typical usage includes import attribute, which imports the specified Java classes or packages to be used elsewhere in the JSP page (similar to importing Java classes or packages in the Java source file header). An example page directive that imports the java.util package is included in the following code snippet:

```
<%@ page import="java.util.*" %>
```

Table 3-3 defines all available attributes for the page directive.

***Table 3-3.** The Attributes for the page Directive*

Attribute	Definition
language="scriptingLanguage"	Tells the server which language will be used to compile the JSP file. (Java is currently the only available JSP language.)
extends="className"	Defines the parent class from which the JSP will extend.
import="importList"	Defines the list of Java packages that will be imported into this JSP. It will be a comma-separated list of package names.
session="true|false"	Determines whether the session data will be available to this page. The default is true.
buffer="none|size in kb"	Determines whether the output stream is buffered. The default value is 8KB.
autoFlush="true|false"	Determines whether the output buffer will be flushed automatically, or whether it will throw an exception when the buffer is full. The default is true.

Attribute	Definition
isThreadSafe="true|false"	Tells the JSP engine that this page can service multiple requests at one time. By default, this value is true. If this attribute is set to false, the SingleThreadModel is used.
info="text"	Represents information about the JSP page that can be accessed by invoking the page's Servlet.getServletInfo() method.
errorPage="error_url"	Represents the relative URL to a JSP that will handle JSP exceptions.
isErrorPage="true|false"	States whether the JSP is an errorPage. The default is false.
contentType="ctinfo"	Represents the MIME type and character set of the response sent to the client.

The include Directive

The include directive is used to insert text and/or code at JSP translation time. The syntax of the include directive is shown in the following code snippet:

```
<%@ include file="relativeURLOfTheFile" %>
```

The file attribute contains the path of the file to be included relative to the current JSP file. The included file can reference a file with HTML content, or it can reference a JSP file, which is evaluated at translation time. This resource referenced by the file attribute must be local to the web application that contains the include directive. Typically, you would use this directive to include reusable page snippets, like in the following example:

```
<%@ include file="header.jsp" %>
```

■ **Note** Because the include directive is evaluated at translation time, this included text is evaluated only once. This implies that, if the include resource changes, these changes are not reflected until the JSP/servlet container is restarted.

The taglib Directive

The taglib directive states that the including page uses a custom tag library, uniquely identified by a URI and associated with a prefix that distinguishes custom tags for each separate tag library. The syntax of the taglib directive is as follows:

```
<%@ taglib uri="tagLibraryURI" prefix="tagPrefix" %>
```

The attribute uri specifies the URI of the tag library, which must exist on the web applications classpath. Parameter prefix is used to specify the library in the JSP code. In the examples throughout the book, we are using JSP Standard Tag Library a lot.

JSP Standard Tag Library (JSTL) contains the core functionality often used on JSP pages. It has support for common programming patterns, like conditional statement (if-then-else), loop iterations, internationalization, and even SQL statements. The current version of JSTL is 1.2, and it can be downloaded from the JSTP project web site (http://jstl.java.net/).

To use JSTL, you will have to package the jstl.jar library file to your web applications WEB-INF/lib directory. Each JSP file where you want to use JSTL tags should contain a taglib directive like the code snippet here:

```
<%@ taglib prefix="c" uri="http://java.sun.com/jsp/jstl/core" %>
```

Here, we're importing the core JSTL tag library with unique URI that represents the JSTL (and resolves to JSTL class library on our classpath), and we are configuring prefix c, which is commonly used prefix for core JSTL library.

Now we can add JSTL tags to your JSP code. For example, to have if-then conditional if JSP, we can use the <c:if> tag, like this:

```
<c:if test="${5 > 3}"/>
    5 is greater then 3
</if>
```

To iterate through a collection of objects, we can use the <c:forEach> tag, like this:

```
<c:forEach items="${users}" var="u">
    User: ${u.username}
</c:forEach>
```

The syntax element starting with dollar sign and enclosed in curly brackets (${something}) are JSP Expression Language constructs. We will explain JSP Expression Language in the following sections of this chapter.

JSP Scripting

Scripting is a JSP mechanism for directly embedding Java code fragments into an HTML page. Three scripting language components are involved in JSP scripting: declarations, expressions, and scriptlets. Each of these components has its appropriate location in the generated servlet. In this section, we look at each of these components.

Declarations

JSP declarations are used to define Java variables and methods in a JSP. A JSP declaration must be a complete declarative statement.

JSP declarations are initialized when the JSP page is first loaded. After the declarations have been initialized, they are available to other declarations, expressions, and scriptlets within the same JSP. The syntax for a JSP declaration is:

```
<%! declaration %>
```

A sample variable declaration using this syntax is declared here:

```
<%! String name = new String("BOB"); %>
```

A sample method declaration using the same syntax is declared here:

```
<%! public String getName() { return name; } %>
```

Expressions

JSP expressions are JSP components whose text, upon evaluation by the container, is replaced with the resulting value of the container evaluation.

JSP expressions are evaluated at request time, with the result being inserted at the expression's referenced position in the .jsp file. If the resulting expression cannot be converted to a string, a translation time error occurs. If the conversion to a string cannot be detected during translation, a ClassCastException is thrown at request time. The syntax of a JSP expression is:

```
<%= expression %>
```

A code snippet containing a JSP expression is shown here:

```
Hello <B><%= getName() %></B>
```

A sample JSP document containing a JSP expression is listed in the following code snippet:

```
<HTML>
<BODY>

<%! public String getName() { return "Bob"; } %>

Hello <B><%= getName() %></B>

</BODY>
</HTML>
```

JSP Expression Language (EL)

JSP Expression Language (EL) is the powerful feature of JSP introduced with version 2.0. It enables developers to easily access Java objects available to the current JSP page.

These objects can exists in one of the four scopes:

- pageScope: Maps current page attributes names to their values

- requestScope: maps HttpServletRequest attributes names to their values

- sessionScope: maps session attributes names to their values

- applicationScope: maps ServletContext attributes names to their values

For example, if you have a "username" attribute in the HttpServletRequest, you can render it on the current page using the following syntax:

```
${requestScope .username}
```

You can also access properties of the rich objects stored as attributes, if they conform to the JavaBean convention.

JavaBean is the class that, for every field property, contains accessor methods, so-called getters and setters. Here is an example of User class, which is JavaBean:

```
public class User implements Serializable{
    private String username;

    public String getUserame(){
```

```
        return username; //getter
    }
    public void setUsername(String username){
        this.username = username; //setter
    }
}
```

If you have an User object stored as a request attribute, with name "user," you can access it's properties simply by referencing them by name, with the dot(.) as separator, like this:

```
${user.username}
```

The same approach can be applied for nested properties as well:

```
${user.address.city}
```

In addition to any scoped attributes, EL gives developers access to common properties of the HttpServletRequest directly. Table 3-4 shows the available implicit variables available in JSP EL expressions.

Table 3-4. *Implicit Objects Available in JSP EL Expressions*

EL Expression	Result
${param.NAME}	Returns a single string request parameter with the name NAME.
${paramValues.NAME}	Returns an array of all values for the request parameter NAME.
${header.NAME}	Returns the string value of the request header with the name NAME.
${headerValues.NAME}	Returns the array of the request headers with the name NAME.
${cookie.NAME}	Returns the java.servlet.http.Cookie object with the name NAME from the current request.

You can also perform arithmetic and boolean operations in JSP EL, so the following examples are EL-valid syntax:

- ${1+2} outputs value 3

- ${requestScope.username == sessionScope.loggedinuser} outputs true/false

- ${requestScope.count > 5} true/false

- ${!empty param.product_id} checks if the request parameter with name "product_id" exists, outputs true/false

You can use EL expressions to output any value in the JSP page, and as part of other JSP components.

EL expressions are used in JSP tags, like we saw in the JSTL example earlier in this chapter. To compare values using EL in the if-then conditional statement, you will use <c:if> standard JSP tag, as shown here:

```
<c:if test="${empty param.productId}">
        Please select a product!
</c:if>
```

Scriptlets

Scriptlets are the JSP components that bring all the JSP elements together. They can contain almost any coding statements that are valid for the language referenced in the language directive. They are executed at request time, and they can make use of all of the JSP components. The syntax for a scriptlet is as follows:

```
<% scriptlet source %>
```

With the first request of a JSP containing scripting code, the JSP is converted to servlet code and then compiled and loaded into resident memory. The actual source code, which is found between scriptlet tags <% ... %>, is placed into the generated service() method that was created by the JSP compiler. The following code snippet contains a simple JSP that uses a scripting element to print the text "Hello Bob" to the requesting client:

```
<HTML>
<BODY>

<% out.println("Hello Bob"); %>

</BODY>
</HTML>
```

Implicit Objects

As a JSP developer, you have implicit access to certain objects that are available for use in all JSP documents. These objects are parsed by the JSP engine and inserted into the generated servlet as if you defined them yourself.

out

The implicit out object represents a JspWriter, which is derived from a java.io.Writer that provides a stream back to the requesting client. The most common method of this object is the out.println() method, which prints text to be displayed in the client's browser. Listing 3-5 provides an example using the implicit out object.

Listing 3-5. The Source Code of out.jsp

```
<%@ page errorPage="errorpage.jsp" %>

<html>
    <head>
        <title>Use Out</title>
    </head>
    <body>
        <%
```

```
        // Print a  simple message using the implicit out object.
        out.println("<center><b>Hello Bob!</b></center>");
        %>
    </body>
</html>
```

To execute this example, copy this file to the CATALINA_HOME/webapps/apress/ directory and then open your browser to the following URL:

```
http://localhost:8080/apress/out.jsp
```

You should see a page with the "Hello Bob!" text displayed.

request

This object represents the javax.servlet.http.HttpServletRequest object, which we discussed earlier. The request object is associated with every HTTP request.

One of the more common uses for the request object is to access request parameters. You can do this by calling the request object's getParameter() method with the parameter name you are seeking. It returns a string with the value matching the named parameter. An example using the implicit request object can be found in Listing 3-6.

Listing 3-6. The Source Code of request.jsp

```
<%@ page errorPage="errorpage.jsp" %>

<html>
    <head>
        <title>UseRequest</title>
    </head>
    <body>
        <%
        out.println("<b>Welcome: "+
        request.getParameter("user") + "</b>");
        %>
    </body>
</html>
```

You can see that this JSP calls the request.getParameter() method passing in the parameter user. This looks for the key user in the parameter list and returns the value, if it is found. Enter the following URL into your browser to see the results from this page:

```
http://localhost:8080/apress/request.jsp?user=Bob
```

response

The implicit response object represents the javax.servlet.http.HttpServletResponse object. The response object is used to pass data back to the requesting client. This implicit object provides you with all of the functionality of the HttpServletResponse, just as if you were executing in a servlet. One of the more common uses for the response object is writing HTML output back to the client browser; however, the JSP API already provides access to a stream back to the client using the implicit out object.

session

The implicit `session` object represents the `javax.servlet.http.HttpSession` object, which is used to store objects in between client requests providing an almost stateful HTTP interactivity. You can read more about user sessions in Chapter 5.

application

The `application` object represents the `javax.servlet.ServletContext`, and it is most often used to access objects that are stored in the `ServletContext` to be shared between web components. It is an agreed place to share objects between JSPs and servlets. In the following example, we use the application object to store and access our application's specific information. An example using the application object can be found later in this chapter in the section "Understanding ServletContext."

config

The implicit `config` object holds a reference to the `ServletConfig`, which contains configuration information about the JSP/servlet engine containing the web application in which this JSP resides.

page

The page object contains a reference to the current instance of the JSP being accessed. You use the page object just as you would `this` object in standard Java code: to reference the current instance of the generated servlet representing this JSP.

Standard Actions

JSP standard actions are predefined custom tags that can be used to easily encapsulate common actions. Six standard actions are available to JSP developers. Each group is defined and used in the following sections.

<jsp:include>

The `<jsp:include>` standard action provides a method for including additional static and dynamic web components in a JSP. The syntax for this action is as follows:

```
<jsp:include page="urlSpec" flush="true">
        <jsp:param name="name" value="value"/>
</jsp:include>
```

The nested `<jsp:param>` action is used to provide parameters and values to the JSP standard actions.

■ **Note** It is important to note the difference between the `include` directive and the `include` standard action. The directive is evaluated only once, at translation time, whereas the standard action is evaluated with every request.

This syntax description does a request-time inclusion of a URL that is passed an optional list of param sub-elements that are used to argument the request.

<jsp:forward>>

The `<jsp:forward>` standard action enables the JSP engine to execute a run-time dispatch of the current request to another resource existing in the current web application, including static resources, servlets, or JSPs. The appearance of `<jsp:forward>` effectively terminates the execution of the current JSP.

A `<jsp:forward>` action can contain nested `<jsp:param>` action, which act as parameters that are forwarded to the targeted resource. The syntax of the `<jsp:forward>` action is as follows:

```
<jsp:forward page="relativeURL">
        <jsp:param name="name" value="value"/>
</jsp:forward>
```

This action contains a single attribute, page, which represents the relative URL of the target of the forward.

Relationship Between Servlets and ServletContext

We've seen that it's possible to configure and deploy multiple servlets within the same web application (for example, by configuring multiple `<servlet>` elements in the web.xml file).

From the previous chapters we know that each web application is represented in a single context within servlet container, like Tomcat. In Servlet API, context is defined using javax.servlet.ServletContext interface. Servlets deployed in the same web application (same context), can share the information between them using the shared ServletContext object. ServletContext maintains the collection attributes that can be accessed by any servlet belonging to the same ServletContext.

You can access a ServletContext object from the underlying ServletConfig object in your servlet. If your servlet extends the convenient HttpServlet class, like all our examples, or the GenericServlet class, then you can get the ServletContext instance by using following code snippet:

```
ServletContext servletContext = getServletConfig().getServletContext();
```

The getServletConfig() method is conveniently available in the GenericServlet class, which HttpServlet extends. For convenience, the GenericServlet class offers the method getServletContext(), which you can use to get the underlying ServletContext instance directly. We will use this convenient method in our examples that follow.

Let's take an example of two servlets, servlet1 and servlet 2, deployed within the same context, apress. If one of the servlets sets the attribute on its ServletContext object, the same attribute will be available to the other servlet as well.

Servlet1 sets the attribute of the ServletContext object:

```
/apress/servlet1: getServletContext().setAttribute("foo", "bar");
```

Servlet2 reads the attribute with the same name from the same underlying ServletContext:

```
/apress/servlet2: getServletContext().setAttribute("foo");//equals bar
```

The value read by the servlet2 will be "bar," matching the value set by the servlet1.

■ **Note** Objects stored in the `ServletContext` remain available for the life of the Web application.

Using `ServletContext` attributes, servlets from the same context can communicate between each other, by sharing the same `ServletContext` instance. Any servlet deployed in another context will get different `ServletContext` object, with the completely separate collection of attributes.

Let's, as another example, deploy another servlet to the same context instance (servlet3), but under a different context (let's say the context with path /av for example). If the server3 tries to access an attribute with the same name "foo," used by servlet1 and servlet2, the read value will be null.

`/av/servlet3: getServletContext().setAttribute("foo");//equals null`

Figure 3-3 illustrates relationship between servlets and the `ServletContext` objects that servlets belong to.

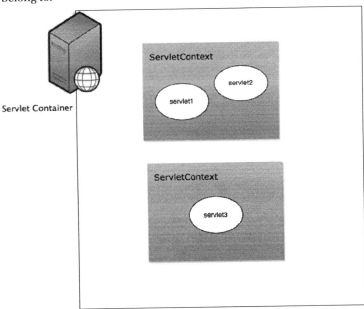

Figure 3-3. Servlets deployed in the same context share the same ServletContext instance

Summary

In the first part of this chapter, we explained Java servlet architecture, its lifecycle, and the details of servlet development and configuration. We also covered some of the new features of the Servlet API 3.0, which is the version supported by Apache Tomcat 7.

The second part of the chapter was dedicated to JSP. We described JSP architecture and its lifecycle within the servlet container. Next, we discussed a number of JSP components and syntax constructs that will be useful for the code samples throughout the book.

In the final section, we explained the relationship between web applications and the underlying ServletContext.

From the next chapter, we are going to dig into the Tomcat configuration and features, starting with the Tomcat's Manager web application in Chapter 4.

CHAPTER 4

Using Tomcat's Manager Web Application

In previous chapters, we have learned, among other things, how to deploy Java web applications to Apache Tomcat server. In our examples, we copied the directory or WAR file of the web application to Tomcat's /webapps directory, and started (or restarted) the server. However, in a production environment, it may be inconvenient to stop the running server with existing applications – that's where Tomcat's Manager web applications come in handy. Using Manager web application bundled with the Apache Tomcat distribution, you can deploy new applications, undeploy existing ones, and perform various other server management tasks from your browser.

In this chapter, we will:

- Define the Tomcat Manager web application, and discuss its usage

- Describe how to access the Tomcat Manager web application using its HTML web interface

- Explain the steps involved in accessing Manager's text-based interface using Ant scripts

What Is the Manager Web Application?

The Tomcat Manager web application is packaged with the Tomcat server. It is installed in the context path of /manager and provides the basic functionality to manage Web applications running in the Tomcat server. Some of the provided functionality includes the ability to install, start, stop, remove, and report web applications. Using Manager web application, you can easily deploy web applications on the local or remote server, without the need for FTP access to the server itself – all commands are invoked over HTTP protocol – using your favorite browser or the command line.

Tomcat Manager web application shipped with Apache Tomcat 7 and has a web-based interface, so it can be accessed via any browser and commands issues by simply clicking on the links in the web page.

Although a web-based browser is convenient and easy for human access, sometimes we need to manage web applications using external scripting tools. For that reason, commands to the Manager web application can be issued using the text-based interface.

For advanced access when security is critical, Manager web application can be accessed via Java Management Extension (JMX) proxy. JMX is a standard Java technology created for the management of applications, devices, or networks using standardized Java API. Because JMX is beyond the scope of this book, we won't be getting into the details of JMX access to Tomcat Manager web application. For more information about JMX, see the JMX home page at www.oracle.com/technetwork/java/javase/tech/javamanagement-140525.html. You can find details about JMX access to the Tomcat Manger application on Tomcat project's web site at http://tomcat.apache.org/tomcat-7.0-doc/manager-howto.html#Using_the_JMX_Proxy_Servlet.

Finally, accessing status information of the Tomcat instance is also part of the Manager web application. You can see basic server stats from Tomcat's status page, including the Tomcat version, Java version, OS version, and basic JVM memory and thread information.

For convenience and easier access and security management, these four ways of accessing Tomcat's Manager web application are accessible on separate contexts (all sub-contexts of the main /manager context). Table 4-1 shows the contexts for accessing different parts of Manager web application.

Table 4-1. Manager Web Application Components and Their Context Paths

Component	Context Path
HTML-based web application	/manager/html
Text-based script access	/manager/text
JMX proxy access	/manager/jmxproxy
Status request	/manager/status

In the following sections we will demonstrate issuing commands to the Manager web application using its HTML web-based interface, as well as using Ant script to access Manager web application from the command line.

Gaining Access to the Manager Web Application

Before you can use the Manager, you must set up a new user with the appropriate privileges to access the Manager web application. If you try to access any part of the Manager web application without setting up security privileges, you will be presented with a Tomcat error page, with standard HTML status code 403 - forbidden, as Figure 4-1 illustrates.

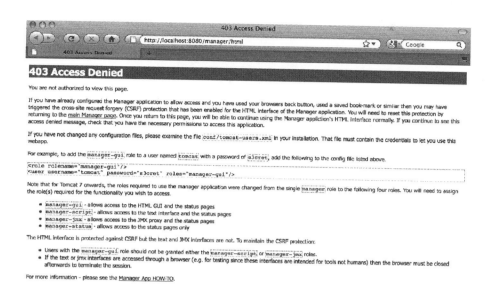

Figure 4-1. *Error page displayed if user tries to access Manager web application without required privileges*

Prior to Tomcat version 7, there was one user role required to access it, which was simply called "manager." From version 7, Tomcat introduced four different roles for accessing Manager web application – one for each component described in the previous section. Table 4-2 shows the roles required to access each of the components:

Table 4-2. *User Roles Required to Access Manager Web Application Components*

Component	Required User Role	Description
HTML -based web application	manager-gui	Allows access to HTML interface and status pages only.
Text-based script access	manager-script	Allows access to the text-based scripting engine and status pages only.
JMX proxy access	manager-jmx	Allows access via JMX proxy and status pages only.
Status request	manager-status	Allows access to status pages only.

> ■ **Note** For security reasons, a user shouldn't be given more than one of the following roles: `manager-gui`, `manager-script`, or `manager-jmx`.

> ■ **Note** Users with the role of `manager-gui`, `manager-script`, or `manager-jmx` will have access to status pages, even if they don't have the `manager-status` role set explicitly.

Now we need to create a couple of users with required roles, so we can demonstrate what can be done using Tomcat's Manager web application. Although we will cover Tomcat's security in more depth in Chapter 6, we will cover a few details now so we can proceed with Manager web application. Tomcat's users' usernames, passwords, and roles are stored in file `CATALINA_HOME/conf/tomcat-users.xml`. If you open this file in your favorite text editor, you will see that it's empty. It would be quite dangerous if Tomcat shipped with pre-configured users and roles – someone might, by mistake, use the default configuration in production, allowing management of any web application deployed to anyone who knows Tomcat's default user configuration.

So, we will have to add a couple of lines to `tomcat-users.xml`, so we can create users that can access Manager web application. Listing 4-1 shows the configuration that we will use in the examples that follow.

Listing 4-1. Tomcat Users Configuration, Allowing Access to the Manager Web Application

```
<?xml version='1.0' encoding='utf-8'?>
    <user username="managerGui" password="abc123" roles="manager-gui"/>      #1
    <user username="managerScript" password="abc123" roles="manager-script"/> #2
</tomcat-users>
```

In the line marked #1, we have defined a user with the username managerGui and the role of manager-gui. In the next line (#2), we created the user managerScript with the role of manager-script. User managerGui therefore can only access Manager web application's HTML interface, and user managerScript can only issue commands using a text-based script engine.

As we explained before, both users can access status pages.

Accessing the Manager Web Application Using Web Interface

The most common way to access Manager web application is using its rich web interface. Once you have a privileged user, you can go to the home page of the Manager web application by entering the following URL in your browser's address bar: `http://localhost:8080/manager/html`. Because Manager web application is a protected web page, you will be presented with the BASIC authentication login dialog box, similar to Figure 4-2.

Figure 4-2. Login page after requesting Apache Tomcat Status component

---

■ **Note** Tomcat uses the BASIC authentication mechanism for login, so the look and feel of the login box will depend of the OS and browser you are using. You will learn more about BASIC authentication in Chapter 6.

Now let's enter the username and password for the user we configured with the role of manager-gui. We will enter the username as managerGui, and the password as abc123, as per Listing 4-1.

After entering the correct credentials, you will see the Manager web application's home page. Figure 4-3 shows how this page looks in the browser. Note that, due to the screen size, part of the page is not visible in the figure.

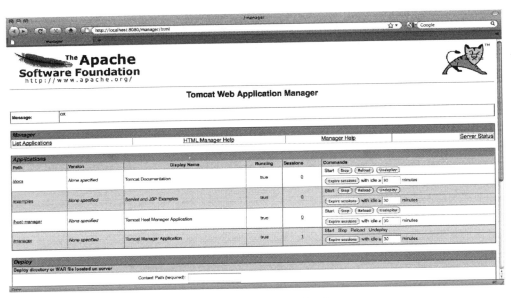

Figure 4-3. *Tomcat's Manager web application – web interface home page*

Just below the famous Tomcat logo and the page title in Figure 4-3, you can see the box titled "Message" and the text "OK." In this message box, you will see the response from Tomcat after every action. Each action or command performed by Tomcat's Manager web application will provide a response. If everything worked as expected, response message will be short – OK. In case of an error, the response message will be conveniently displayed in the message box for easy and quick troubleshooting of the problem. When using Tomcat' Manager web application, make sure to check the message box often, so you can see the relevant information about any operation you perform.

Below the message box, you will see the table with four links: the List Applications link, two Help page links, and the Server Status link.

The Help pages give useful information about Manager web application, and specifically its web interface. The Server Status link shows the Tomcat status page, as you'll see later in this chapter. Let's now explore the List Applications link in the Manager section.

Listing Deployed Web Applications

The List Application link performs the list command on the Tomcat instance. The command results in a list of all web applications currently deployed on the server. The list command is the invoked by default when using the web interface of the Tomcat Manager. So, when we loaded the Tomcat Manager's home page, we actually invoked list command. If you click the List Applications link, you will actually be invoking list command, resulting in the same page being reloaded in the browser. The message box will contain message the message "OK" to notify you that the list command has been invoked successfully.

You can see the result of the list command in the section Applications, which is just below the four links in the Manager section. All web applications shipped with Tomcat are in the list by default, including the Examples web application, which we used before, and the Manager web application – the one we are using to see this information. For each web application deployed to Tomcat, you can see its context path in the first column. The next two columns show the version and the display name of the web application. The Running column indicates whether it is running. The Sessions column shows the number of active sessions for the web application, so you can see how many users are currently accessing the application. Clicking the number in the Sessions column gives you more information about the specific application's sessions, which we will see in more detail later in this chapter. Finally, the Commands column shows all the commands you can perform on each single web application – all of which will be covered in more detail later in this chapter.

Below the Applications list, you'll see deploy box, with the HTML form for invoking the deploy command.

Now that we have access to the home page of the Manager web application, you can begin looking at the functionality that's associated with the Manager web application, which currently has the following available commands:

- List web application currently deploy on the server with the list command, as we've seen in this section

- Check server status, using the status command

- Deploy new web application to the Tomcat, using the deploy command

- Reload selected web application, using the reload command

- Check server sessions for each web application with the sessions command

- Start web application, using the start command

- Stop running web application, using the stop command

- Remove the web application from the server, using the remove command

We will discuss each of these commands in relation to our sample web application packaged in the apress.war file, which was created in Chapter 2. All commands will be performed from your browser with just a few mouse clicks, using the web interface of the Manager web application.

▪ **Note** Before you begin using these commands, make sure you have backed up and removed the /apress web application from your current Tomcat installation.

Checking Server Status

The first component of the Manager web application we're going to use is the server status. To access the Apache Tomcat status, click on the Server Status link in the top right area of the Manager web application's home page. Or, you can enter the following URL to your browser: http://localhost:8080/manager/status. You will see the Apache Tomcat Status page. Figure 4-4 shows how the status page looks in the browser.

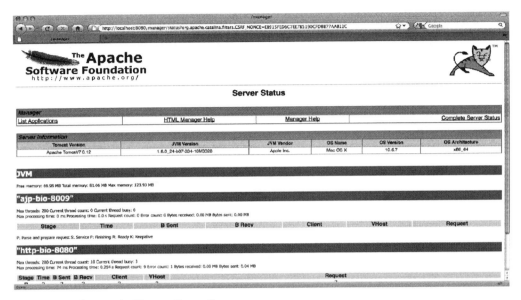

Figure 4-4. The Apache Tomcat Server Status page

On the Server Status page, you can see details about your operating system (the name, architecture, and version), your Java virtual machine (vendor and version), and the version of Apache Tomcat you are running.

In addition, at the bottom of the screen, you can see the JVM memory status and the status of AJP and HTTP Tomcat connectors – thread status, and status of active requests.

Deploying a New Web Application

The first command we are going to use is `deploy`, which is used to deploy new web applications. To deploy a new web application using the web interface, you will use the HTML form of the Manager's home page. There are two HTML forms available: one to deploy a web application for a file or directory already available on the server where the Tomcat instance is running, and one that allows you to deploy a web application from the WAR file located on your local machine.

Figure 4-5 shows the Deploy section of the home page, with the deployment HTML forms.

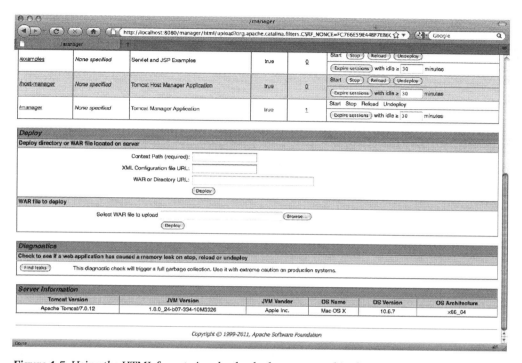

Figure 4-5. *Using the HTML form to invoke the deploy command in the Manager web application*

The most common usage of the Manager web application for deployment to Tomcat is the remote deployment – where you have the web application packaged in the WAR file on your local machine, and you want to deploy it to a remote Tomcat server. To achieve that, we will use second form in the Deploy section of the Manager web application home page, titled "WAR file to deploy" and shown in Figure 4-5. All you have to do is to select the file located on your disk's file system (by clicking on the "Browse…" button), and click the Deploy button below the file selection field. The web application will be deployed under a context path matching the name of the WAR file, excluding the .war extension – in our case, the context path will be /apress, as we will be uploading apress.war file.

▨ **Note** The deploy command takes the referenced WAR file and extracts it into the /webapps directory during this process.

When the command completes, the Manager web application web page will be reloaded in the browser, and you will see a success message (simply saying "OK") in the message box. In addition, you will see newly a deployed application listed along with the other applications deployed on the Tomcat server. Figure 4-6 shows the web page after the successful deployment of the new application.

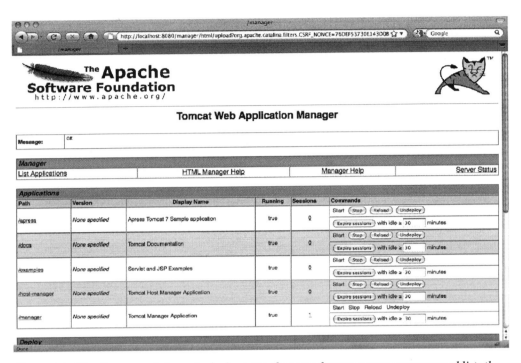

Figure 4-6. *After the successful remote deployment, the page shows a success message and lists the new web application.*

▪ **Note** The web application is automatically started after deployment, as you can see in the Running column, which displays true for the /apress application.

You can also use the Manager web application to deploy a web application located on the server's file system. This is done using the top form in the Deploy section shown in the Figure 4-5. The form has three input fields: Context Path, "XML configuration file URL," and "WAR or directory URL." The first parameter, Context Path, is, as its name suggests, a context path that the web application will be deployed to. We are going to deploy our web application under the /apress context path, so we enter that in the Context Path text input field in the HTML form. The Context Path field is mandatory when deploying a web application from the local path. You should populate one of the other two parameters, depending of the location of the web application you're deploying. If you know the location of the WAR file, or the directory of the web application on the local file system, you should specify it in the "WAR or directory URL" field – and leave the "XML configuration URL" field empty. On the other hand, if you have a deployment descriptor XML file, enter its file location in the "XML Configuration file URL" field, and leave the field for the WAR file location empty. When you have entered all the details, you can submit the form by clicking the Deploy button.

■ **Note** You'll have to upload the web application files (either the WAR file or the exploded directory) to the machine where the Tomcat is running – for example via FTP – before you can deploy it using this approach.

If the deployment was successful, you will see the screen shown in Figure 4-6, and the new application will be listed along with the other deployed applications.

If, for some reason, an error occurs during the deployment, the error message explaining the problem will be displayed in the message box as a response. Table 4-3 shows the common error messages received during deployment, and their causes.

Table 4-3. Common Error Messages That Can Occur During Deployment

Response Message	Cause
Application already exists at path /apress.	Context path specified is already used on the server.
Document base does not exist or is not a readable directory.	The value passed as a value of war parameter is incorrect – it must be either unpacked web application directory, or an absolute path to the WAR file.
Invalid application URL was specified.	The value passed as a value of war parameter is incorrect – it must start with file: and end with .war in case of absolute war path.
Invalid context path was specified.	The value of path parameter is wrong – context path must start with slash /.
Encountered exception.	An exception was thrown while deploying application. Check the Tomcat logs for details.

Reloading an Existing Web Application

The reload command is used to reload all of the web components, including servlet, JSPs, and dependent classes, associated with the named web application. You can invoke reload command by clicking the Reload button for the selected web application, which is located in the Commands column in the Applications list (see Figure 4-3). If any of the files of the selected web application have changed on the server, the changes will be reloaded after you invoke this command.

Once all of the components have been reloaded, the Manager web application responds with a page similar to that shown in Figure 4-7.

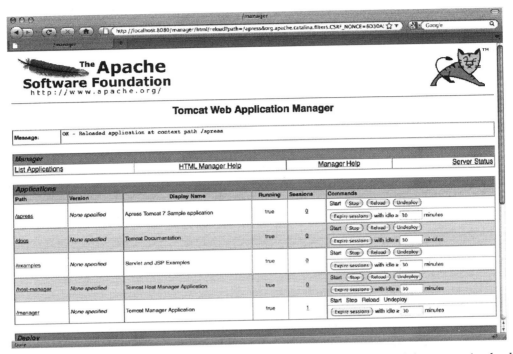

Figure 4-7. After invoking the reload *command, the Manager web application's home page is reloaded in the browser.*

As you can see, the response message is displayed in the message box. The response has the usual success message ("OK"), but also contains information about the reloaded web application – more specifically, its context path.

Sessions

The HTTP protocol that we use to communicate with server web applications is stateless. This means that the protocol treats each request independently, with no information about previous requests from the same user for example, or from the same Internet address. All that is important is the current request, and the server's response to it. A servlet container, such as Tomcat, uses user sessions to maintain the state between the requests. Tomcat associates each client with the session id, and then maintains the stateful information in the session. Every request contains the session id and, when it reaches the server, the session with that id is loaded and attached to request. Usually, session information contains information such as whether user has already logged in, so we don't need to ask for username and password on every request. The shopping cart is usually stored in the session as well, so we can browse the online shop without losing the data we added to the cart previously. We will cover sessions in more depth in Chapter 5.

You can see the number of associated user sessions for each web application on the Manager's home page. This information is presented as the number in the Sessions column of the list of deployed applications. You should see value 1 in the Sessions column of the Manager web application (context path /manager) – this is actually your session, as you're accessing the Manager web application at the moment. If haven't accessed other applications recently, the value of the Sessions column for other listed applications will be zero.

If you do the same from another computer (or from a different browser on the same computer – say from Firefox and Internet Explorer) and then reload the Manager's home page again, the number of sessions displayed for the Manager web application will now be 2.

Sessions are stored for a limited amount of time, configurable in your web application's web.xml file. The default value is 30 minutes. This means that if a user does not access web application for 30 minutes, the session information associated with that visit will be cleared (for example, the user will need to log in to the web site again). You can invalidate all sessions for a particular web application by clicking the "Expire sessions" button in the Commands column. You can also filter the session to invalidate, and invalidate only sessions that are inactive for the selected number of minutes, by entering the desired value to the text box next to the "Expire sessions" button.

Finally, you can get detailed information about each session for a selected web application by clicking on the number of sessions in the Sessions column. The number is actually a link, and by clicking on it, you will be presented with the detailed session information page. Figure 4-8 shows detailed information about the Manager web application sessions.

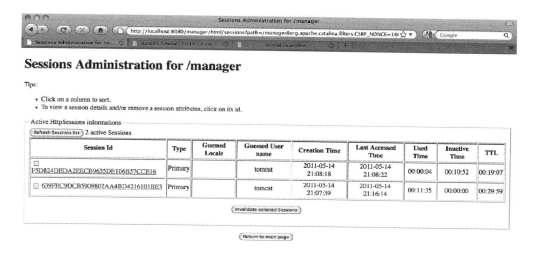

Figure 4-8. Detailed session information page for Manager web application displayed in the browser

The page shows a list of all active sessions, with basic information about each session. Table 4-4 explains the columns displayed on this page.

Table 4-4. The Session Information Page Columns on the Details Session Page

Column	Description
Session Id	The identifier for the session – a string that is unique for the Tomcat instance.
Type	Used in a clustered environment where the same session is available on multiple Tomcat instances. In the instance where the session is created, it is considered as primary. In single instance environments, like our examples, all sessions will be primary.
Guessed Locale	User locale, if it can be determined from the request attributes.
Guessed Username	Username of the logged-in user (if any), if it can be determined from the request.
Creation Time	The date and time when the session is created.
Last Accessed Time	The date and time the session was accessed last.
Used Time	The amount of time between the session's creation and its last use.
Inactive	The time passed since the session has been last accessed.
TTL	Time To Live – the time left until the session is invalidated (if it stays inactive).

You can invalidate a single session by clicking on its Session Id link. If you want to invalidate multiple sessions, you can check the checkboxes for the sessions you want to invalidate and click the "Invalidate selected sessions" button.

Stop

The stop command does just what you think it does: it stops the named web application. When the web application is stopped, it cannot be accessed anymore. You can stop a web application by clicking the Stop button in the Commands column for the selected web application. Once you click the button, the Manager's home page will be reloaded and, if the command was executed successfully, you should see a page similar that shown in Figure 4-9. We stopped our /apress web application in this example.

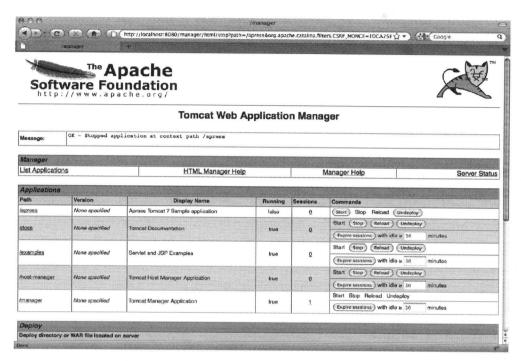

Figure 4-9. *The Manager web application after the selected web application is stopped*

You can see the response message displayed in the usual message box. In addition, the status of the /apress application now shows that it has stopped – you can see the value false in the Running column. If you try to access our sample application by entering http://localhost:8080/apress/index.jsp URL, you will see Tomcat's error page with HTML status 404 – Not Found in the browser. Figure 4-10 shows the error page.

Figure 4-10. 404 – Not Found error page when trying to access stopped web application

In order to have our application up and running, we have to start it again.

Start

The start command also does just what you'd expect: it starts a named web application that has been previously stopped. All you have to do is to click the Start button (in the Commands column) for the previously stopped web application.

■ **Note** The buttons for the commands that cannot be performed for each application will be disabled by the Manager web application. So, you won't be able to try to start the application that is already started, or stop the application that is not running.

Once all of the components have been reloaded, the Manager web application's home page reloads with the following response text in the message box: OK - Started application at context path /apress. The status of the web applications will be changed again: the Running column will display value true.

If you try to access our sample application again, you will see the welcome page, meaning that our web application is running and accepting requests again.

Undeploy

The last command that you will use, appropriately enough, is the undeploy command. It is used to stop and remove the named web application from the Tomcat server. It does not remove the directories and files associated with the web application, however; it simply removes the application from the internally maintained list of deployed applications.

You can undeploy application by clicking on the Undeploy button for the selected web application. Once all of the components have been removed, the Manager web application responds with a page similar to that shown in Figure 4-11, with expected text message: OK - Undeployed application at context path /apress.

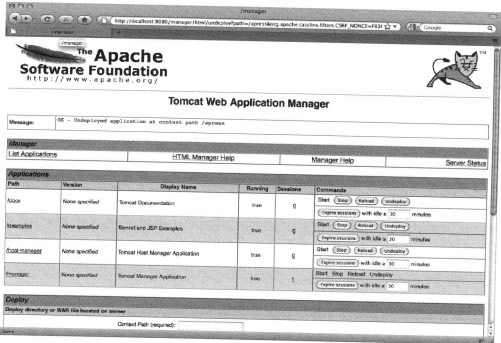

Figure 4-11. After you undeployed a web application, the Manager's home page is reloaded with an updated list of deployed applications.

You will notice that the list of applications of the Manager's home page does not show the undeployed web application anymore.

Using the web interface of the Manager web application is an easy and convenient way to perform basic administration tasks for web applications deployed to Tomcat server. However, the administration tasks often need to be performed by other computers and not humans, using executable scripts. For that

89

reason, Tomcat Manager web application is accessible using the text-based interface, in addition to the HTML web interface described in this section. In the next section, we are going to show you how you can use Ant scripts to invoke the Tomcat Manager commands, using this text-based interface.

Using a Text-Based Interface to Access Manager Web Application

Manager's text interface can be used directly from the browser by typing the commands in the form of URLs and getting the text response directly back to the browser. However, in practice, text-based access to the Tomcat's Manager web application is usually done using Ant scripts.

Ant is a popular building tool for Java, and ships with a number of Tasks you can use to control different stages of Java project builds. These tasks include compiling Java classes, running unit tests, packaging, copying artifacts to target directories, and many more.

In addition to being a useful build tool with its out-of-the-box Tasks, Ant is extremely flexible and extensible. You can easily implement your own Tasks (in Java) to satisfy specific requirements of your build process. A lot of other popular libraries and frameworks supply their own Ant Tasks libraries, to help building projects using that particular product. Apache Tomcat supplies its own Ant Tasks that you can use to access Manager web application from your Ant command line scripts.

■ **Note** Ant is an open source project, and it's part of Apache's open source community. You can find out more about Apache Ant on its project's home page at http://ant.apache.org.

Installing Ant

We'll start with quick instructions for how to install Apache Ant to your computer. The first step is to download the Ant binary distribution from the project's web site (http://ant.apache.org/bindownload.cgi). Ant is distributed as a platform-independent archive (ZIP or TGZ file), so you will download same version of the file regardless of your operating system. The latest version of Apache Ant at the time of writing is 1.8.X. After downloading the ZIP file, unpack it to the location of your choice; this will be the ANT_HOME directory of your ANT installation. For the purposes of this example, we will unpack the archive to the /opt/ant directory.

To complete the installation, you'll need to set environment variables for the ANT_HOME directory, and add ANT_HOME/bin to the global PATH environment variable so you can invoke Ant commands regardless of the working directory you're in. You can do this in the same way we set Tomcat's environment variables in the Tomcat installation section of Chapter 1.

And that's it! To test the installation open your command prompt window (on Windows) or terminal window (on Linux), type ant and press enter. If everything is working correctly, you should see following message:

```
ant
Buildfile: build.xml does not exist!
Build failed
```

This message means that the ant command has been executed, and tried to build the project in the current directory. We haven't configured any project, so we see the error message from Ant.

If Ant wasn't installed correctly, you would see a "Command not found" error when trying to execute the ant command.

Now that we have Ant installed and ready to use, we need to configure Tomcat's Ant tasks for accessing Manager web application.

Configuring Tomcat's Ant Tasks

Tomcat's Ant tasks are shipped with Tomcat 7, in a single library catalina-ant.jar. You can find this library in the CATALINA_HOME/lib directory of your Tomcat 7 installation. In order to use Ant tasks from the catalina-ant.jar library, you have to copy it to the Ant's libraries directory, located in the ANT_HOME/lib directory.

▪ **Note** The Tomcat's Ant tasks classes need to be available on the Ant's classpath during execution, so without copying the catalina-ant.jar file to ANT_HOME/lib directory (which is on Ant's classpath), you won't be able to execute Tomcat's Ant tasks to invoke Manager web application's commands.

To build any Java project using Ant, you have to write build.xml file. This file contains all the instructions for Ant about the structure of your project, and about the tasks it needs to perform on it. You should place the build.xml file in your projects directory and invoke Ant commands from the same directory, so Ant can locate the build.xml file.

Our project contains of one single WAR file, and for the purposes of this example, we are going to assume our project path is /apresstomcat7/project/chapter4 – the code accompanying this book has the example on this path.

The first step is to create build.xml in this directory, and configure Tomcat's tasks in that file. You can use any text editor you like, or an IDE, like Eclipse, to create this file. Listing 4-2 shows how the build.xml file should look.

Listing 4-2. Ant's Build File with Tomcat's Ant Tasks Definitions

```
<project name="Apress Tomcat 7 Sample Web Application" basedir=".">      #1
  <property name="managerUrl"
            value="http://localhost:8080/manager/text"/>                 #2
  <property name="username" value="managerScript"/>                      #3
  <property name="password" value="abc123"/>                             #4

  <property name="contextPath"    value="/apress"/>                      #5
  <property name="warFileName"    value="apress.war"/>                   #6

  <!-- Configure the custom Ant tasks for the Manager application -->    #7
  <taskdef name="deploy"    classname="org.apache.catalina.ant.DeployTask"/>
```

```
<taskdef name="list"      classname="org.apache.catalina.ant.ListTask"/>
<taskdef name="reload"    classname="org.apache.catalina.ant.ReloadTask"/>
<taskdef name="start"     classname="org.apache.catalina.ant.StartTask"/>
<taskdef name="stop"      classname="org.apache.catalina.ant.StopTask"/>
<taskdef name="undeploy"  classname="org.apache.catalina.ant.UndeployTask"/>

<target name="list" description="List deployed web applications">          #8
  <list url="${managerUrl}"
        username="${username}" password="${password}"/>                   #9
</target>

<target name="deploy" description="Install web application">              #10
  <deploy url="${managerUrl}" username="${username}" password="${password}"
          path="${contextPath}" war="file:${basedir}/${warFileName } "/>  #11
</target>

<target name="reload" description="Reload web application">
  <reload  url="${managerUrl}" username="${username}" password="${password}"
          path="${contextPath}"/>
</target>

<target name="undeploy" description="Remove web application">
  <undeploy url="${managerUrl}"
            username="${username}" password="${password}"
          path="${contextPath}"/>
</target>
<!- The rest of the targets is omitted for clarity →

</project>
```

The build.xml file's root element is <project>, where we specify the project's name and the base directory (#1). Next, we configure a few properties relating to the Tomcat's instance and the Manager web application we are going to access. The first property we set is the managerUrl, where the Manager web application is running (#2). We're running the Tomcat instance locally for this example, so the URL points to the localhost. Note that the managerUrl points to the text-based interface of the Manager web application: http://localhost:8080/manager/text. Next, we configure the username and password of the user we're going to use to access Manager web application. We configured user managerGui, with password abc123, to have access to text-based interface (see Table 4-2), so we configure username and password to these values (#3 and #4 in Listing 4-2).

Finally, we configure the properties for the web application we're going to deploy using this Ant script – the context path we're going to deploy it to (#5), and the name of the packaged web application's WAR file (#6).

The properties we defined can now be used instead of their values for the rest of the build.xml file, making the build script easier to write, and also easier to read and maintain later.

Next step is to configure the Tomcat tasks for accessing Manager web application (#7). For each task we are going to use, we need to add <taskdef> element, specifying the task name, and the class where the task is implemented. You can choose your own names for each task, but for this example our tasks' names match the commands that they invoke. The task classes specified are located in the catalina-ant.jar library. Although catalina-ant.jar library contains implementations for every command available, you will only be able to use those commands that you defined in the <taskdef> elements in the build.xml file.

The Ant command, ant, when executed from the command line, actually invokes targets defined in the build.xml file. Each target performs specific task, and we are going to create Ant target for each of the tasks we defined previously.

Target is defined using <target> XML element, and needs only the name attribute, and optionally the description. The first target we're going to configure is the list target (#8). Target by itself doesn't do anything; it is the elements that are enclosed within the <target> element that do the actual work. For this target, we're going to invoke the list command using the list task defined previously (#9). As you can see, the task we defined using <taskdef> can now be used as an XML element directly. We specify three attributes: the URL of the Manager web application, and the username and password we use to access it. All three attributes are specified using the properties we defined at the top of the build.xml file.

The next target we're going to configure is the deploy target (#10). It encloses the deploy task, which in turn deploys a new application to the Tomcat server (#11). The <deploy> element requires more attributes than we used for listing web applications. In addition to the Manager web application's URL, username, and password, it requires the context path under which we want to deploy our web application, and the path to the WAR file to deploy. We specify these two attributes using the properties we defined earlier in the build.xml file (#5 and #6).

You can configure the rest of the tasks on your own for practice; they are all configured in exactly the same way. The code that accompanies this book contains the configuration for all the tasks as well.

Now we have all the tasks configured, and we can run them from the command line.

Running Ant Scripts

All Ant tasks are executed by running the ant command from the projects base directory, and specifying one or more targets you want executed.

So, to list all the applications deployed on the configured Tomcat instance, go to the project's directory and type **ant list**. This is the text response you will see in your terminal window:

```
apress-apache-tomcat7/project/chapter4$ ant list
Buildfile: /Users/aleksav/Sandbox/apress-apache-tomcat7/project/chapter4/build.xml

list:
    [list] OK - Listed applications for virtual host localhost        #1
    [list] /manager:running:0:manager                                 #2
    [list] /docs:running:0:docs
    [list] /examples:running:0:examples
    [list] /host-manager:running:0:host-manager

BUILD SUCCESSFUL
Total time: 0 seconds
```

The information returned is the same as we saw when using HTML web interface, only in text format. The "OK" success message is displayed (#1), followed by all applications deployed on the Tomcat instance. Instead of a table and columns, the text response contains the usual information delimited with the colon (#2). The part until the first colon is the context path of the web application (/manager), followed by the status (running), followed by the number of active sessions, and finally followed by the application name. The same format is used for all listed application.

Let's now deploy our apress.war application using Ant. All you have to do is execute the deploy target from our build script, by running following command: ant deploy. The result of this invocation is the same status message that was displayed when using web interface earlier in this chapter. This is the success message you should see in your terminal window:

```
Buildfile: /Users/aleksav/Sandbox/apress-apache-tomcat7/project/chapter4/build.xml
Trying to override old definition of datatype resources

deploy:
    [deploy] OK - Deployed application at context path /apress

BUILD SUCCESSFUL
Total time: 2 seconds
```

In case of any errors during deployment, you will see one of the messages from Table 4-3 instead of the success message.

The same approach applies for executing any other command – you can play with those yourself. In addition, you can execute multiple ant targets at the same time. For example, by running the ant undeploy list, the application will be undeployed first using undeploy task, then the list command will be executed – so you can quickly confirm that the application is not listed anymore. The usual scenario in automated scripts that are part of continuous integration is to undeploy the old version of the web application, build the WAR file, deploy it to Tomcat (using deploy task), and finally run automated test scripts against the deployed web application. By specifying all tasks to be executed, the entire process executed as a single ant command, making it repeatable and easy to automate.

As you can see, using Ant scripts to access the text-based interface of the Manager web application is not as pretty as the HTML web interface, but it's more convenient to execute as part of the project build, and to automate as part of the bigger build and test scripts.

Summary

In this chapter, we covered using the Tomcat Manager web application to install and manage our own web application. We explained the role of the Manager web application and configured security privileges so we are able to access it. We discussed how to execute each of the available commands using Manager web application's HTML interface. Finally, we used Tomcat's Ant tasks to perform all available commands from the command line. In the next chapter, we cover HTTP sessions and their persistence in Tomcat.

CHAPTER 5

Persistent Sessions

So far, we have covered the basics about the HTTP protocol and how it's used in a servlet container, like Tomcat. The HTTP protocol, like the Servlet API, has its foundations in the simple request/response mechanism. The state of the conversation between client and server is not maintained in such cases. In this chapter, we will see how the Java Servlet specification overcomes that challenge, and becomes stateful if required, using user sessions. In addition, we will learn how to configure Tomcat to store the session information for users accessing the site, so that it isn't lost when the server crashes, for example.

In this chapter, we

- Discuss HTTP sessions servlet implementation and their uses

- Implement a sample web application to demonstrate usage of HTTP sessions

- Configure Tomcat to store sessions to a file

- Use a SQL database to store session information

HTTP Sessions

Before we can start examining HTTP sessions, we must first understand their purpose. When the HTTP protocol—the transport mechanism of all World Wide Web traffic—was first introduced, it was intended to be only a simple request/response protocol, and no state was required to be maintained between autonomous requests. Based on the HTTP protocol specification, the client needs to establish a new TCP connection on every request; therefore, no state information about previous requests is available. This was fine until the Web's popularity exploded.

One of the biggest demands as the Web's popularity grew was the ability to maintain—between requests—a state that is specific to each client. For example, online shops required to maintain the customer's shopping basket between requests. Or, for secured web sites, the mechanism was required to remember the user's login details for a period of time so the user doesn't have to log in every time the protected page is required.

Several solutions to this problem are currently available: request parameters, cookies, and session management.

Using request parameters to pass information about the request state is a workaround to simulate statefullness of the request. This is achieved by either by adding hidden form fields to the current form, or by appending request parameters to the URL (usually called URL rewriting). If using hidden form fields, the user won't see any difference in the browser; but the content of these parameters can be seen if the user opens the HTML source of the web page, making this approach a security risk. In addition, in order to make a web application stateful using this approach, hidden fields need to be added to all forms on the site, and the additional request parameters need to be added to all URLs. For a large site, this makes the web application much more complex to develop and maintain. Finally, this approach increases the bandwidth usage, as information about all previous requests is sent to the server with each subsequent request, affecting the server performance.

Cookies are simple text fields, which are stored on the user's browser machine. The content of the cookie is controlled by the web application, and with each user request, the browser sends all the cookies for the accessed web application to the server as HTTP headers. By reading the information about the request state in the cookie, the web application can maintain the state for each browser. The web application can store anything to a cookie that relates to the user's web application access–shopping cart details, login information, and the like. Because the content of cookies is just text, a web application on the server must parse the text in order to understand it. As simple text files, cookies do not pose security risks (such as accessing a user's private files) because they cannot be executed on the client's machine. However, as they are sent to the server on each request, they can be malicious if used as spyware. That's why all modern browsers allow users to disable cookies for web browsing. If security is a concern, the cookies' content can be encrypted as well. As with hidden form fields, using cookies for maintaining state increases the bandwidth and affects the server's performance in case there is a lot of data stored in a cookie (for example, large shopping carts).

The biggest issue with request parameters and cookies as mechanisms for maintaining states is that that in both cases state information is stored on clients' machines—either in the HTML code of the web page or in the text file on the file system. The consequences are security concerns (if secured resources need to be part of the state, storing them on clients' computers is risky) and the performance (the state information needs to be sent to the server with each request, and the server needs to process it before reading).

However, as the HTTP protocol is natively stateless, the described solutions are the only two native HTTP mechanisms to maintain states in the HTTP request/response communication. Therefore, a better solution is required, one that will enable web applications to store the state information on the server. That's why web developers came up with the session management solution: a way to maintain the request state on the server, and still use the stateless HTTP protocol.

The idea behind session management is simple: a web server stores the stateful information for each client locally. It is identified by a session identifier (session id), which is a unique identifier for each client accessing the web application. A server can store this information however it wants – as a hash table in memory, with session identifiers as keys; or in a file or even a SQL database table, with the session id as the primary key. When the client accesses the server for the first time, the server allocates a session id to the client, and creates a new session. The client will then pass its unique session id with each subsequent request to identify itself to the server. The server will find the existing session for the received session id, and match it to the request, making it available for further processing on the server.

The question here is how does the client store the session id that the server allocates to it? And how then does the client send its session id to the server with each subsequent request? The answer is simple: it uses cookies, or hidden form fields. We said before that cookies and request parameters are the only native HTTP features available to simulate statefulness—and session management uses just that. If request parameters are used, every form in the web application has a hidden field for the session id, which is then passed to the server just like any other request parameter. If using cookies, a server sends a cookie with session id after first request. The cookie is then sent back to the server with each request, and that's how the server gets the session identifier from the client. Because only the identifier is ever stored in the browser, there is no fear that confidential data can be left unprotected in the user's browser. In addition, the amount of information sent with the cookie is small, so there is no performance trade-off.

Session management (or HTTP session, as it's usually called) quickly became the de-facto standard for stateful HTTP communication. Most web servers implement session management, including Microsoft's IIS, Apache Web Server, and Apache Tomcat. Using HTTP session mechanism, all the user session information is stored on the server, which is more secure and much more performant. In this chapter, we focus on HTTP sessions, specifically HTTP sessions in the Java servlets context with Tomcat.

Now that we understand more about session management in general, we can take a look at the session implementation in the Tomcat servlet container.

The Servlet Implementation of HTTP sessions

The Java Servlet API implements HTTP sessions using an interface named, appropriately enough, `javax.servlet.http.HttpSession`. Every servlet container must implement this interface, including Tomcat 7. The class that implements this interface will use a unique identifier, the session id, to look up a user's session information. This identifier is stored in the client's browser (in the cookie, or as a request parameter) and is part of every HTTP request.

The `HttpSession` interface defines several methods for accessing and modifying a user's session information. Table 5-1 describes the some most commonly used of these methods.

Table 5-1. Commony Used Methods of the `HttpSession` Object

Method	Description
`getId()`	The `getId()` method returns a `java.lang.String` representing the unique identifier assigned to this user's session.
`getAttribute(String name)`	The `getAttribute()` method takes a `java.lang.String` parameter, name, and returns the object bound with the specified name in this session, or `null` if no object is bound under the name.
`getAttributeNames()`	This method returns a `java.util.Enumeration` of `java.lang.String` objects containing the names of all the objects bound to this session.
`setAttribute(String name, Object value)`	The `setAttribute()` method takes a name/value pair and binds the object referenced by the value parameter to this session. The name parameter is used as the key to access object. If an object is already bound to the name parameter, the object is replaced with the most recent value.
`removeAttribute(String name)`	This method removes the attribute stored in the session and specified by name argument. In case the attribute is not present, it doesn't do anything.
`getCreationTime()`	This method returns the long value of the time when the session was created. The value represents the milliseconds passed since January 1, 1970, 00:00:00 GMT.
`getLastAccessedTime()`	This method returns the long value of the time when the session was last accessed. The value represents the milliseconds since January 1, 1970, 00:00:00 GMT.

Method	Description
invalidate()	This method is used to invalidate this user's session, which will in turn remove all session attributes from the invalidated session.

By default, the servlet container uses cookies for session tracking. The cookie stored in the browser is named JSESSIONID by default, as per Java Servlet specification. Since Servlet API 3.0, this name can be customized in the web.xml file. In order to see the cookie with session information, we're going to access Tomcat's Manager web application, which we discussed in Chapter 4. If you start your Tomcat instance, and access Tomcat's Manager web application on the URL http://localhost:8080/manager/html, a session will be created for you. You will see the Manager web application under Applications in the Manager home page, and the value in the Sessions column will be 1. If you now take a look at the cookies stored in your browser (you can search cookies by host name localhost), you will see the JSESSIONID cookie with the session id as its content. Figure 5-1 shows the cookie in the Firefox web browser.

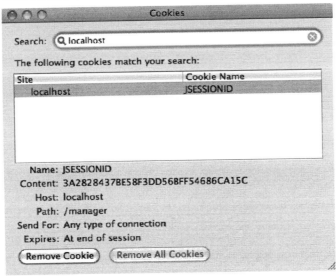

Figure 5-1. JSESSIONID cookie stored in the Firefox browser

Every time you click on any of the links in the Manager web application, this cookie will be sent to Tomcat, and based on the session id stored in the cookie, Tomcat will identify the session as belonging to you and match it to the request.

If cookies are disabled in your browser, the session id will have to be sent along with every request as a request parameter (whether as a hidden form parameter or as part of the URL). We can demonstrate this by disabling cookies in your browser. Consult your browser documentation to find out how can this be achieved (or just search the web for "BROWSER_NAME disable cookies," replacing BROWSER_NAME with the name of your browser). In Firefox, you can go to Options > Privacy, select "Custom history settings," and uncheck the "Accept cookies from sites" check box. Restart your browser and Tomcat server after the changes so all other sessions are cleared.

If you now access the Manager web application like before, you will see one session—just like with the cookies. But now if you click on any link on the Manager's home page, you will see that the URL in the browser address bar has changed, and now includes the jsessionid request parameter, with a long String value, representing the session id. Figure 5-2 illustrates the browser's address bar after we clicked on the "List applications" link from the Manager's home page.

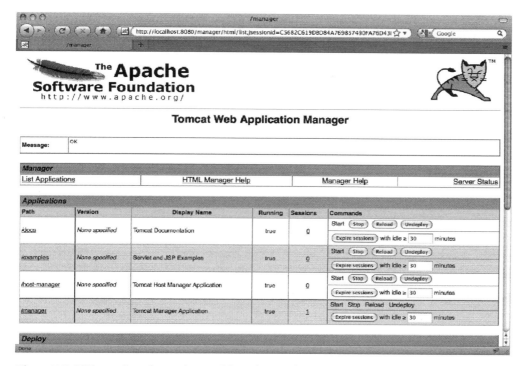

Figure 5-2. URL rewritten for session tracking when cookies are disabled

We have seen how Tomcat employs cookies and URL rewriting for session tracking. For the rest of the examples in this chapter, we will assume cookies are enabled and used for session tracking. Let's now see session in action, using a real-world example.

Shopping Basket Session Example

To demonstrate the HTTP session usage with servlets, we will introduce an example that we will use throughout this chapter. We will implement a session-stored shopping basket, with the typical functionality used on online shopping web sites.

Firstly, let's introduce the HTTP shopping basket object model in Java. We will need two classes to model the shopping basket: class Item, which will represent a single product that can be bought (and added to shopping basket), and the shopping basket itself, modeled in HttpShoppingBasket class. Listing 5-1 shows the Java implementation of the Item class.

Listing 5-1. *Class Item, Representing the Single Product Added to the Shopping Basket*

```java
public class Item implements Serializable{
    private String name;
    private double price;

    public Item(String name, double price) {
        this.name = name;
        this.price = price;
    }

    public String getName() {
        return name;
    }

    public double getPrice() {
        return price;
    }
}
```

As you can see, we are using a simple implementation, storing only the name of the product and its price, which will be sufficient for our example.

Listing 5-2 shows the HttpShoppingBasket class, which contains the collection of products (Items), and the total value of the order.

Listing 5-2. *Simple Shopping Basket Implementation*

```java
public class HttpShoppingBasket implements Serializable{

    private List<Item> items = new ArrayList<Item>();
    private double totalValue = 0;

    public void addToBasket(Item item){
        this.items.add(item);
        this.totalValue+=item.getPrice();
    }

    public List<Item> getItems() {
        return items;
    }

    public double getTotalValue() {
        return totalValue;
    }
}
```

We have two simple properties: items, representing the collection of all items added to the basket by the customer, and totalValue, a double property that represents the total sum of the entire basket. The method addToBasket(..) simply adds Item to the basket's items collection, and increases the totalValue for the Item's price.

■ **NOTE** Java code for this example can be found in the source code distributed with this book, along with all other examples in the book. The directory of the source code represents the chapter number, so all examples can be found in the BookCode/chapter5 directory.

Now that we have the basic object model for a shopping basket, we need to implement the servlet that will update the basket when the user clicks on the "Add to basket" button for the product he or she wishes to buy.

We will implement the AddToBasketServlet servlet, using the Servlet API 3.0 style, introduced in Chapter 3. Listing 5-3 shows the servlet class implementation.

Listing 5-3. AddToBasketServlet Java class, Implemented Using the Latest Servlet API 3.0

```java
@WebServlet(urlPatterns={"/addToBasket.html"})                          #1
public class AddToBasketServlet extends HttpServlet{                    #2

    protected void doPost(HttpServletRequest request,
                          HttpServletResponse response)
                throws ServletException, IOException {                 #3

        HttpSession session = request.getSession(true);                #4
        HttpShoppingBasket basket = (HttpShoppingBasket)
            session.getAttribute("SHOPPING_BASKET");                   #5
        if(basket == null){
            basket = new HttpShoppingBasket();                         #6
        }

        String productName = request.getParameter("productName");      #7
        double price = Double.parseDouble(request.getParameter("price"));

        Item item = new Item(productName, price);
        basket.addToBasket(item);                                      #8

        session.setAttribute("SHOPPING_BASKET", basket);               #9
        response.sendRedirect("/chapter5/jsps/products.jsp");          #10
    }
}
```

■ **NOTE** At the time of writing, Apache Tomcat 7 and Apache GlassFish 3 are the only released application servers that support the Servlet API 3.0.

Based on the Servlet API 3.0 specification, we have set the urlPattern for this servlet using @WebServlet annotation (#1). The Servlet API 2.X style would require the servlet metadata, including urlPattern, to be configured in a web.xml file. However, Servlet API 3.0 allows this to be set on the servlet class itself, using @WebServlet annotation. This annotation is the only Java Servlet 3.0 specific feature we are using in this example; the rest of the AddToBasketServlet class is typical servlet implementation, regardless of the Servlet API you are using.

The servlet class extends standard HttpServlet from Java Servlet API library, and extends its doPost(..) method, that handles HTTP POST method (#3).

Next, we take the currently active session (#4). The HttpSession object that represents current session can be extracted from the HttpServletRequest by calling HttpServletRequest.getSession(boolean createNew). The boolean argument of this method specifies what the method should return in case no HttpSession has yet been associated with the user. If the argument passed in is false, the method will return null in case no session is found. We are passing value true as the argument—meaning that a new HttpSession will be created if no active session is found for the user.

To get the object previously stored in the session, all we need to do is call HttpSession.getAttribute(String attributeName) method (#5). The method will return the object stored with the key specified as the attributeName argument. If no object is found for the given key, this method will return null. We are trying to find an existing shopping basket in the session, using the "SHOPPING_BASKET" attribute name. In case the user's shopping basket is empty (for example, when the user tries to add the first item to the basket), this will return null, and we need to construct new HttpShopingBasket for that user (#6).

Now we have a reference to the user's shopping basket, and we want to add the new Item to it. We will assume that the item's details are passed as standard request parameters, and we are going to extract them from the request, using HttpServletRequest.getParameter(String paramName) method (#7). Using the values extracted, we will instantiate a new Item object, and add it to the existing basket (#8).

At this point, our shopping basket has been updated to contain the new Item. If the basket has been empty before, we create a new one (#6), and then add the first Item to it (#8). In case we found an existing basket (#5), we just add another Item to its items collection (#8).

All we have to do now is to store the shopping basket to the session again (#9). Simply enough, all we have to do is call HttpSession.setAttribute(String attributeName, Object value), passing the attribute name ("SHOPPING_BASKET") and the object we want to store (basket instance of HttpShoppingBasket). In case there is a "SHOPPING_BASKET" object stored in the session already, this method will simple overwrite it with the newer value—which is the behavior that we expect.

Finally, after the session has been updated, we redirect the user to our online store web page, so he can buy more stuff (#10). We are using the HttpServletResponse.sendRedirect(..) method to do this, passing the relative URL of the page we want to redirect the user to.

To make sure our servlet is loaded correctly by the Tomcat 7 servlet container, we need to configure its web.xml file. Because we have configured the servlet's urlPattern using annotation metadata, the web.xml will be quite simple. Listing 5-4 shows the contents of the web.xml file, which should be located in the /WEB-INF/ directory of the web application's WAR file.

Listing 5-4. Web Deployment Descriptor (`web.xml`) for a Servlet API 3.0 Web Application

```
<?xml version="1.0" encoding="ISO-8859-1"?>
<web-app xmlns="http://java.sun.com/xml/ns/javaee"
  xmlns:xsi="http://www.w3.org/2001/XMLSchema-instance"
  xsi:schemaLocation="http://java.sun.com/xml/ns/javaee
                                     http://java.sun.com/xml/ns/javaee/web-app_3_0.xsd"
version="3.0">

  <display-name>Chapter 5</display-name>
    <description>Http Session Demo</description>
    <metadata-complete>false</metadata-complete>                    #1
</web-app>
```

In addition to the standard `displayName` and `description` elements, all we need to set is the `metadata-complete` element with value false (#1). This will tell Tomcat that the servlet configuration in this `web.xml` file is not complete, and that it should scan all the loaded classes for servlet metadata annotations (like `@WebServlet` from our servlet class). If you don't configure this element in the `web.xml` file, the Tomcat won't recognize the `AddToBasketServlet` class as the servlet that needs to be deployed, and you will see 404 Page Not Found page displayed in your browser.

Finally, in order to complete this sample web application, we will need JSP page that will list all the products available in our online shop, and which will show the content of the user's shopping basket.

Listings 5-5 and 5-6 show the JSP file we will use, and it should be located in the `/WEB-INF/jsps/products.jsp` location within our project. Let's first take a look at the list of products available for shopping.

Listing 5-5. JSP File That Lists All Products Available for Shopping

```
<%@ taglib prefix="c" uri="http://java.sun.com/jsp/jstl/core" %>

<html>
  <head>
  <title>Apress Demo Store</title>
  <meta http-equiv="Content-Type" content="text/html; charset=UTF-8">
  </head>
  <body>
    <div class="content">
      <b>Welcome to Apress store </b>
        Select product: <br/>
        <table>
            <tr>
                <td>Product Name</td>
                <td>Price</td>
                <td>Actions</td>
            </tr>
            <tr>
                <td>Apache Tomcat 7</td>
                <td>$34.99</td>
                <td>
                    <form action="/chapter5/addToBasket.html"
                        method="POST">                              #1
```

```
                            <input type="hidden"
                                    name="productName" value="Apache Tomcat 7"/>        #2
                            <input type="hidden" name="price" value="34.99"/>            #3
                            <input type="submit" value="Add to basket" />                #4
                        </form>
                    </td>
                </tr>
                <tr>
                    <td>Pro Spring 3</td>
                    <td>$39.99</td>
                    <td>
                        <form action="/chapter5/addToBasket.html" method="POST">
                            <input type="hidden"
                                    name="productName" value="Pro Spring 3"/>
                            <input type="hidden" name="price" value="39.99"/>
                            <input type="submit" value="Add to basket" />
                        </form>
                    </td>
                </tr>
                <tr>
                    <td>Android Development for Beginners</td>
                    <td>$24.99</td>
                    <td>
                        <form action="/chapter5/addToBasket.html" method="POST">
                            <input type="hidden" name="productName"
                                    value="Android Development for Beginners"/>
                            <input type="hidden" name="price" value="24.99"/>
                            <input type="submit" value="Add to basket" />
                        </form>
                    </td>
                </tr>
            </table>
    </body>
</html>
```

We are just listing a few books that are available for adding the to basket, in the HTML table. For each row in the table, in the Actions column, we add an HTML form for adding that product to the basket. The form's action URL is the one we configured for our servlet's urlPattern before—/chapter5/addToBasket.html—and the form method is set to POST to match our doPost(..) method implementation (#1). The form has two input fields, matching the request parameters we extracted in our servlet (#2 and #3). Finally, we add a submit field that will show in our web page as an Add to basket button.

Now that we have the storefront page, we need to display the content of the basket for the user browsing the store. Listing 5-6 shows the JSP part that does it, which we will add to the bottom of the product list from Listing 5-5.

Listing 5-6. JSP Showing the Contents of the Shopping Basket

```
<c:set var="basket" value="${sessionScope.SHOPPING_BASKET}"/>                     #1
        <c:if test="${basket != null && not empty basket.items}">                #2
            <b>Your shopping cart:</b> <br/>
            <table>
```

```
<tr>
    <td><b>Product</b></td>
    <td><b>Price</b></td>
</tr>
<c:forEach  items="${basket.items}" var="item">          #3
    <tr>
        <td><c:out value="${item.name}"/></td>
        <td><c:out value="${item.price}"/></td>     #4
    </tr>
</c:forEach>

</table>
<tr>

        <td><b>Total:</b></td>
        <td>
          $<c:out value="${basket.totalValue}"/>         #5
        </td>
</tr>
</c:if>
<c:if test="${basket ==null || empty basket.items }">    #6
    <b>Your basket is empty</b>
</c:if>
```

In order to get access to the session attribute in the JSP page, we are using the sessionScope implicit argument (#1). This argument is implicitly made available on all JSP pages by the servlet container (Tomcat 7 in our case), and you can access any session attribute by specifying the attribute name after the dot. Using the c:set directive from standard JSP tag library, we store the value of the "SHOPPING_BASKET" session attribute to the local variable basket, for easier access on the JSP page.

Next, we check if the basket has any content, to be safe from unexpected exceptions on the page (#2). If basket is not empty, we simply list its content using JSP's c:forEach directive (#3), and render the name and price for each item in the basket (#4); and the total basket value at the bottom (#5).

Finally, in case the basket is empty (when user accesses the store for the first time), we display the appropriate message (#6).

Let's now try our example in the browser. If you package the web application in the WAR file (we will call it chapter5.war) and deploy it to Tomcat—either by copying it to Tomcat's webapps directory, or using the Manager web application—you should see the products list with empty basket when you navigate to http://localhost:8080/chapter5/products.jsp. Figure 5-3 shows how the page should look when opened in the browser.

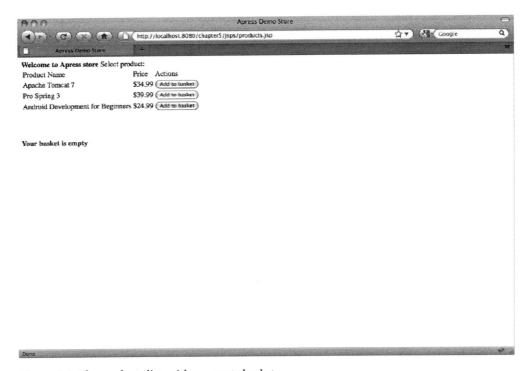

Figure 5-3. The products list, with an empty basket

If you add a couple of products to the basket (by clicking the "Add to basket" button), you will see the basket updated after adding each product. Figure 5-4 shows the page after two products have been added to the shopping basket.

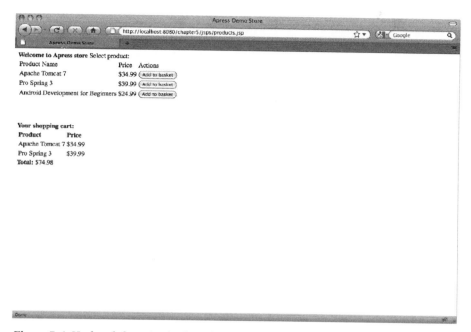

Figure 5-4. *Updated shopping basket after adding two products to it*

This example demonstrates how the browsing becomes stateful when using sessions. After each reload, the page will show the content of the shopping basket, although the products are added to the basket in the previous requests.

In case cookies are disabled, session tracking will be done using URL rewriting, which requires that a session identifier is encoded in every URL. In order to render links with a session id in your JSP files, you have to encode every URL, using the `HttpServletResponse.encodeURL(String url)` method. For example, in the previous above, the form will have to have an encoded action attribute, like in the following code snippet:

```
<form action="<%=response.encodeURL("/chapter5/addToBasket.html")%>" method="POST">
```

You should use the same approach in case you need to use URL rewriting for session tracking.

Invalidating a Session

The `HttpSession` object is stored on the server and remains active for the duration of the user's browsing of the site. If the user becomes inactive for a period of time, his session will be invalidated. By default, this time is set to 30 minutes on Tomcat, but it can be configured for each web application in the `web.xml` file. To configure the session timeout, just add the following snippet to the web.xml:

```
<session-config>
      <session-timeout>60</session-timeout>
 </session-config>
```

The value set using the session-timeout element is in minutes, so the previous configuration will extend the user's session to one hour. Setting the session timeout to -1 will make the session active indefinitely.

The session is also invalidated when the browser is closed. You can easily demonstrate this by closing the browser after adding a few products to the basket in our sample shopping basket web application (after Figure 5-4, for example). After the browser is shut down, open it again, and navigate to the products.jsp page once more—you will see that the basket is empty again.

Finally, HttpSession can be invalidated programmatically, by calling the HttpSession.invalidate() method. You will call this method from your servlet code when you implement the logout mechanism for your web application, for example.

You can extend our shopping basket example by adding the "Clear basket" button, which will remove all products from the current basket. All you need to do is implement another servlet, which will simply call request.getSession(true).invalidate(), and redirect the user to the products.jsp page again. You can get inspiration from our AddToBasketServlet. After you have the servlet implemented, just add a link to the basket page, pointing to the URL matching the servlet's urlPattern. We don't have enough space to show you the solution here, but this chapter's sample code that is distributed with the book has the solution fully implemented, in case you need any guidance.

Session Management in Tomcat

Session management in Tomcat is the responsibility of the session manager, defined with interface org.apache.catalina.Manager. Implementations of the Manager interface manage a collection of sessions within the container. Tomcat 7 comes with several Manager implementations. Table 5-2 describes all concrete Manager implementations available in Tomcat 7.

Table 5-2. Session Manager Classes Available in Apache Tomcat 7

Session Manager	Description
org.apache.catalina.session.StandardManager	Default manager implementation, with limited session persistence, for a single Tomcat instance only.
org.apache.catalina.session.PersistentManager	Configurable session manager for session persistence on a disk or relational database. Supports session swapping and fault tolerance.
org.apache.catalina.ha.session.DeltaManager	Replicates session across the cluster, by replicating only differences in session data on all clusters. Used in a clustered environment only.
org.apache.catalina.ha.session.BackupManager	Replicates session across the cluster by storing backup of all sessions for all clustered nodes on a single, known, backup node. Used in a clustered environment only.

Session manager for the Tomcat instance is configured in the TOMCAT_HOME/conf/context.xml file.

All session managers are responsible for generating unique session ids, and for managing session lifecycles (to create, inactivate, and invalidate sessions). In addition to these main responsibilities, each manager has more specific features and options.

■ **Note** All Tomcat session managers serialize session data using Java object serialization before persisting its binary representation. Therefore, in order for session persistence to work correctly, all Java objects that are stored in the session should implement the `java.io.Serializable` interface.

In the following sections of this chapter, we will cover the configuration and usage of StandardManager and PersistentManager. We will not be covering configuration of session managers in clustered environments (using DeltaManager or BackupManager). You can find more information about cluster session managers at http://tomcat.apache.org/tomcat-7.0-doc/config/cluster-manager.html.

StandardManager

StandardManager is the default session manager implementation on Tomcat 7. This means that if you don't configure any session manager in the Tomcat's context.xml file, Tomcat will instantiate and use the StandardManager for you. If you are using Tomcat as it was downloaded from the Internet, you can see that there is no manager configuration in the Tomcat's context.xml file—so you are using the default StandardManager.

Using the Default StandardManager

StandardManager stores user sessions on disk between server restarts by default. After the server is restarted, all sessions are restored to the state they were in before the server was stopped.

The sessions are stored in the work directory for each web application, in the file SESSIONS.ser. Only active sessions are persisted to this file; all inactive sessions are lost after every Tomcat restart, if you are using StandardManager. Because StandardManager persists sessions only on graceful server shutdowns, in the case of an unexpected server crash, no session will be saved.

To demonstrate the usage of StandardManager, you can start Tomcat, load our sample shopping basket web application, and add a few books to the basket. Then, without closing the browser, stop the server gracefully (by running a shutdown script in CATALINA_HOME/bin directory). After the server is stopped, you should see the SESSIONS.ser file on your disk, where Tomcat saved all active sessions. The file will be located in the directory that matches the context name where the web application is deployed. We have deployed a shopping basket application under /chapter5 context, so the saved sessions file will be located at CATALINA_HOME/work/Catalina/localhost/manager/SESSIONS.ser. If you see this file, it means that StandardManager persisted the sessions for your web application successfully.

Now start Tomcat again (by running /CATALINA_HOME/bin/startup.sh on Linux or startup.exe file on Windows), and load the shopping basket web application again. You will see that the basket still contains the items you added before the server was stopped.

Let's now demonstrate what happens when the server crashes unexpectedly. You will need to stop Tomcat without using the shutdown script. On Windows, list all processes in Task Manager, find the java process belonging to Tomcat and kill it. On Linux based operating systems, you can just run killall -9 java in the terminal. That will kill all java processes, including Tomcat.

Now start Tomcat again, using the standard startup script, and load the shopping basket sample application. The basket will be empty this time. In addition, you won't be able to locate SESSIONS.ser file on the disk anymore; all the shopping you did before the server crashed has been lost.

Configuring StandardManager

We have seen Tomcat's StandardManager in action, without even configuring it, due to the convenience of the default manager configured by Tomcat automatically. But if you need to customize the behavior of the StandardManager, you will need to configure it manually in Tomcat's context.xml file. The session manager is configured using the <Manager> element, within the <Context> element in the context.xml file. Listing 5-7 shows a sample StandardManager configuration.

Listing 5-7. Simple Configuration of StandardManager in context.xml File

```
<Manager
        className="org.apache.catalina.session.StandardManager"    #1
        maxActiveSessions="-1"                                     #2
        pathname="/var/sessiondata/mysessions.ser"                 #3
        sessionIdLength="32">                                      #4
</Manager>
```

We set className attribute to the fully qualified class name of the StandardManager (#1). This tells Tomcat to use the StandardManager implementation as session manager. Next, we configure the maximum number of sessions allowed for the Tomcat instance by setting the maxActiveSession attribute (#2). The negative value means that the number of sessions in unlimited. We can also configure the path of the file where the session information is stored on server shutdown (#3). The path can be absolute, like in our sample configuration, or relative, when the file is created relative to the web application's work directory. Finally, we configure the length of the session id in bytes (#4). The session ids must be unique on the Tomcat instance, so the value of this attribute should be configured in relation to the maxActiveSessions attribute value.

If you add the code snippet from Listing 5-7 to your Tomcat's context.xml file, and restart the server, you will be using customized StandardManager for session management. If you access our shopping basket web application again, and shutdown Tomcat gracefully, you will see that the sessions are now stored in the newly configured file on disk.

There are a number of attributes available for the <Manager> element in context.xml file. Some of the attributes are common for all Manager implementations. Table 5-3 shows those attributes that can be used to configure any concrete Manager implementation available on Tomcat.

Table 5-3. Common <Manager> Configurable Attributes

Attribute	Description
className	The className attribute represents the fully qualified class name of the Manager to use.
distributable	Sets whether the manager should enforce distributable application restriction, as specified in the Servlet API—meaning that all session attributes implement java.io.Serializable interface. Default is false.

Attribute	Description
maxActiveSessions	Configures the maximum number of sessions that can be created. By default, there is no limit (value is -1)
maxInactiveInterval	The maximum time interval after which session can be marked as inactive, in seconds. The default value is 60. This attribute is overridden by Tomcat's or the specific web application's session-timeout value configured in web.xml.
sessionIdLength	The length of the session identifier, in bytes.

In addition to these generic Manager configuration attributes, Table 5-4 describes the attributes specific to the StandardManager implementation.

Table 5-4. StandardManager's Configurable Attributes

Attribute	Description
pathname	The absolute or relative path of the file where session information is stored. Relative paths are relative to the web application's work directory. Default is SESSIONS.ser.
processExpiresFrequency	Configures how often the background process for checking the session expiration is going to run. The lower the amount, the checks will be more often. The default value is 6.
secureRandomClass	The class that is used to generated session ids; must extend java.security.SecureRandom, which is the default option as well.
secureRandomAlgorithm	Defines what random algorithm to use, default value is SHA1PRNG.
secureRandomProvider	Configures the provider for random numbers generation; defaults to the default provider for the platform where Tomcat is running.

Disabling Session Persistence on Server Shutdown

In some cases, you don't need persistence of active sessions on server restart. For example, if you want to force all users to create new sessions after you deploy a completely new version of the web application. Because StandardManager by default stores active session on server shutdown, even if you don't configure it at all, you may get this feature out of the box, without needing it.

In order to achieve this, you need to configure the <Manager> element in the context.xml file, and set the pathname attribute value to empty String (""). You don't need to specify any other attribute, including the className—all other attributes will use default values. So in case you want to disable session persistence entirely, the session manager configuration should look like the following code snippet:

```
<Manager pathname="" />
```

And that's all. Although quite simple, this configuration has been the cause of a lot of confusion in the Tomcat community; that's why we have demonstrated it here specifically.

StandardManager is useful for development and prototyping, and in cases you don't need sessions persistence at all. But, usually, real-world web applications require some form of session persistence, so that the online users don't lose their session data in case of planned or unplanned server restarts. Let's see how we can achieve that using Tomcat's PersistentManager.

PersistentManager

Session persistence became an issue when session objects needed to be swapped in and out of memory based upon activity, load, and during container restarts. Tomcat servers configured in a clustered environment also are required to store and load session information from other instances in the cluster. There needed to be a way to save and retrieve the session information when these events occurred.

For example, applications with thousands of concurrent users may require too much memory to keep all session data in memory. Since activity patterns between users are different, memory can be managed by backing up idle sessions to some persistence store, like disk or database, and load them when needed.

In addition to standard session creation, access, and maintenance responsibilities, PersistentManager has the ability to swap out idle sessions to external storage. Idle sessions are those that are still active, but are not accessed for a configured period of time (the default is 60 seconds), so they can be stored away temporarily while session of the users currently active can be loaded to memory.

To use session persistence you have to configure Tomcat's PersitentManager as session manager in the context.xml file.

Configuring PersistentManager

PersistentManager persists session data using the org.apache.catalina.Store interface. Tomcat currently comes bundled with two implementations of the Store interface: the org.apache.catalina.session.FileStore, for persistence to file on disk, and org.apache.catalina.session.JDBCStore, for persisting session data to the relational database. We will discuss both of these implementations in this section.

But first we need to configure the <Manager> element in the Tomcat's context.xml file to use PersistenceManager. Table 5-5 shows the allowed attributes that can be configured for PersistentManager and their default values.

Table 5-5. PersistentManager's *Configurable Attributes*

Attribute	Description
saveOnRestart	The saveOnRestart attribute, if true, signifies that all active sessions will be saved to the persistent store when Tomcat is shut down. All sessions found in the store are reloaded upon startup. All expired sessions are ignored during shutdown and startup.
minIdleSwap	The minIdleSwap attribute represents the minimum length of time, in seconds, that a session can remain idle before it is swapped out to the persistent store. If minIdleSwap equals -1, then there is no minimum time limit before a swap can occur.
maxIdleSwap	Opposite to the minIdleSwap, this attribute specifies the maximum length of activity after which the session should be swapped to disk. The default value is -1, which disables this feature entirely
maxIdleBackup	The maxIdleBackup attribute represents the length in time, in seconds, that a session can remain idle before it is backed up to the persistent store. When a session is backed up, it remains active as opposed to being swapped out, in which it is removed from the collection of active sessions. If the maxIdleBackup attribute is set to -1, no sessions are backed up.
processExpiresFrequency	This configures how often the background process for checking the session expiration is going to run. The lower the amount, the more frequent the checks will be. The default value is 6.
secureRandomClass	The class that is used to generated session ids, must extend java.security.SecureRandom, which is the default option as well.
secureRandomProvider	This configures the provider for random numbers generation; defaults to default provider for the platform where Tomcat is running.
secureRandomAlgorithm	Defines what random algorithm to use, default value is SHA1PRNG.

In order for `PersistentManager` to perform correctly, based on configuration, Tomcat will need to track the active requests for each session. This is required to determine valid sessions; a session is valid if it has at least one active request. Tomcat does not do this by default, in order not to affect performance and memory footprint unnecessarily, especially since `PersistentManager` isn't configured by default. In order to tell Tomcat to start tracking active requests for each session, you need to set at least one of the following Java environment properties:

- `org.apache.catalina.session.StandardSession.ACTIVITY_CHECK`, or

- `org.apache.catalina.STRICT_SERVLET_COMPLIANCE`

You can set any of these variables in the `JAVA_OPTS` environment variable:

- `JAVA_OPTS="`
  `org.apache.catalina.session.StandardSession.ACTIVITY_CHECK=true"`, or

- `JAVA_OPTS=" org.apache.catalina.STRICT_SERVLET_COMPLIANCE=true"`

In addition to attributes configuration, `PersistentManager` requires the `Store` element be configured as a nested element. The `Store` element configures one of the two implementations that we will describe in the next sections.

FileStore

The `FileStore` uses a file as the storage mechanism for session data. Unlike `StandardManager`, which saves all sessions in one configured file, `FileStore` stores session data in one file per session. The filenames are not configurable, but you can configure the directory where the files will be stored.

Listing 5-8 shows the sample `PersistentManager` configuration using `FileStore` for storage.

Listing 5-8. PersistentManager Configured with FileStore

```
<Manager
      className="org.apache.catalina.session.PersistentManager"
      saveOnRestart="true"
      maxActiveSessions="-1"
      minIdleSwap="-1"
      maxIdleSwap="-1"
      maxIdleBackup="-1">
      <Store className="org.apache.catalina.session.FileStore"
            directory="/var/mysessionsdata"/>
</Manager>
```

Table 5-6 shows all the available attributes for configuration of the nested `FileStore`.

Table 5-6. FileStore Configurable Attributes

Attribute	Description
className	This configures how often the background process for checking the session expiration is going to run. The lower the amount, the checks will be more often. The default value is 6.
directory	The directory where the session data files will be saved to. If relative, it will be relative to the web application's work directory, which is the default directory if this attribute is not specified.
checkInterval	The number of seconds between checks if any of the swapped sessions is expired.

PersistentManager with FileStore is easy to configure, and convenient to demonstrate how the swapping of idle sessions works. However, since it stores session data in one file per session, in case a large number of sessions are used, a lot of files will be saved and loaded on the file system, and the disk IO operations (save and load) can quickly become a performance issue. That's why FileStore-based session persistence should be only used for prototyping and demonstration purposes. For production level session persistence, session data should be store to relational database, using JDBCStore.

JDBCStore

The JDBCStore acts much the same as the FileStore does, with the only difference being the storage location of the session information. In this store, Tomcat reads and writes session information from the database defined in the <Store> sub-element.

Before you begin configuring Tomcat to use a JDBC persistent session, you must first create a database to hold your collection of session objects. For the purpose of this section, we'll create a MySQL database.

Creating a Database for JDBCStore

We will create the database called tomcatsessions. The database that we can be use with JDBCStore, has to have one table for storing session data, with well defined columns for specific data types. The table name, and the column names are fully configurable, so you can decide on which names to use. We will use the table name tomcat_session_data for our sample. Table 5-7 shows the column names we will use in this section, and describes the data stored in each column.

Table 5-7. The Definition of Columns for Session Data Table

Column	Description
session_id	This column contains a string representation of the unique session ID. The id has a type of varchar(100), and is primary key for tomcat_session_data table.
application_name	The name of the web applications engine, host, and context are stored in this context, separated by forward slash; for example /Catalina/localhost/chapter5. The column's datatype is varchar(255).
valid	The valid column contains a single character that represents whether the session is valid or invalid. The valid column has a type of char(1).
maxinactive	The maxinactive column contains an integer representing the length of time that a session can remain inactive before becoming invalid. The maxinactive column has a type of int.
last_access	The last_access column contains an integer that represents the length of time since the session was last accessed. The last_access column has a type of bigint.
session_data	This column contains the serialized representation of the HTTP session. The data column has a type of mediumblob.

Listing 5-9 shows the SQL scripts that can be executed to create the required database and table for storing session data.

Listing 5-9. SQL Script for Creating the tomcatssessions Database and the tomcat_session_data Table

```
create database tomcatsessions;
use tomcatsessions;
create table tomcat_session_data (
    session_id         varchar(100) not null primary key,
    valid              char(1) not null,
    maxinactive        int not null,
    last_access        bigint not null,
    application_name   varchar(255),
    session_data       mediumblob
);
```

To be able to access the tomcatsessions database, you need to create user first, and grant access to the required database to the user created. You can do that with following two SQL commands:
```
CREATE USER 'tomcatuser'@'localhost' IDENTIFIED BY 'abc123';
```

grant all privileges on tomcatsessions.* to tomcatuser@localhost ;

We now have a MySQL database that can be used as a storage container for HTTP sessions objects.

Configuring Tomcat to use JDBCStore

The configuration of JDBCStore with PersistentManager is very similar to the FileStore configuration from the previous section—all you need to do is use JDBCStore to configure the <Store> nested element. Listing 5-10 shows the sample PersistentManager configuration.

Listing 5-10. PersistentManager *Configured to Use* JDBCStore *for Session Persistence*

```
<Manager
  className="org.apache.catalina.session.PersistentManager"
  saveOnRestart="true"
  maxActiveSessions="-1"
  minIdleSwap="-1"
  maxIdleBackup="-1">
    <Store className="org.apache.catalina.session.JDBCStore"          #1
        driverName="org.gjt.mm.mysql.Driver"                          #2
        connectionURL=
 "jdbc:mysql://localhost/tomcatsessions?user=tomcatuser; password=abc123"  #3
        sessionTable="tomcat_session_data"                            #4
        sessionIdCol="session_id"                                     #5
        sessionAppCol="application_id"
        sessionDataCol="session_data"
        sessionValidCol="valid"
        sessionMaxInactiveCol="maxinactive"
        sessionLastAccessedCol="last_access"
        checkInterval="60"/>
</Manager>
```

The attributes configured for the <Manager> element are exactly the same as for the PersistentManager application used with FileStore in previous section. The store element this time references JDBCStore as className (#1). The driver name is the fully qualified class name of the driver class for the configured database, in our case the MySQL database driver (#2). The connectionName attribute specifies the database JDBC connection string, with the username and password to use (#3). Attribute sessionTable specifies the name of the table where session data is stored (#4). After specifying the table name, we can configure the name for each column used with corresponding attributes (#5).

■ **NOTE** Make sure that the JAR file containing the JDBC driver referenced by the driverName attribute is placed in Tomcat's CLASSPATH. This is done easily by placing the jar file to the CATALINA_HOME/lib directory.

And that's it. After Tomcat restarts, we will store all session information in the configured MySQL database. You can access our sample shopping basket application, and create a session by adding few products to the basket. You can now log in to the database tomcatsessions, using SQL console for MySQL and see the session data stored by issuing the SQL command:

```
select * from tomcat_session_data;
```

The JDBCStore with PersistentManager is a robust and scalable solution for session persistence on Tomcat, usable for web applications with a large number of concurrent users whose idle sessions can be swapped easily to a database to lower the memory print of the Tomcat server.

Summary

In this chapter, we discussed HTTP sessions and how they are used. First we explained how are HTTP sessions used to keep the state of the request/response conversation with the server, and we described the details of HTTP session implementation in Apache Tomcat. We have implemented a shopping basket example to demonstrate the usage of user sessions in Java web applications. Next, we introduced session persistence with Tomcat, using the default StandardManager for session management. Finally we configured Tomcat's PersistentManager to persist HTTP session objects to a file on disk using FileStore and to a SQL database using JDBCStore.

In the next chapter, we cover Tomcat security realms.

CHAPTER 6

Configuring Security Realms

So far, we have learned about the basics of Tomcat architecture, and how to run servlets and JSP pages in Tomcat. In this chapter, we cover some of the methods that Tomcat provides for protecting resources. First, we talk about using security realms to protect a resource. Then, we move on to the common security realms used with Tomcat. Finally, we cover the basics of Tomcat container security using BASIC and FORM-based authentication.

In this chapter, we will

- Introduce security realms

- Describe `MemoryRealm` and `UserDatabaseRealm` and their usage with BASIC authentication

- Describe `JDBCRealm` and `DataSourceRealm` and their usage with FORM-based authentication

- Introduce `JNDIRealm`

- Discuss how you can access user data after authentication

Security Realms

A security realm is a Tomcat's mechanism for protecting web application resources. It gives you the ability to protect a resource with a defined security constraint, and then define the user roles that can access the protected resource. More specifically, Tomcat's realm can be defined as a collection of usernames, corresponding passwords, and the user roles associated with each user integrated with Tomcat server.

Tomcat's abstraction of a security realm is defined by the `org.apache.catalina.Realm` interface. This interface provides a mechanism by which a collection of usernames, passwords, and their associated roles can be integrated into Tomcat. If you downloaded the Tomcat source, you can find this interface in the following location:

`<CATALINA_HOME>/src/catalina/src/share/org/apache/catalina/Realm.java`

Tomcat 7 provides several implementations of `Realm` interface. Table 6-1 lists the implementations and their usage.

Table 6-1. Realm Implementation Available in Tomcat

Concrete Realm class	Description
MemoryRealm	Simple implementation that uses an xml file as a user store (typically tomcat-users.xml).
JDBCRealm	Realm that support storing usernames, passwords, and roles information in the SQL database.
JNDIRealm	Implementation backed by the Java Naming Directory Interface (JNDI).
DataSourceRealm	Realm backed by a JNDI-configured JDBC data source.
UserDatabaseRealm	Realm backed by a custom UserDatabase configured via JNDI.
JaasRealm	Security authentication using Java Authentication and Authorization Service (JAAS).
CombinedRealm	Realm implementation that allows usage of multiple realms at the same time.
LockOutRealm	Extends CombinedRealm, to lock out users if too many incorrect login tries are detected – prevents brute force server attack.

In addition to the Realm implementations available out of the box with Tomcat, you can provide your own custom implementation. All you have to do is implement Realm interface, package your implementation with all required classes into jar file, and copy file to CATALINA_HOME/lib directory. As discussed in previous chapters, all libraries in the lib directory will be available to Tomcat on startup, so you can start using your implementation straight away.

In this chapter, we will cover MemoryRealm and JDBCRealm in more detail. With MemoryRealm, we will cover its more advanced version, UserDatabaseRealm, and similarly JDBCRealm will be further explained with JNDI version DataSourceRealm. Finally, we will introduce JNDIRealm, which is used for authentication with LDAP directory server. For more information about other Realm implementations available with Tomcat 7, take a look at Tomcat's online resources (http://tomcat.apache.org/tomcat-7.0-doc/realm-howto.html).

MemoryRealm

Let's take a look at the simplest realm available in Tomcat: MemoryRealm. The MemoryRealm (contained in package org.apache.catalina.realm.MemoryRealm) uses an in-memory user database, which is read from an XML file on server startup. The root of the XML structure is the <tomcat-users> element, which holds the <user> elements. Each <user> element contains the required attributes for each user – name (username for authentication), password (plain text password), and roles (comma-separated list of roles that the user belongs to, used for authorization).

Listing 6-1 shows an example of the XML file containing four users.

Listing 6-1. XML Defining Four Users, with Usernames, Passwords, and User Roles

```
<tomcat-users>
        <user name="tomcat" password="tomcat" roles="tomcat" />          #1
        <user name="role1" password="tomcat" roles="role1" />
        <user name="both" password="tomcat" roles="tomcat,role1" />      #2
        <user name="bob" password="password" roles="apressuser" />
</tomcat-users>
```

Most user definitions are simple, with username, password, and a single role (#1), but one common scenario involves users that have two or more roles, which can be specified as comma-separated values in XML (#2).

■ **NOTE** The default location of the MemoryRealm's XML file is the <CATALINA_HOME>/conf/tomcat-users.xml. You can change the location of this file in the Tomcat's XML configuration, as we will show later in this section.

Now that we have discussed how user information is stored for usage with MemoryRealm, we can protect access to our sample web application.

Protecting a Resource with a MemoryRealm

To actually see how a MemoryRealm works, let's create a realm that protects our sample web application /apress, which we introduced in previous chapters.

The first step is to enable MemoryRealm in the Tomcat configuration file CATALINA_HOME/conf/server.xml. All we need to do to achieve this is to add the following line under the <Engine>, <Host>, or <Context> element of server.xml. We will configure it for our /apress web application under <Context> element, as Listing 6-2 shows.

Listing 6-2. MemoryRealm Configuration in server.xml file

```
<Context path="/chapter6" docBase="chapter6">
            <Realm className="org.apache.catalina.realm.MemoryRealm" />
        </Context>
```

If the <Realm> element is added under the <Engine> element of server.xml, all web applications served by the engine will have the realm enabled. That usually means that all web applications deployed on the Tomcat instance can use the configured realm. If the <Realm> element is within the <Host> element, all web applications within that host will have the realm enabled, but the web applications belonging to other hosts defined won't see the realm at all. Finally, if the <Realm> element is within the <Context> XML element, only web applications that are defined for that context can use the configured realm.

Only one realm is active for each web application at any given time. Therefore, the realm defined in <Engine> will apply to all web applications deployed on the server, unless it's overridden by the <Realm>

element under <Host>. Similarly, a realm defined under the <Engine> or <Host> elements can be overridden by a single web application-configured realm, under <Context> element. To avoid confusion and to keep configuration as robust as possible, it is a recommended approach to configure a realm on the web application level, within <Context> element, as our example shows.

However, just configuring the realm in this way won't make the web application secure; adding the <Realm> element to server.xml simply enables the realm for the web application. The web application must also be configured to use the realm's security features to complete the configuration. You can test this by starting the Tomcat server after this change is made and trying to access /examples, /apress, or any other application deployed – all of them will still be accessible as before, without any username or password required.

The next step is to configure the /apress sample web application to use the configured MemoryRealm implementation by editing web.xml file for our web application (located in CATALINA_HOME/webapps/apress/WEB-INF/web.xml). We need to add the <security-constraint> element to the web.xml, and define the protected resource. Listing 6-3 shows the web.xml configuration.

Listing 6-3, Definition of a Secured Resource in web.xml

```
<?xml version="1.0" encoding="ISO-8859-1"?>
<web-app version="2.4" xmlns="http://java.sun.com/xml/ns/j2ee"
xmlns:xsi="http://www.w3.org/2001/XMLSchema-instance"
        xsi:schemaLocation="http://java.sun.com/xml/ns/j2ee
http://java.sun.com/xml/ns/j2ee/web-app_2_4.xsd">

    <display-name>Chapter 6</display-name>
    <description>Security Realms Demo</description>

    <security-constraint>                                             #1
        <web-resource-collection>                                     #2
            <web-resource-name>Memory Realm Sample</web-resource-name> #3
            <url-pattern>/*</url-pattern>                             #4
        </web-resource-collection>
        <auth-constraint>                                             #5
            <role-name>apressuser</role-name>                        #6
        </auth-constraint>
    </security-constraint>
</web-app>
```

▪ **NOTE** The order of XML elements in web.xml is important. If your application does not start, check the error messages in the log files, and make sure that the order of XML elements is correct.

First, we define the <security-constraint> element, which acts as a holder for all security configurations for this web application. This element has two required child elements: <web-resource-collection>, which defines the URL path of the web applications that are to be protected (#2), and <auth-constraint>, which defines authorization roles that a user accessing the protected URLs must have (#5).

Within the `<web-resource-collection>` element we define its name (#3) and the URL pattern that matches all web application URLs that we want to protect (#4). It this example, we want to protect all pages of our sample application, so we use the wildcard character to match all URLs (/*).

As for the authorization part, we set the role name that is required for the access pages specified (#6) – the role name is "apressuser." If you take a look at Listing 6-1, you will notice that we have configured user "bob" to have role "apressuser."

If you now restart Tomcat and navigate to our web application's home page (http://localhost:8080/chapter6/jsps/index.jsp), you will see an error page with HTML status code 403 Forbidden – which means that access to the page is restricted successfully. Figure 6-1 shows the page in the browser.

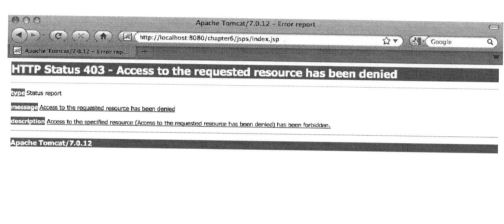

Figure 6-1. *Accessing a protected page in the browser without the required role*

So we have secured our web application, but when we tried to access it, we got the error page straight away. We should be offered a chance to enter a username and password and, if we log in successfully and have the required role, we should see the actual page.

The configuration so far only protected the page – we need a few more lines of XML code in order to tell Tomcat to render a login page if a user is not logged in.

For that, we are going to add the `<login-config>` element to web.xml file, after the `<security-constraint>` element. Listing 6-4 shows the additional configuration we need to add to the web.xml file of our web application.

Listing 6-4. Login Configuration for Secured Resources in `web.xml`

```
<login-config>
    <auth-method>BASIC</auth-method>          #1
    <realm-name>Apress</realm-name>           #2
</login-config>
```

For login configuration, we need to set the authentication method to use. For this example, we will use basic authentication supported by Tomcat (#1). With basic authentication, the server will display a popup window when you try to access a secure resource. In this window, you can type a username and password. The username and password are then transported (in plain text) to the Tomcat's built-in authentication mechanism, which will check your credentials against a configured user database (in our case, `tomcat-users.xml` file, as defined by `MemoryRealm`). We also configure the authentication realm name, which will be displayed in the login window (#2).

In addition to BASIC authentication, Tomcat supports other types of authentication: FORM, DIGEST, and CLIENT_CERT. FORM authentication will be covered with the `JDBCRealm` sample in the next section. For more information about other authentication methods, consult the Tomcat online manual. Table 6-2 lists authentication types supported by Tomcat.

Table 6-2. Authentication Types Supported by Apache Tomcat.

Authentication	Description
BASIC	Client authenticates by entering a username and password to a built-in browser login window. The browser sends the username and password in HTTP header in plain text, Base64 encoded. The username and password are then decoded on the server.
FORM	This is the most common authentication type. Client authenticates using HTML form by entering a username and password. The sending mechanism, password encoding, and the style of the HTML form are customizable by the user. The form attributes (input field names and form action attributes) are defined as part of Java Servlet specification.
DIGEST	Similarly to BASIC authentication, this uses the browser's login window to collect credential details and send them to the server as HTTP header. Unlike with BASIC authentication, usernames and passwords are digested – encoded using MD5 algorithm, which is a one-way hash function, so the username and password cannot be decoded – making authentication more secure. Some older browsers do not support DIGEST authentication.
CLIENT_CERT	This authentication type uses Secure Socket Layer (SSL), where both the client (user) and the server have their own SSL certificates, which are used for mutual authentication. This type of authentication does not require a username and password, and is the most secure of all the types mentioned. You can learn more about SSL configuration of Tomcat in the next chapter.

After finishing with the configuration, you'll have to restart Tomcat in order to apply the changes. After you restart, navigate the browser to the same URL as before (`http://localhost:8080/chapter6/jsps/index.jsp`), and you will see a login window displayed, asking you to enter your username and password. Figure 6-2 shows how the login window looks in the browser.

Figure 6-2. BASIC authentication login window

If you enter a username or password that is not contained in the tomcat-users.xml file, you will see the login dialog displayed again. This will repeat until you enter a valid username and password. Tomcat handles the flow of BASIC authentication process, and displays the login prompt until the correct details are entered; there is no special configuration for this functionality.

Now enter the username and password of the user that has required role "apressuser" – which is our user "bob" with password "password" – and you will be presented with our sample web application home page. Figure 6-3 shows the page rendered in the browser after a successful authentication and authorization.

Welcome to Apress

Figure 6-3. After a successful login, the home page of the application is displayed

If you entered credentials for the existing user, but without required role, you will see the same page as shown in Figure 6-1: the 403 Forbidden error page.

No matter what authentication method you use, you are always at risk of malicious users discovering your usernames and passwords and being able to access secured pages. That is the reason the tomcat-users.xml file does not have any users entered by default – imagine if an inexperienced user downloaded Tomcat and deployed it to a public server – anyone who knows the default usernames and passwords would be able to access all the pages deployed on the server!

Even with all standard protection methods, malicious users can still attempt brute force attacks on your server. In the next section we will cover some options available within Tomcat to avoid such attacks.

Protection Against Brute Force Attacks

Brute force attacks are usually performed by other programs, which try huge numbers of usernames and passwords to attempt to gain access to the server. These malicious programs are usually written so they try words that are known to be used as usernames and often used as passwords (names, dates of birth, names followed with year of birth, and the like). Although there are millions of combinations available, it is still possible – given time – for the usernames and passwords to be guessed, especially on web sites with millions of users. A common approach for preventing this is to lock out users for a given period of time if they enter an incorrect password too many times.

Tomcat's solution that is available out of the box is LockOutRealm, which we mentioned before as one of the realms available out of the box in Table 6-1. The LockOutRealm is a simple CombinedRealm, which encapsulates any other realms we can use. It needs to be configured in as a default Realm, replacing the realm we defined in listing 6-2. Listing 6-5 shows the LockOutRealm configuration.

Listing 6-5. Configuring LockOutRealm for Brute Force Attack Protection

```
<Context path="/chapter6" docBase="chapter6">
    <Realm className="org.apache.catalina.realm.LockOutRealm"
        failureCount="3 lockoutTime="3600">                        #1
            <Realm className="org.apache.catalina.realm.MemoryRealm" />   #2
    </Realm>
</Context>
```

The LockOutRealm is configured as any other realm (#1). The MemoryRealm we want to use is configured within the LockOutRealm (#2). LockOutRealm has two important properties:

- failureCount: Defines how many failed attempts a user can have before being locked out. The default value is 5.

- lockoutTime: Defines how long (in seconds) the user will be locked out if the failureCount has been exceeded. The default is 300.

Although not the prefect solution, the user lock out strategy is simple and usually good enough to protect against brute force attacks to your server.

UserDatabaseRealm

UserDatabaseRealm is an advanced version of the MemoryRealm. It has the same capabilities as MemoryRealm, and the users database is backed with the same XML file (which defaults to CATALINA_HOME/conf/tomcat-users.xml by default). The advantage of the UserDatabaseRealm is that it's configurable via the Java Naming Directory Interface – the standard Java API that allows clients to look up objects by a known name. Don't worry if you don't understand every bit about JNDI configuration at this point; it will be covered in much more detail in Chapter 11. The configuration for the UserDatabaseRealm is very similar to that of the MemoryRealm, with the addition of JNDI resource configuration. Listing 6-6 shows the UserDatabaseRealm configuration within <Context> element in a server.xml file.

Listing 6-6. Configuring UserDatabaseRealm in the Tomcat's server.xml file

```
<GlobalNamingResources>"                                          #1
        <Resource name="UserDatabase" auth="Container"            #2
            type="org.apache.catalina.UserDatabase"
            description="User database that can be updated and saved"
            factory="org.apache.catalina.users.MemoryUserDatabaseFactory"
            pathname="conf/tomcat-users.xml" />                   #3
</GlobalNamingResources>
```

```
<Context path="/chapter6" docBase="chapter6">
        <Realm className="org.apache.catalina.realm.UserDatabaseRealm"
              resourceName="UserDatabase"/>                                          #4
</Context>
```

The JNDI resource is configured within the `<GlobalNamingResources>` element in server.xml (#1). All JNDI resources for the server instance will be listed here. Next, we configure our `UserDatabase` resource (#2) with some basic properties. The configuration and properties of the JNDI resource configuration will be covered in more detail in Chapter 11. The one attribute to notice is the pathname attribute, which points to the XML file, which contains the user database (#3). The XML file used is the same `tomcat-users.xml` file we used for our `MemoryRealm` example. You can configure the custom path for your user database file, but it has to have same XML format as Listing 6-1 shows. Finally, we configure the actual `Realm` implementation, referencing the configured JNDI resource via `resourceName` attribute (#4).

Using a JNDI-backed resource allows us to access it easily – either programmatically (using JNDI API) or using JMX, and potentially change the user's details without needing to change the XML file on the disk. We can change `UserDatabase` resource instead.

`MemoryRealm` and `UserDatabaseRealm` security are easy to set up and configure; therefore, they are good to use for prototyping. Also, if your web application uses another authentication mechanism and does not use realms at all, `MemoryRealm` (or `UserDatabaseRealm`) can be handy for occasional Tomcat administration. However, user information is still stored in unsecure file, with passwords in plain text, making it potentially dangerous. In addition, the XML file can become difficult to maintain if you have hundreds or thousands of users. Because information about users in large systems is usually stored in some kind of relational database, in the next section we will demonstrate how to configure `JDBCRealm`, which will authenticate users against SQL database.

JDBC Realms

The second `Realm` implementation provided with Tomcat that we are going to cover is a JDBC realm, which is implemented by the `org.apache.catalina.realm.JDBCRealm` class. This class is much like the `MemoryRealm` discussed in the previous section, with the exception that it stores its collection of users. A `JDBCRealm` stores all of its users in a user-defined and JDBC-compliant database. Setting up a JDBC realm involves several steps, but it is really simple to manage once it is configured.

Creating the Users Database

Before you begin configuring Tomcat to use a `JDBCRealm`, you must first create a database to hold your collection of users. For this example, we will be configuring a MySQL database.

▪ **NOTE** If you already have a database of users, you can substitute the values we are using here with the appropriate values relating to your database. If you do not have an existing database, you can find the SQL scripts to create the MySQL database with the rest of the source code for this book.

In order to store user information in the SQL database and use `JDBCRealm` with the data, you will need to have two tables in the database schema.

The first table will store the usernames and passwords of all users, and must contain at least two text columns: one for usernames and one for passwords. For the sake of clarity, let's call this table the users table. The names of the database, tables, and columns are not important, as they can be configured as part of JDBCRealm configuration. Table 6-3 shows the users table definition, as we will use it for our examples.

Table 6-3. Users Table Definition

COLUMN	DESCRIPTION
user_name	Contains a string representing the username that will be used in the login form. It has a type of varchar(12).
user_pass	Contains a string representing the user's password. It also has a type of varchar(12).

The second table will store the roles for every user; let's call it the user_roles table. It must have two text columns. One column will contain usernames, and it will be a foreign key column referencing usernames in the first table (with usernames and passwords). The other column will contain single role for the user. The user_roles table will have a many-to-one relationship to the users table. Again, the name of the table or columns is not important. You can call these tables and columns whatever you want, as long as you configure the relevant names with the <Realm> element configuration in server.xml file. Table 6-4 shows the column definitions for the user_roles table.

Table 6-4. The user_roles Table Definition

COLUMN	DESCRIPTION
user_name	Contains a string referring to a user in the users table. It has a type of varchar(12).
role_name	Contains a string referring to a role in the roles table. It also has a type of varchar(12).

■ **NOTE** the columns specification discussed is the minimal requirement. Tables can contain other columns as well, as required for the application. For example, most users tables will contain information like last login, full name, email address, and other. Other columns in your tables will not be read or used by JDBCRealm.

Listing 6-7 shows the SQL script for the creation of the MySQL database with tables required for the JDBCRealm example.

Listing 6-7. Create Database SQL Script

```
create database tomcatusers;
use tomcatusers;
create table users
(
user_name varchar(12) not null primary key,
user_pass varchar(12) not null
);
create table users_roles
(
user_name varchar(12) not null,
role_name varchar(12) not null,
primary key(user_name, role_name)
);
```

Before you can create the users database in MySQL, you need to have downloaded and installed the MySQL server, which can be found at www.mysql.com. You should also download the latest JDBC driver for MySQL, which can also be found at the same Web site.

After you have MySQL installed, you need to complete the following steps to create and configure a MySQL Users database:

1. Start the MySQL client found in the <MYSQL_HOME>/bin/ directory.

2. Create the tomcatusers database, and the users and user_roles tables, by executing the SQL script from Listing 6-7.

3. Create the user that we will use to connect to the database from Tomcat, and grant this user permission to access the tomcatusers database. To keep things simple, we will create a user with username "test" and the password "test." You will need to execute the SQL script from the following code snippet to create the "test" user and grant the required permissions:

    ```
    create user 'test'@'localhost' identified by test;
    grant all privileges on tomcatusers.* to test@localhost
    ```

4. Finally, we'll need to insert few users to the database so that we can run our sample application. Listing 6-8 shows the insert SQL script, which populates the database with the same usernames, passwords, and roles that we used for the MemoryRealm example in the previous section (see Listing 6-1).

Listing 6-8. SQL Script Used to Populate the tomcatusers Database

```
insert into users values("tomcat", "tomcat");
insert into users values("role1", "tomcat");
insert into users values("both", "tomcat");
insert into users values("bob", "password");
insert into user_roles values("tomcat", "tomcat");
insert into user_roles values("role1", "role1");
insert into user_roles values("both", "tomcat");
insert into user_roles values("both", "role1");
```

```
insert into user_roles values("bob", "apressuser");
```

Now we have a MySQL database of users ready and we can proceed with JDBCRealm configuration.

Configuring Tomcat to Use a JDBCRealm

Now that we have a collection of users stored in a relational database (MySQL), let's configure Tomcat to use the JDBC container instead of the previously configured MemoryRealm. Here are the steps involved in configuring a JDBCRealm:

1. Open the <CATALINA_HOME>/conf/server.xml and place a comment around the previously uncommented <Realm> element.

   ```
   <!-- <Realm className="org.apache.catalina.realm.MemoryRealm" /> -->
   ```

   We mentioned before that only one realm can be active for each web application, so we are removing the old MemoryRealm configuration in order to introduce the new JDBCRealm.

2. Replace the commented out <Realm> element with the JDBCRealm configuration, as Listing 6-9 illustrates.

Listing 6-9. JDBCRealm Configuration in server.xml

```
<Realm className="org.apache.catalina.realm.JDBCRealm"          #1
        driverName="org.gjt.mm.mysql.Driver"                     #2
        connectionURL="jdbc:mysql://
            localhost/tomcatusers?user=test;password=test"       #3
        userTable="users"                                        #4
        userNameCol="user_name" userCredCol="user_pass"          #5
        userRoleTable="user_roles"                               #6
        roleNameCol="role_name"                                  #7
    />
```

To enable JDBCRealm, the className attribute of <Realm> element must specify its class, org.apache.catalina.realm.JDBCRealm (#1). The next required attribute is driverName, which specifies the JDBC driver class name for the selected database – in our case, MySQL driver (#2). The connectionURL attribute specifies the database connection URL (#3). It starts with jdbc:, and contains the host name or IP of the server where the database is running (in our case, localhost), as well as the database name, and username and password of the database user (these details are configured outside Tomcat, within the selected database administration console).

These properties conclude the general database configuration. The next step is to tell JDBCRealm which tables and columns to use in the configured database to load users, their passwords, and roles. Attribute userTable specifies the table, which contains usernames and passwords, and in our case it has the value "users" (#4). The columns of the table specified with userTable attribute are defined with the attributes userNameCol (username column) and userCredColumn (password column) (#5). Finally, we specify the table, which contains user roles using attribute userRoleTable (#6) and its column for storing user role (#7). The column of userRoleTable that contains the username and is referencing userTable will be automatically detected by Tomcat, and doesn't need to be configured.

░ **NOTE** Make sure that the JAR file containing the JDBC driver referenced by the `driverName` attribute is placed in Tomcat's CLASSPATH. To do so, download the driver jar file from the MySQL web site, and copy it to CATALINA_HOME/lib directory.

To complete this configuration change, stop and restart the Tomcat server.

A `JDBCRealm` is now configured so it can secure resources your Web applications. At this point, you should be able to log in to the /apress Web application by selecting from the users table the user who has a role of apressuser. The login process and screens in the browser will be exactly the same as with the `MemoryRealm` examples from the previous section.

BASIC authentication is just what it name implies: basic. It uses the built-in browser form, which you cannot customize using CSS. The password is sent in plain text, encoded using the Base64 algorithm, which is easy to decode. Because of this, BASIC authentication is not often used on production systems. FORM-based authentication is probably the most common type of authentication used on the Internet, including by global web giants, like Google, Facebook, or Yahoo. In the next section, we will take a look at a sample using FORM-based authentication with `JDBCRealm` configured earlier.

Configuring FORM-Based Authentication with JDBCRealm

Let's first describe how FORM-based authentication works. A user requests a protected resource – a web page that requires login. If the user is not already logged in, the login form is displayed where the user can enter a username and password. After entering these credentials, the container (in our case, Tomcat) checks the entered details against configured database of users (in our case, `JDBCRealm` checks the database columns for username and password). If the username and password do not match the stored records, an error page is displayed.

If the entered user credentials are matched in the database, user is *authenticated*. Now that the container knows who the user is, it checks the user's roles to see if the user can access the requested resource. This is called *authorization*. If the authenticated user has the required role, the requested page is displayed in the browser. If user does not have the role, an error page is displayed, with HTML status code 403 Forbidden.

Now that we know how the FORM-based authentication works, we can configure our web application to use it. The first step is to implement a login page. Listing 6-10 shows the JSP page with the login form.

Listing 6-10. Login Form for FORM-Based Authentication

```html
<html>
  <head>
   <title>Apress Demo</title>
   <meta http-equiv="Content-Type" content="text/html; charset=UTF-8">
  </head>
  <body>
    <div class="content">
      <b>Please login to continue</b>
        <form action="j_security_check" method="POST">          #1
            <table>
                <tr>
```

```
            <td><label for="username">Username:</label></td>
            <td><input id="username" type="text" name="j_username"
value=""/><td>                                                              #2
        </tr>
        <tr>
            <td><label for="password">Password:</label></td>
            <td><input id="password" type="password" name="j_password"
/><td>                                                                      #3
            <td><input type="submit" value="Login" /></td>                  #4
        </tr>
    </table>
  </form>
 </div>
 </body>
</html>
```

We are rendering the form using the HTML `<form>` tag (#1). The action attribute is set to j_security_check, which is the Java Servlet specification naming convention for FORM-based authentication action. Next, we add a text input field for the username (#2). The name of the field must be j_username – again, Java Servlet specification naming convention for the username field. Then we add password field, input with type password (#3) – and named j_password – another convention. These conventions are agreed as part of Java Servlet specification, so all servlet containers (like Tomcat, Jetty, JBoss, and so on) that conform to the specification have well defined configuration for FORM-based authentication. Finally, we need a submit field (#4).

Apart from form action and the names of input fields, a user can customize all other parts of this form. Labels, HTML elements and attributes, JavaSsript handlers, and CSS styles all can be edited to match the look and feel requirements of your web application. This is something we couldn't do with BASIC authentication.

▪ **NOTE** FORM-based authentication is not more secure by itself then the BASIC authentication, but it's much more customizable. You can configure SSL certificates and set up the authentication rules so the username and password are sent encrypted using more secure encoding algorithms.

Let's save the login page in the separate directory, on path /WEB-INF/secure/login.jsp. Remember that our index page is stored in the /WEB-INF/jsps/index.jsp. We'll discuss these paths shortly.

Now that we have the login form, we need to implement a page that will be rendered when a user cannot be authenticated – a login error page. Listing 6-11 shows the simple login error JSP page.

Listing 6-11. Login Error JSP page

```
<html>
  <head>
  <title>Apress Demo</title>
  <meta http-equiv="Content-Type" content="text/html; charset=UTF-8">
  </head>
  <body>
    <div class="content">
```

```
        <b>Login error, please go back to <a href="login.jsp">login page</a>.</b>
      </div>
    </body>
</html>
```

Let's save the error page in the same directory as the login page, so its path looks like this: /WEB-INF/secure/login-error.jsp.

We have the views that will be rendered in the browser. The last step we have to complete is the configuration of the FORM-based authentication in the web.xml file. As you can see in Listing 6-12, the changed web.xml has a few more lines of XML configuration than the BASIC configuration example.

Listing 6-12. Configuration of FORM-Based Authentication in the web.xml file

```
<security-constraint>
      <web-resource-collection>
          <web-resource-name>JDBC Realm Sample</web-resource-name>
          <url-pattern>/jsps/*</url-pattern>                              #1
      </web-resource-collection>
      <auth-constraint>
          <role-name>apressrole</role-name>                              #2
      </auth-constraint>
</security-constraint>

<login-config>
      <auth-method>FORM</auth-method>                                    #3
      <realm-name>Apress</realm-name>
      <form-login-config>
          <form-login-page>/secure/login.jsp</form-login-page>          #4
          <form-error-page>/secure/login-error.jsp</form-error-page>    #5
      </form-login-config>
</login-config>
```

Similarly, as with the BASIC authentication example from the previous section, we first need to configure security-constraint, which consists of the URL pattern (#1) and the role required to access it (#2). Note that we configured the URL pattern using the wild character (*) to match all pages under the /jsps/ directory.

Next, we configure the login-config element. This time we are configuring an authentication method to be FORM based (#3). For FORM-based authentication, two new elements must be set, which haven't been used in the BASIC authentication example. Those elements are:

- <form-login-page>: Defines the page to be rendered when a user requests a secure resource, but is not authenticated – our login page (#4).

- <form-error-page>: Defines the page to be rendered when user credentials are not recognized – our login error page (#5).

One thing to point out here is how we configured the URL pattern for the secured pages. The URL pattern we configured security for (#1 in code Listing 6-11) should match all URLs that we want to protect. On the other hand, the actual login page (and login error page) *must not* be protected – so un-authenticated user can access those pages to log in.

Now you understand why we saved the login pages (login.jsp and login-error.jsp) and content pages (index.jsp) in the separate directories, /WEB-INF/secure/ and /WEB-INF/jsps, respectively. It is a common mistake to have a login page that matches the secure URL pattern, so you end up with a login page that requires a user to log in, creating an infinite loop that can never be resolved, and resulting in a server crash. However, all modern browsers can detect infinite redirect loop, and display the error page before the server crashes.

Let's now see how FORM-based authentication with JDBC realm works in practice. Build the web application into WAR archive, and deploy it to the server using any of the methods we covered in this book so far. For the purpose of this example, we will name our WAR file chapter6.war. Once you have Tomcat started up, navigate to your application in the browser by entering the following URL: http://localhost:8080/chapter6/jsps/index.jsp. Because of our security setup, instead of the welcome page you will be redirected to the login page. Figure 6-4 shows the login page rendered in the browser.

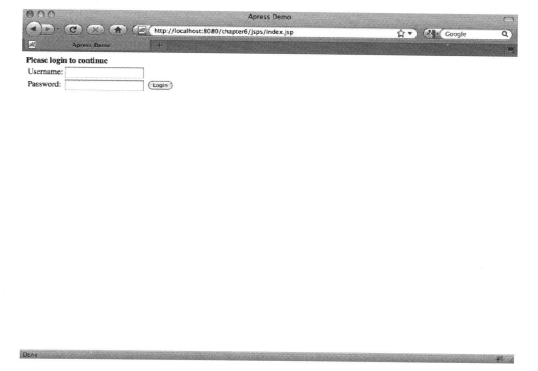

Figure 6-4. *Login page in the browser for FORM-based authentication*

The form in our example looks pretty basic – but there is nothing stopping you from adding CSS styles to the HTML form in Listing 6-10 to make it look however you want.

The next step is to actually log in using username and password. Enter the credential that we inserted in the database for the JDBCRealm; we have one user with required role "apressuser", with username "bob" and password "password" (as Listing 6-8 shows). After submitting the form, you will be authenticated and authorized to see the requested page, and the welcome page shown in Figure 6-3 will be displayed in the browser.

In case you enter invalid credentials in the form from Figure 6-4 (an unknown user or username and password that do not match), you will be redirected to the login-error page. Figure 6-5 illustrates the login error page rendered in the browser.

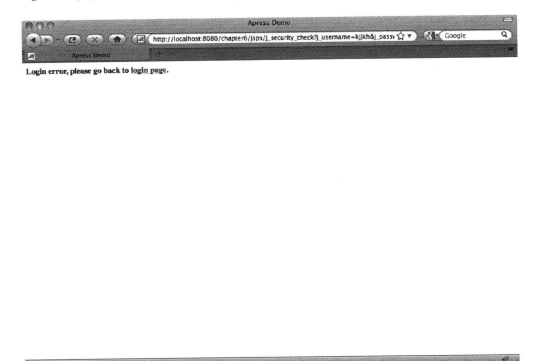

Figure 6-5. *Login error page displayed in the browser after unsuccessful login*

If you log in as a user that does not have required appressuser role, you will see Tomcat's standard error page with HTML status 403 forbidden, as Figure 6-1 shows.

In the previous section, we discussed that, to logout using BASIC authentication, a user has to close the browser, or to clear the browser history – which can be inconvenient. When using FORM-based authentication, a user can be logged out by invalidating the user's session. You can use that from the Tomcat's Manager web application as we saw in Chapter 4, or you can do it programmatically, from your servlet code. For more information about sessions and how to access them, read Chapter 5.

DataSourceRealm

DataSourceRealm is the upgraded version of the JDBCRealm, which allows configuration of the database connection as the JNDI resource. JNDI configuration offers more flexibility and easier management – either programmatically (using JNDI API) or via JMX access. Similar to UserDatabaseRealm, which is a JNDI configurable version of MemoryRealm, DataSourceRealm configuration is very similar to JDBCRealm configuration, with the addition of JNDI resource configuration. The functionality it offers is the same as that of JDBCRealm, with database tables and columns defined in the same way. To configure DataSourceRealm, you only need to configure JNDI data source resource, and use that resource with the security realm configured in the usual way. Listing 6-13 shows the server.xml file with the configured DataSourceRealm.

Listing 6-13. Configuring DataSourceRealm in Tomcat's server.xml File

```
<GlobalNamingResources>
        <Resource name="jdbc/tomcatusersdb" auth="Container"          #1
                type="javax.sql.DataSource"
                maxActive="100" maxIdle="30" maxWait="10000"
                username="test" password="test"
                driverClassName="com.mysql.jdbc.Driver"
                url="jdbc:mysql://localhost:3306/tomcatusers"/>
</GlobalNamingResources>
<Context path="/chapter6" docBase="chapter6">
    <Realm className="org.apache.catalina.realm.DataSourceRealm"      #2
        dataSourceName="jdbc/tomcatusersdb"                           #3
        userTable="users"
        userNameCol="user_name" userCredCol="user_pass"
        userRoleTable="user_roles"
        roleNameCol="role_name"
        />
</Context>
```

Similarly to the configuration of the UserDatabase JNDI resource in Listing 6-6, first we need to configure the JDBC data source as a global JNDI resource (#1). The attributes of the resources are similar to the database connection parameters we used for the JDBCRealm configuration, including database URL, driver class, and username and password credentials. Next we configure the DataSourceRealm for the chapter6 <Context> element (#2). We set the same attributes as we did for the JDBCRealm – namely names of the database tables in which we store the users' details, and the relevant column names in those tables. The only new attribute we need to add is the dataSourceName, defining the name of the JNDI resource we want to use (#3). The value of the dataSourceName attribute is set to jdbc/tomcatusersdb, same as name attribute of the <Resource> element (#1).

And that's it – we have fully configured DataSourceRealm. The examples we used with JDBCRealm earlier will all work without any changes.

The Benefits of Using a JDBCRealm

JDBCRealm and DataSourceRealm provide advantages over simple MemoryRealm (and UserDatabaseRealm) for managing Tomcat users. Using a JDBCRealm makes it possible for you to leverage your application's database as users storage, whereas, in most previously existing web applications, the container of users exists in some proprietary web server database. The management of a user database with more than a dozen users quickly becomes impossible when using MemoryRealm and store users in the file. On the other hand, every relational database ships with an administration console with which user information can be easily managed. You can even implement the user management functionalities within your own web application deployed in the same Tomcat instance.

In addition, you can make changes to the SQL user database and have the changes take effect without restarting the Tomcat server. The changes you make to the user data will be visible to the user when he or she logs in. For BASIC authentication, that is when the browser is restart. If using FORM-based authentication, the changes will take effect once a user's current session expires. When using a

MemoryRealm, you must restart the Tomcat server after adding new users, or modifying user information (passwords or roles) in any way.

As a note, the production systems usually don't use MemoryRealm and JDBCRealm directly. The common practice is to use one of the JNDI versions of realms – UserDatabaseRealm instead of MemoryRealm and DataSourceRealm instead of JDBCRealm. These two realms provide exactly the same functionality as the two we discussed earlier in this chapter, with the addition of managing the user database as a JNDI resource, treating is as abstract, reusable resource, managed by the Tomcat itself. You can read more about JNDI in Chapter 13.

Finally, the production systems will usually use some of the advanced realms available in Tomcat, such as CombinedRealm (if you have multiple database of users, or want to use both MemoryRealm and JDBCRealm at the same time); or LockOutRealm, which we demonstrated earlier – allowing the built-in protection against brute force attacks from malicious software or users.

JNDIRealm

When discussing large production systems, you will often find LDAP server is used for user information storage and management. LDAP stands for Lightweight Directory Access Protocol, and it's a protocol for accessing directory-based resources over IP networks. The resource, in LDAP terminology, can be anything that is organized as a set of hierarchical records (students at a university, organized across departments, for example; or a list of IP addresses across networks). LDAP is most often used as a user data storage and authentication system within large organizations. LDAP is usually accessed via a JNDI provider, where a JNDI API is used to access LDAP information, analogous to how relational databases are accessed via JDBC.

Tomcat supports authentication using LDAP server via its JNDIRealm implementation.

JNDIRealm is configured to access an LDAP directory via a JNDI provider and provide data for the authentication and authorization of users in Tomcat. Detailed discussion about LDAP directory server and its configuration is beyond the scope of this book, but we will demonstrate a simple JNDIRealm configuration without going into depth of LDAP settings.

Similarly to other security realm configurations, all we need to do it add a <Realm> element in the CATALINA_HOME/conf/server.xml file. Listing 6-14 illustrates the JNDIRealm configuration in the server.xml file.

Listing 6-14. Sample JNDIRealm Configuration for LDAP Authentication

```
<Realm className="org.apache.catalina.realm.JNDIRealm          #1
       connectionURL="ldap://apress.com:389                     #2
       userPattern="uid={0},ou=users,dc=apress,dc=com"          #3
       roleBase="ou=groups,dc=apress,dc=com"                    #4
       roleSearch="(uniqueMember={0})" />                       #5
```

Firstly, we configure the <Realm> element with the JNDIRealm full class name (#1). Next, we set the connectionURL attribute, which sets the URL where the LDAP server is running. Then, we set the userPattern attribute, which contains the pattern for the *distinguished name* directory entry for locating the records (#3). In the pattern, {0} will be replaced by the actual username. Attribute roleBase specifies the LDAP directory entry where information about user roles can be retrieved (#4). Finally, the roleSearch attribute defines the LDAP filter for searching the user roles (#5).

There are numerous LDAP servers implementations available, such as Microsoft Active Directory and Apple Directory. If you are looking to to explore LDAP in more detail, we suggest looking at the most popular open source implementation OpenLDAP (www.openldap.org). With its large user base and open source support, you can find a lot of online resources and configuration examples for Apache Tomcat. In addition, Apache Tomcat's online documentation has a good example of the LDAP setting for OpenLDAP server and corresponding JNDIRealm configuration (http://tomcat.apache.org/tomcat-7.0-doc/realm-howto.html#JNDIRealm).

Accessing an Authenticated User

Once a user has been authenticated, it is very easy to access the user's information using the HttpServletRequest interface. Because the user's information is stored in the HttpServletRequest object, it is available to all JSPs and servlets existing in the same request. To see how this information is accessed, we are going to edit the index.jsp page we used in throughout this chapter. The modified index.jsp can be found in Listing 6-15.

Listing 6-15. The Modified index.jsp Page

```
<html>
  <head>
   <title>Apress Demo</title>
   <meta http-equiv="Content-Type" content="text/html; charset=UTF-8">
  </head>
  <body>
    <div class="content">
      <b>Welcome to Apress, <%= request.getRemoteUser() %></b>          #1
    </div>
  </body>
</html>
```

To illustrate the access of the authentication information on the JSP page, we have embedded a bit of Java code in the JSP page to print the logged in user on the screen (#1). The request variable used is a reference to the current HttpServletRequest object. It's implicitly available to all JSP pages (by Tomcat), so we can access it, and all of its properties within the JSP page.

This code uses the request.getRemoteUser() method to retrieve the authenticated user's username. It then outputs the returned username. After you have made the changes to this JSP, copy it to the <CATALINA_HOME>/webapps/apress/ directory and point your browser to the following URL: http://localhost:8080/apress/index.jsp.

If you have already been authenticated, you should see the screen shown in Figure 6-6 with the username with which you were authenticated following the Welcome to Apress text. If you have not been authenticated in the /apress Web application, enter bob and password in the BASIC authentication dialog box.

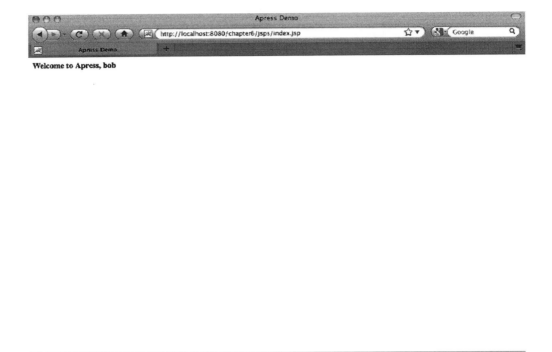

Figure 6-6. The Modified welcome.jsp page shows the effect of retrieving the username from a security realm.

In case you call this method when there is no authenticated user, it will return null.

In addition to username of the authenticated user, you can also check if the user is in the required role programmatically, by querying HttpServletRequest object. The method HttpServletRequest.isUserInRole(String roleName) returns true if the authenticated user had the role specifies with argument, and false otherwise.

Summary

In this chapter, we discussed security realms and how they are used. We also covered the most common types of security realms that are packaged with Tomcat, including their configuration and use. In addition, through realm configuration examples, we demonstrated Tomcat container authentication, specifically BASIC and FORM-based authentication. Finally, we demonstrated how to access the information about authenticated user within your Servlet or JSP code. In the next chapter, we cover securing a Web application using the Secure Sockets Layer (SSL).

CHAPTER 7

Securing Tomcat with SSL

In the previous chapter, we learned how to protect web applications in Tomcat from unauthorized access by configuring security realms. However, securing web resources with usernames and passwords can still leave a web application vulnerable to malicious access. If anyone eavesdrops on the communication between client and server, they can get access to the username and password of the legitimate user and compromise the web application's security.

In this chapter, we will learn how SSL protocol works, and demonstrate how we can employ SSL protocol to encrypt the traffic between browsers and Tomcat, making sure that information passed to and from Tomcat cannot be intercepted or changed in any way.

In this chapter, we will do the following:

- Introduce SSL protocol and its secure mechanism

- Describe how to generate SSL certificates using Java tools

- Configure Tomcat and a web application for secure access over SSL

- Demonstrate how to use SSL for secure session tracking

Introduction to SSL

Secure Socket Layer (SSL) is a secure transfer protocol used for communication on the Internet using cryptographic methods. SSL was first developed by Netscape to make its own products secure. After its public release, it was quickly adopted by a number of big players in the IT industry, including Microsoft, and it became the de-facto standard for Internet traffic encryption.

■ **Note** More recently, the Internet Engineering Task Force (IETF), the organization that develops and promotes Internet standards, developed Transport Level Security (TLS) based on SSL. TLS is a community-standardized protocol and will probably eventually replace SSL. Because almost all current server and client applications support both TLS and SSL, you can decide which one to use. Although there is little difference between the SSL and TLS protocols, TLS is backward compatible with SSL, and thus a safer option. However, due to its widespread usage, SSL is still the more commonly used secure protocol for web applications. For that reason, and to avoid confusion, we're using the term SSL to refer to the secure communication protocol throughout this chapter.

What SSL Does

The main purpose of the SSL protocol is to guarantee that no one can eavesdrop on or tamper with the communication between a browser and the server where the web application is deployed. When accessing the web sites secured by SSL, a user can be sure that no one can intercept and read the information passed to the remote server; for example, usernames and passwords or credit card information when using e-commerce web sites. In addition, the user is safe to send and receive any sensitive information to and from web server, knowing that no one could have tampered with the information during transport, or can change the transported content in any way.

Another purpose of secure communication is the ability to authenticate the server and its owner based on the SSL information – so that a user can be certain that the server that it's accessing is the one that it's saying it is. This has become very important in today's Internet-dependent society, so that we are sure that we are accessing our bank's web site, for example, and not some malicious web site representing itself as our bank. The term for a site that is masquerading itself as another, tricking a user to pass sensitive information to it, is phishing.

How SSL works

SSL is a cryptographic protocol, using symmetric pair of keys to encrypt and decrypt traffic sent over the Internet.

In a common SSL scenario, when the user accesses the web server for the first time, the server sends its SSL certificate, or public key, to the client. The SSL certificate contains the information about the server, its owner, company, and its validity period. A user can reject a certificate if it does not trust its authenticity, effectively terminating the connection.

If the user accepts the certificate, the certificate itself is stored in the browser, and is used to initiate a secure connection with the issuing server. This key is public, as the server sends it to anyone that asks for it.

The information encoded using the public key can only be decoded using the symmetric private key. The private key is, as its name suggests, private, and kept safely on the server. A client generates the symmetric key, with which both client and server will encrypt all traffic sent to the other side. With the symmetric key, content is encoded and decoded using the same key known to both parties in the communication, which is less secure than the asymmetric public/private key communication. That's why it's important that the exchange of the symmetric keys is secure. Therefore, a client encodes the symmetric key using the server's public key (received in the certificate), and the server encodes it using its private key.

When a server receives the symmetric key, the connection between server and client is secure, and all traffic sent from the browser to the web application, and response content from the web server to the browser, will be encrypted using the generated symmetric key known to client and server only. The exchanged symmetric key is valid only for the duration of the current session, and needs to be re-generated every time a user initiates a new session.

The security of SSL depends on how secure the key used to encrypt data is. SSL is not unbreakable in theory, but with the amount of time required to break standard 128-bit key, in practice it is often assumed as safe from brute-force attacks. For the industry-standard 128-bit key, there are 2^{128} combinations possible to generate the key. The value of 2^{128} calculates to 340,282,366,920,938,463,463,374,607,431,768,211,456, or roughly 240 trillion trillion trillions! To put things into perspective, today's super computers can break the DES encryption algorithm, which uses 56-bit long keys, in around one day. If, in the future, man develops a machine that can perform the same task of breaking a 56-bit key in one second, it would still take 149.7 trillion years to brute force a 128-bit key!

SSL protocol communication over HTTP protocol is referred to as HTTPS (secure HTTP). The web sites that are using SSL encrypted connections display https as the protocol name in the browser's address bar, for example https://www.mybank.com.

Ensuring that the connection is secure from eavesdropping and tampering, using asymmetric and symmetric cryptography methods is the main purpose of using SSL. However, there is another useful purpose of SSL-certificate protected web sites: the ability to authenticate that the site is what it says it is. SSL certificates, sent by the secure server as public keys to the client, contain basic information about the site to which they belong, such as the domain name, owner name, and company name. Organizations called Certificate Authorities (CA) can authenticate the details of the SSL certificate, so if the user trusts the CA, they can be sure that the secure web site is certified, and its details are correct. There is a number of CAs that can issue a certified SSL certificate. Modern browsers automatically recognize the largest and best-known CAs, and allow connections to the sites providing SSL certificates certified by these organizations automatically.

The secure icon and the registered domain name are displayed in the browser's address bar if the SSL connection is active. Figure 7-1 shows an example in the Firefox web browser. (Note that the company name is not a mandatory field, as indicated by the "unknown" reference in Figure 7-1.)

Figure 7-1. The secure connection icon and the registered domain name from the certificate are displayed in the browser's address bar.

If the SSL certificate is not certified by a CA, or is certified by the CA but not recognized by the user's browser, the user will be presented with a warning screen, where he or she can decide whether to trust the certificate. Figure 7-2 shows the warning received if the certificate is not automatically accepted by the browser.

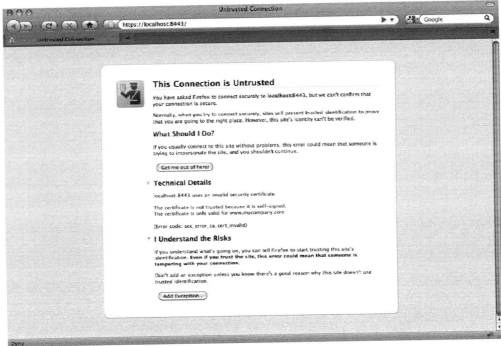

Figure 7-2. If the SSL certificate cannot be accepted automatically, a warning is displayed to the user.

Configuring Tomcat with SSL

In order to use SSL for server access, we need to create our own public key, which we will use as a certificate. The certificate we are going to create is usually called a self-signed certificate, as it will not be verified with an independent CA, so we cannot authorize as web site owners with it. But, having self-signed certificate is sufficient enough to have SSL encrypted communication with our server. For development and testing purposes, or for internal applications not accessible outside the company's network, this is often enough to provide a usable, secure environment.

Creating Keystore with SSL Certificate

All publicly known certificates are stored in a repository called the keystore. The keystore is a file that contains the public and private key data required to encode and decode information using SSL or TLS. Applications that are using SSL must be able to read the keystore file, and use its data as keys to encrypt and decrypt information. The key data in the keystore file can be stored in a number of formats that depend on the tool used to create keystore. Apache Tomcat 7 can read keystores in one of the following formats: PKCS11, PKCS12, and JSK. PKCS11 and PKCS12 formats belong to the standards called Public-Key Cryptography Standards, developed by the RSA Laboratories, which is one of the leading network security companies in the world. JKS format stands for Java KeyStore, which is a Java-specific keystore format. JKS keystore can be created and manipulated using the keytool utility application, distributed as part of Java SDK from version 1.4. Because JKS is simple enough to use and easily accessible as part of Java SDK, we will be using its keytool application to create JKS keystores, which we will use to configure SSL on Tomcat.

Keytool, which we will use to create a self-signed SSL certificate, is located in the JAVA_HOME/bin/ directory. The file name is keytool.exe (on Windows systems), or just keytool, with no extension (on Unix-based systems). Because JAVA_HOME/bin is on the systems path by default after Java installation, you can execute it from any directory on the file system. In order to check if the keytool is available on your system, just type keytool on the command line in the terminal window. You should see the list of all required and optional command line arguments you can use to invoke the application.

Table 7-1 shows the commands with the required arguments that you should execute for Windows and Unix-based systems, respectively.

Table 7-1. The Commands to Generate a New, Self-Signed Certificate in a JKS Keystore

OS	Command
Windows	`keytool -genkeypair -alias tomcat -keyalg RSA -keystore C:\mykeystore`
Unix	`keytool -genkey -alias tomcat -keyalg RSA -keystore /home/aleksav/mykeystore`

We are using the keytool to generate a new SSL certificate by specifying the -genkeypair argument. The genkeypair argument was named genkey in earlier versions of the Java SDK (earlier than version 1.6), and it is still supported for backward compatibility. Because one keystore can contain multiple public/private key pairs, we will be using the alias "tomcat" to identify our new certificate within the keystore (by specifying the command argument -alias tomcat). We can also specify the algorithm used to generate the key pair, using the –keyalg argument. We will be using the RSA algorithm, a commonly used cryptography algorithm for public and private key generation. Finally, we will specify the file where our keystore will be saved using the -keystore argument. If you omit this argument, new file named .keystore, will be created in the home directory of the user running the command.

When you press Enter, you will first be prompted for the keystore password. This password will be used to access any certificate stored in the created keystore, so use the usual precaution when deciding on the keystore password. For the purpose of this example, we will set the keystore password to **abc123**.

After that, you will be prompted to enter some information about the certificate, the owner's name, the company, and location (country). You are first asked to enter your first and last name. The information you enter is stored in the keystore as the common name (CN) of the certificate. Although it looks confusing, you should enter the host name for the server for which you are generating a certificate. The reason for this is that, according to HTTPS specification, browsers should match the CN of the provided certificate to the domain name of the requested URL. If they do not match, the user will be presented with a warning in the browser that states that the certificate does not match the domain name of the site they are accessing. Because this decreases the amount of trust users have in the web site, the warning is not something that is desired for the public web site. To avoid this, make sure that any certificate you generate has a valid domain name as the CN, confusingly set as the first and last name value in the keytool interface (see the first question in Figure 7-3).

■ **Note** You can only have one SSL certificate for one IP address. If you host multiple domains on the same IP, only one of these host names can have a valid SSL certificate that matches its domain name. If you try to use SSL for any other domain name on the same IP, the browser will display a warning that the domain name does not match the certificate. This is a known limitation of SSL, because an SSL protocol handshake must happen before the hostname is extracted from the HTTP request.

Once you enter all the required details, you will be asked for another password, this time the password for this particular certificate within the keystore. For this example, we will set this password to **tomcat123**. Both the keystore password we set earlier and the certificate password are used for Tomcat configuration later, so remember them or write them down.

Once completed, you will have the chance to confirm all details entered. Once these are confirmed, you will have your certificate generated and stored in the file you specified as the –keystore argument. Figure 7-3 shows the terminal window with the keytool executed.

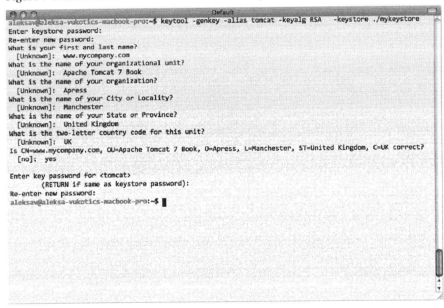

Figure 7-3. Running a keytool from the terminal command line

Now that we have the SSL certificate generated, we can configure Tomcat to use it for SSL server access.

Configuring Tomcat's SSL Connector

The first step in configuring SSL with Tomcat is to configure Tomcat's Connector, which will handle SSL connections over HTTPS. To configure the <Connector> element for SSL, all you have to do is set the SSLEnabled attribute to true, and set the scheme and secure attributes in order that the SSL information is correctly interpreted by the servlets deployed in Tomcat. Along with these basic attributes, you can configure additional details for your SSL configuration relating to the keystore and certificate we generated in the previous section. Listing 7-1 shows typical Tomcat SSL Connector configuration in the server.xml file.

Listing 7-1. Tomcat's SSL Connector Configuration Using Non-Blocking Java SSL Implementation

```
<Connector
    SSLEnabled="true"                                                #1
    scheme="https" secure="true"                                     #2
    port="8443"                                                      #3
    protocol="HTTP/1.1"                                              #4
    clientAuth="false"                                              #5
    keystoreFile="/Users/aleksav/mykeystore" keystorePass="abc123"   #6
    keyAlias="tomcat" keyPass="tomcat123"                           #7
/>
```

We first set the SSLEnabled attribute to true, telling Tomcat that this connector handles SSL connections (#1). In addition, we set the scheme attribute to value https, so that all SSL-secure URLs are recognized by the standard https:// protocol identifier; and we need to set secure attribute to true, if we wish to check for an SSL connection within Java servlet code, by calling HttpServletRequest.isSecure() method (#2). Next, we set the port on which the SSL connector will accept incoming connections (#3). Because 443 is the common port number for HTTPS connections, Tomcat itself uses the slight variation 8443 (using the same convention for port 8080 for standard HTTP request, as opposed to the "common" port 80, adding 8000 for the standardized port).

The next bit is the protocol configuration. We used standard HTTP/1.1 protocol, which is implemented in Tomcat's class org.apache.coyote.http11.Http11Protocol (#4). Http11Protocol is the standard blocking Java HTTP protocol. It is blocking because it uses a single thread to process the incoming requests and dispatch the response back to the browser. You have a choice to use a non-blocking version of Java Tomcat protocol instead, or even an APR Tomcat native protocol. Non-blocking Java protocol must reference its implementing class as the protocol attribute value: org.apache.coyote.http11.Http11NioProtocol. To use Tomcat's native APR protocol, you must make sure you have Tomcat's native library on the Tomcat classpath, and reference the APR HTTP connector class name as protocol attribute value: org.apache.coyote.http11.Http11AprProtocol.

▪ **Note** In order to use the Tomcat native library, you must compile it from the source code for your specific operating system. The native library compilation is beyond the scope of this book, but you can consult Tomcat's native documentation about the required steps at http://tomcat.apache.org/native-doc/.

The next attribute we configure is the clientAuth attribute (#5). This attribute specifies whether we are using one-way secure certificate authentication or if the client needs to present the valid SSL certificate to the server as well. When using SSL for web applications publicly accessible on the Internet, we don't require users to authenticate to the server using SSL certificate; to establish a secure connection, it is enough that the client accepts the certificate from the server. However, sometimes the server requires the client to be authenticated as well, usually in a business-to-business scenario, where both client and server are actually computer programs, without any human influence. For this example, we will configure standard public web site SSL connectivity by setting the `clientAuth` attribute to `false`.

Finally, we need to set the attributes relating to the keystore and the certificate our Tomcat server will use to encrypt and decrypt SSL traffic. We configure the keystore file path by specifying the `keystoreFile` attribute, setting it to the absolute path of the keystore file we created in the previous section (#6). At the same time, we specify the password we used for the keystore. And, as the last step, we specify the alias of the actual SSL certificate that can be used to identify it within the specified keystore (#7). We must use the same alias used when creating the certificate, as well as the password for the certificate itself. As you can see, we used the same values as specified when running the keytool application in the previous section.

Now we need to start Tomcat (or restart it if it's already running). After the startup is completed, you will be able to access Tomcat's home page by typing `https://localhost:8443` URL to your browser's address bar.

■ **Note** Make sure you start the web address with `https` for the protocol name to access the application correctly. If by mistake you use http (for example `http://localhost:8443`), you will end up with the error page in the browser, because Tomcat expects any URL with HTTP protocol to use port 8080 (and at the same time, any URL with HTTPS protocol must use port 8443). Any other combination will not be recognized by Tomcat as a valid URL.

When you do that for the first time, you will be presented with a warning, exactly the same as the warning shown in Figure 7-2. This is expected, for two reasons. First, we are using a self-signed certificate that has not been validated by any CA, so the browser will warn the user about that. Second, we created the certificate by specifying CN record as www.mycompany.com, and now we access it using the localhost domain name. As expected, the browser is displaying a warning that the CN domain name and the domain name used to access the site do not match.

In order to proceed, you will need to add exception for this certificate by confirming to the browser that you indeed trust this site. After adding the SSL exception, you will be presented with the familiar Tomcat home page, but this time using HTTPS secure protocol on the configured port 8443.

Figure 7-4 shows the browser windows when you access the Tomcat's home page using the HTTPS secure protocol.

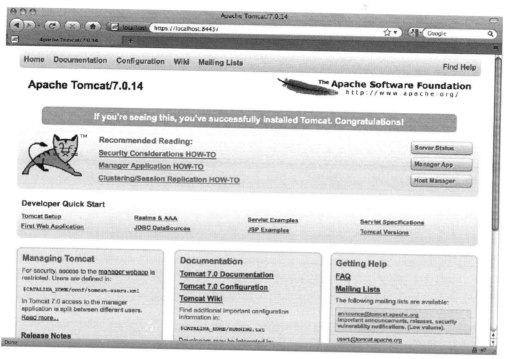

Figure 7-4. Tomcat's home page access over SSL on port 8443

If you change the port name to 8080 and the protocol to HTTP, you will notice that you can still access Tomcat's home page using the standard HTTP protocol as before on http://localhost:8080. With the configuration so far, we have enabled the SSL on Tomcat, and users can choose whether to access the site over HTTP or HTTPS. However, for real-world secure applications, we would like to force users to use the SSL-secured protocol when accessing pages with security-critical information. For example, when users are logging in or when users are typing credit card details in the HTML form. In the next section, we are going to configure our sample web application to do precisely that: force users to use the secure protocol for required pages.

Configuring Secure Resources in the Web Application

To demonstrate forcing the use of the HTTPS protocol, we are going to use the sample web application from the previous chapter, the FORM-based authentication example. We will improve the FORM-based login example by forcing Tomcat to load and submit a login page, with user username and password, over SSL. Our login page is located at /WEB-INF/secure/login.jsp file. All we need to do is to specify a new security constraint in the web deployment descriptor (web.xml). Listing 7-2 shows the updated web.xml file from the FORM-based login example, with the added SSL configuration in bold.

Listing 7-2. Updated Web Configuration to Load Login Pages Using Secure Channel

```
    <security-constraint>
        <web-resource-collection>
            <web-resource-name>JDBC Realm Sample with SSL</web-resource-name>
            <url-pattern>/jsps/*</url-pattern>                              #1
        </web-resource-collection>
        <auth-constraint>
            <role-name>apressuser</role-name>
        </auth-constraint>                                                  #2
         <user-data-constraint>                                            #3
            <transport-guarantee>CONFIDENTAL</transport-guarantee>
         </user-data-constraint>
    </security-constraint>

<login-config>
        <auth-method>FORM</auth-method>
        <realm-name>Apress</realm-name>
        <form-login-config>
            <form-login-page>/secure/login.jsp</form-login-page>
            <form-error-page>/secure/login-error.jsp</form-error-page>
        </form-login-config>
    </login-config>
```

We are adding SSL configuration to the existing web resource collection, matching all JSP pages in the /jsps directory (#1). For all resources in the configured collection, we apply a security constraint using <user-data-constraint> element (#2). This element requires that transport guarantee be configured, which we set to value CONFIDENTAL (#3). By setting transport guarantee to CONFIDENTAL, we are telling Tomcat to force secure channel (HTTPS) for all resources that match the <web-resource-collection> configuration. So, if a user tries to load the login page over HTTP on port 8080 (by typing the address http://localhost:8080/chapter7/jsps/index.jsp), Tomcat will recognize that this URL matches the pattern set in the web.xml, and automatically redirect user to the secure URL https://localhost:8443/chapter7/jsps/index.jsp. The configured realm will kick in and the user will be presented with the login screen. After login, all password-protected pages will be loaded over the SSL protocol.

We used value CONFIDENTAL to specify the transport guarantee for the configured secure pages, which is the most restrictive setting, guaranteeing that the data hasn't been tampered with in transit, and that no unauthorized person has read the content while it was in transit. If your security policy allows more relaxed settings, you can use value INTEGRAL, which only guarantees that the content hasn't been changed while being transported between client and server. The default value is NONE, which disables any security checks.

Although we generated the keystore and the SSL certificate system wide, and configured for the entire Tomcat server, we specified the required security constraints on the web application level, giving developers the freedom to configure web application SSL security as required. SSL encryption and decryption is not a trivial operation, and it adds performance overhead to all requests over HTTPS protocol. By configuring SSL within the web application only for pages that should be secure, leaving access to ordinary public pages without SSL, you can benefit by having secure access to the pages that required such protection, while not affecting the performance of the public pages that have no security-critical content. Common examples of such configuration are using SSL for the password-protected parts of the site, or accessing checkout pages over HTTPS only, so that a user can enter his or her credit card details without fear of someone unauthorized accessing it during transport to the web server.

Installing a Certificate from the Certificate Authority

Using a self-signed SSL certificate will enable us to use the full power of SSL to secure our web application, for development and testing purposes, or for internal web applications used within a private network. However, if we were using self-signed certificate to protect a public web site, we would probably end up with users trusting us less than ever. This is because their browsers will display a warning whenever they access our site, letting them know that the browser cannot determine the authenticity of the certificate. To avoid this, we need to use the certificate signed (therefore authenticated) by the known CA.

Obtaining a CA-Signed Certificate

The first step in the process is to generate the self-signed certificate using the keytool, as we just did in the previous section.

Then, we need to generate a certificate-signing request (CSR) for the generated self-signed certificate, and submit it to the chosen CA. We will use the same keytool to generate CSR. The only difference when generating this self-signed certificate is the different command specified: certreq instead of genkey. The following code snipped shows the example CSR command:

```
keytool -certreq -keyalg RSA -alias tomcat -file mycompany_csr.csr –keystore
/Users/Aleksa/mykeystore.
```

It is important to specify the same keystore where you stored the certificate generated in the previous step. In addition, you have to use the alias with which you stored your self-signed certificate. The CSR will be saved to the file specified with the –file argument, in our case mycompany_csr.csr.

Now you need to submit the generated CSR to your CA, and pay for the service, of course. When the transaction is complete, you will receive your new certificate, signed by the well-known CA.

Importing the CA-Signed Certificate

Before we can import the new certificate to the keystore, we need to import the so-called chained certificate, or root certificate, for the CA we used. The chain certificate is publicly available to download from your CA's web site, and it's used to verify that the CA that will, in turn, authenticate our certificate to the browser. Let's say we downloaded the chain certificate to the /var/chaincert.crt file; you can import this to the keystore using the following command:

```
keytool -import -alias root -keystore /Users/aleksav/mykeystore -trustcacerts –file
/var.chaincert.crt
```

You can pick the alias to import the chain certificate to the keystore, but it is important that it doesn't already exist in the keystore. By specifying the argument –trustcacerts, we are setting this certificate as the "chain trust," so it can be used to certify other certificates.

Finally, we can import the certificate received from the CA using the required alias. The following code snippet demonstrates the command used to import valid certificate:

```
keytool -import -alias tomcat -keystore /Users/aleksav/mykeystore -file /var/myca-cert.crt
```

Now you can restart Tomcat and, assuming the keystore and the certificate alias and passwords are correctly set, your new, signed SSL certificate will be used for HTTPS connections. Because the trusted CA signed the certificate, no warning will be displayed in the browser when users access your web application using HTTPS.

Secure Session Tracking with Tomcat

When we discussed HTTP sessions in Chapter, we described the session-tracking mechanism available in Tomcat, namely cookie session tracking and URL rewriting. When using cookies, which is the default mechanism, the session identifier is stored in the JSESSIONID cookie in the browser, and its value is sent to the Tomcat on every request. With URL rewriting, the session identifier is passed as request parameter with every URL pointing to a web application deployed in Tomcat; it requires that every link displayed on the web page has the session request parameter encoded in the URL.

From version 7, Tomcat supports a third mechanism: using SSL protocol for session tracking. SSL session tracking is actually part of Java Servlet specification 3.0, which Tomcat 7 supports, and can be used for session tracking on web sites that are using SSL protocol to encrypt/decrypt information sent over HTTP. Therefore, if your web application is not using SSL exclusively, you will not be able to use the SSL session-tracking mechanism.

When tracking sessions using SSL, the session identifier actually is the id of the established SSL session, generated by the server at the start of the SSL handshake, when the client (browser) requests the SSL certificate from the server. The SSL session identifier is passed over an encrypted SSL connection along with all other traffic; therefore, this is the most secure way to track a session between server and client.

■ **Note** You can only use SSL session tracking with standard Java connectors, both blocking (BIO) and non-blocking (NIO). The APR Tomcat native connector does not yet support the SSL session tracking.

However, there is a bit of configuration required to enable Tomcat to use the SSL session tracking mechanism.

By default, Tomcat checks all available session-tracking modes before deciding which strategy to use. In addition, cookie strategy and URL rewriting mechanisms take precedence over SSL session tracking. So, to use SSL session tracking with your web application, you must explicitly set this mode as the only one available using custom ServletContextListener. Listing 7-3 illustrates the implementation of this listener, and its configuration in the web.xml file.

Listing 7-3. Configuring ServletContextListener for SSL Session Tracking

```
public class SSLSessionTrackingContextListener implements ServletContextListener {

    public void contextInitialized(ServletContextEvent event) {
        ServletContext context = event.getServletContext();
        EnumSet<SessionTrackingMode> modes = EnumSet.of(SessionTrackingMode.SSL);
        context.setSessionTrackingModes(modes);
    }

    public void contextDestroyed(ServletContextEvent event) {
```

```
        // NOOP
    }

}
…WEB.XML:
<listener>
        <listener-class>
                com.appress.apachetomcat7.chapter7.SSLSessionTrackingContextListener
        </listener-class>
</listener>
```

As per Java Server specification, the configured listener will be instantiated, and its contextInitialized() will be executed before the rest of the web application is configured. This will ensure that Tomcat uses SSL session identifier to track session in our web application.

And that's it. When you deploy the web application to Tomcat, the session tracking will be performed using the SSL session identifier.

To demonstrate this, we will display the session id in our JSP page. The SSL session id is available as request attribute javax.servlet.request.ssl_session. All we have to do is to add the following code snippet to our JSP page:

```
SSL Session ID: <%= request.getAttribute("javax.servlet.request.ssl_session") %>
```

Figure 7-5 shows the SSL session id displayed in the browser.

Figure 7-5. *SSL session id accessed as request attribute in the JSP file*

When using SSL session tracking, you should pay special attention to session invalidation. You have to make sure you invalidate both standard HTTP session and Tomcat's SSL session. At the moment, this can only be done using the Tomcat-specific API. In addition, you will need to explicitly close the connection to the client by sending the Connection=close header, as the low-level SSL session will be active until the connection is closed. Listing 7-4 illustrates the code that you will need to write in order to invalidate SSL session correctly.

Listing 7-4. *Invalidating an SSL Session Using Tomcat's API*

```
        HttpSession session = request.getSession(true);
        // invalidate standard HTTP session
        session.invalidate();
```

```
        // Invalidate the SSL session
        SSLSessionManager mgr = (SSLSessionManager)
request.getAttribute("javax.servlet.request.ssl_session_mgr");
        mgr.invalidateSession();

        // Close the conection
        response.setHeader("Connection", "close");
```

We use Tomcat's SSLSessionManager class to invalidate the underlying SSL session. You need to have Tomcat's jar library tomcat-coyote.jar on the project classpath in order to compile this code.

SSL session tracking has a limitation when used in session replication scenarios, when multiple Tomcat instances are deployed in a cluster. This is because, when a Tomcat instance crashes, session replication will not work when another node takes over users from the failed instance. Because of the way SSL protocol works, SSL session id will be different on each server node, so the existing session id from the client cannot be associated with the replicated session.

Summary

In this chapter we have demonstrated how you can use SSL protocol to secure web applications deployed on Apache Tomcat server. First, we explained what SSL protocol is and how it works. Next, we illustrated how to use Java tools to generate self-signed SSL certificates. We used the generated certificate to demonstrate Tomcat's SSL configuration, including SSL Connector and specific web application settings in the web.xml file. We also illustrated how you can have your certificate signed by a CA and then import the signed certificate to the keystore so it is used by Tomcat. Finally, we described the SSL session tracking, a new feature of Servlet API 3.0 and Tomcat 7.

In the next chapter, we will describe how to intercept and preprocess HTTP requests and responses, using two different technologies with similar ideas: Tomcat valves and servlet filters.

CHAPTER 8

Valves and Servlet Filters

In this chapter, we will discuss two similar technologies: valves and filters. These technologies were invented for the purpose of intercepting requests for one or more web applications. The first, Tomcat Valve, is a proprietary Tomcat technology. The second, servlet filters, is a server-independent technology that was introduced as part of the Java Servlet specification (since version 2.3). Both of these technologies are used to process HTTP requests and response objects.

We will cover the following:

- Define Tomcat valves and servlet filters, their similarities, differences and usage scenarios

- Describe valve implementation and configuration

- Introduce valves shipped with Apache Tomcat 7 and their configuration

- Implement and configure sample filters

- Discuss useful servlet filters shipped with Tomcat

Introduction to Valves and Filters

Since the early adoption of a Java Servlet web application, the need for a HTTP request pre-processor was recognized. Web developers needed a mechanism to pre-process every request before it reaches the web application, and every response before it's dispatched to the calling client (usually a browser). There are numerous use cases for such a feature. A few examples include the following:

- Logging details about every request in one place, without adding log calls to every implemented servlet.

- For security, allowing access from certain remote IPs.

- Setting required content encoding uniformly for every response.

- Data compression, to make content smaller before dispatching it to the browser.

- Localizing request and response to a particular locale (language and country).

The requirement was simply to implement a required functionality in one place (one Java class), and then apply it to all requests/responses for one or many web applications deployed.

What Is a Tomcat Valve?

In 2000, when Tomcat 4 (then called Jakarta Tomcat 4) was developed, it included Tomcat's proprietary technology to enable the pre-processing of the HTTP request and response on the Tomcat's container level. At the time, such a feature wasn't part of the Java Servlet specification 2.2, so Tomcat's developers decided to invent Tomcat Valve to perform the much-required functionality.

A Tomcat Valve allows you to associate an instance of a Java class with a particular Catalina container. This configuration allows the named class to act as a pre-processor for each request. These classes are called valves, and they must implement the org.apache.catalina.Valve interface. To allow easier implementation of valves for web application developers, Tomcat ships with a convenient abstract class that developers can extend to implement various kinds of valves: the org.apache.catalina.valves.ValveBase class. Valves were named after the real-world valves that control flow in a pipeline – just as Tomcat's valves control the request/response flow within the Tomcat server's processing pipeline. After processing, each valve can give control to the next valve in the chain, or stop processing altogether, effectively blocking the incoming request.

Valves can be configured with any of the Tomcat Catalina containers described in Chapter 1: Engine, Host, or Context in the CATALINA_HOME/conf/server.xml configuration file.

If you configure a valve with the Engine container, the configured valve will process all requests to all web applications in all hosts for that engine. For example, if you want to log all request to all web applications deployed to Tomcat instance, you can configure a valve with the Engine container.

Similarly, you can configure a valve with the Host container to process all requests to all web applications belonging to the configured Host.

Finally, if you configure a valve with Context element, it will apply to all requests for that context (the single web application).

As we mentioned before, valves are proprietary to Tomcat and cannot be used in a different servlet container. The Java community noticed that a request pre-processing capability needed to be part of the Java Servlet specification, so it could be used across any servlet container.

What Is a Servlet Filter?

The Java Servlet API 2.3 specification was announced in late 2000 and it was confirmed that the Servlet API 2.3 would include the long-anticipated Server filter specification. A filter is a servlet component responsible for intercepting an HTTP request and response, and manipulating them as required. Similarly to valves, filters can modify the contents of an HTTP request and response (they can change headers, or the actual content), and even decide whether to allow requests to progress to a web application or responses to be rendered in user's browser (in case of security breach, for example). Filters are configured in web deployment descriptors for each web application that uses them. This means you can reuse filters for multiple web applications, but each filter and every web application that uses it must be configured separately. On the other hand, you can configure a valve once for use with multiple applications. The configuration includes the URL pattern configuration to which the filter processing should be applied, so you can easily select only relevant request for filter processing.

▪ **Note** Filters have been available in Tomcat since version 4, which implements Servlet API 2.3. Therefore, the latest Apache Tomcat 7 supports filters as defined in the Servlet API 3.0 specification.

Servlet filter is defined in the Servlet API via the `javax.servlet.Filter` interface. Every filter class needs to implement this interface, so that the servlet container can invoke it. You will learn more about this interface in the section about filter implementations, later in this chapter.

In addition, you can configure multiple filters for a web application. In such a case, the servlet container chains the filters together, in the order in which they should be executed. Using this chaining mechanism, each filter implementation can have well defined responsibility, decoupled from other filters that are responsible for different tasks, and at the same time decoupled from the servlet implementation, so they can be developed and tested independently.

Tomcat Valves vs. Servlet Filters

As you can see, valves and filters have a similar functionality, as they were developed with the same goal: to allow web application developers to implement components that can intercept HTTP requests and responses, and process them independently to the target web application servlet. Because filters are part of the Java Servlet specification, they have gained in popularity – not least because they are platform-independent and can run on any servlet specification compliant server, unlike valves, which are only available on Tomcat. In addition, filter-chaining functionality is very useful when multiple (unrelated) chained processing needs to be applied to requests or responses to a particular web application.

However, being Tomcat-specific technology, valves can be better performing and robust when it comes to web application deployed on Tomcat. This is because they are part of the Tomcat engine API, and are therefore processed on a lower level than filters in the Tomcat's request-response cycle. In addition, valves can be configured on the engine or host level (unlike filters, which can only be configured on a single web application level). This makes it easier to apply request/response pre-processing for all web applications deployed on Tomcat instance, without having to repeat configuration for each web application. In such a case, web applications do not have to know that their requests or responses are pre-processed by valves, which can be a good thing if you don't have access to a web application's configuration files (for example, if you are deploying a third-party web application to your Tomcat server).

We will take a look at the valve and filter configuration in the coming sections.

Configuring Tomcat Valves

Tomcat uses valves internally quite heavily; for example, to manage authentication or to maintain SSL information in a request, or to log request details. Some of these valves are instantiated and configured internally by Tomcat, but some are configurable in Tomcat's configuration files, `server.xml` and `context.xml`. For example, Tomcat's `BasicAuthenticatorValve` is configured automatically for every context that has BASIC authentication configured. Similarly, `FormAuthenticatorValve` is automatically configured for every context with FORM-based authentication

In this section, we will demonstrate how we can implement and configure a custom valve, and how we can take advantage of some of the useful valves available with Tomcat out of the box.

Implementing a Custom Valve

Let's see how we can implement a simple valve that logs the Uniform Resource Identifier (URI) of the requested page, as well as the remote IP of the client accessing it.

We mentioned before that every valve has to implement the `org.apache.catalina.Valve` interface, which is quite complex and requires the defining of no less than the seven methods that need to be implemented correctly in order for valve to work as expected. To ease the developer's life, Tomcat's API has a convenient abstract class, `org.apache.catalina.valves.ValveBase`, which a developer can extend in order to implement a valve. The abstract ValveBase class has only one method that a developer needs to implement: public abstract void invoke(Request request, Response response). By implementing this method, the developer has access to its arguments, which represent Tomcat's implementations of Servlet API's interfaces HttpServletRequest and HttpServletResponse, which you can modify using Tomcat Valve. It is important to note that this method should give control to the next configured valve for Tomcat after successful invocation by calling getNext().invoke(request, response) method.

In our example, we are going to inspect a few properties of the Request argument, and write them to the system log. Listing 8-1 shows the implementation of our SimpleLoggingValve class.

Listing 8-1. Valve Implementation That Logs Request Details to System Log

```
public class SimpleLoggingValve extends ValveBase{
    @Override
    public void invoke(Request request, Response response)          #1
throws IOException, ServletException {
        String remoteAddress = request.getRemoteAddr();
        String requestUri = request.getRequestURI();

        System.out.println("URI " + requestUri
        + " accessed from remote address: "+remoteAddress);        #2
        Valve nextValve = getNext();                                #3
        if(nextValve!=null){
            nextValve.invoke(request, response);                    #4
        }
    }
}
```

In this example, we implemented the invoke(..) method from the abstract ValveBase class (#1), and read HttpServletRequest.requestURI property (the URI of the requested page) and the HttpServletRequest.remoteAddr property (the IP of the client accessing the server) from the request argument. We then logged the property values to system output console (#2).

Finally, we get to the next valve in the pipeline (#3), and if there is any, we give it control over the request and response objects (#4). Once all valves have been executed, the request will reach the target web application.

■ **Note** Be sure to include catalina.jar and servlet-api.jar from the CATALINA_HOME/lib directory to your project CLASSPATH, so that SimpleLoggingValve compiles successfully.

As you can see, in a few lines of code we implemented a valve. Now we need to configure Tomcat to use this valve.

The first step in adding our Valve implementation to Tomcat is to make the SimpleLoggingValve class visible to Tomcat's class loader. In order to achieve that, you need to package the SimpleLoggingValve class in a jar file, using the command jar cvf chapter8-valve.jar chapter8-project-compiled-output, where the chapter-8-project-compiled-output is the directory of the project where the compiled classes are located. If you are using Eclipse or any other IDE, you can create the jar file with few mouse clicks; check your IDE documentation for details.

Once you have built the jar file, copy it to the CATALINA_HOME/lib directory, as that directory is on the Tomcat classpath by default. This means that our valve will be on Tomcat's classpath.

We made our SimpleLoggingValve class visible to Tomcat. Now let's configure our valve to be executed for all requests for all web applications deployed on Tomcat's default host. In order to do that, all we need to do is place a valve configuration element within the <Host> element in the CATALINA_HOME/conf/server.xml file. You should open the server.xml file, locate the <Host> element, and add the <Valve> element to it. Listing 8-2 shows the <Valve> element configuration in the server.xml file

Listing 8-2. *SimpleLoggingValve Configuration in* server.xml *File*

```
<Valve className="com.apress.apachetomcat7.chapter8.SimpleLoggingValve" />
```

The only required attribute for the <Valve> element is the className attribute, where we reference the valve class name to be used – in our case, SimpleLoggingValve. All that is left to do is to restart Tomcat (or start it if it wasn't already running).

We configured our valve, as part of Tomcat's default host, which means that SimpleLoggingValve should process all requests to all web applications under this host. To prove this, log in to a few of the standard web applications shipped with Tomcat (Examples web application, Manager web application, or any of the sample web applications from previous chapters), and check the Tomcat log file (the Tomcat main log file is located at CATALINA_HOME/logs/catalina.out). You should see the log messages from our SimpleLoggingValve in the console output, similar to the following output:

```
URI /manager/html accessed from remote address: 127.0.0.1
URI /manager/html/list accessed from remote address: 127.0.0.1
URI /manager/status accessed from remote address: 127.0.0.1
URI /manager/html/list accessed from remote address: 127.0.0.1
URI /examples/jsp/jsp2/el/basic-arithmetic.jsp accessed from remote address: 127.0.0.1
```

Because we are accessing Tomcat running on the local machine, you will see the localhost IP address logged for every request (127.0.0.1). If you access the Tomcat server from a remote client over the Internet, you will see the public IP of the client browser accessing the server.

We have implemented a simple valve and demonstrated its configuration in the Tomcat's server.xml file. Tomcat, however, comes with a number of ready-to-use valves that you can configure to match your needs, without implementing any Java code. Let's now take a look at few of the useful valves available in Tomcat.

The Access Log Valve

The first of the Tomcat prepackaged valves is the Access Log valve, org.apache.catalina.valves.AccessLogValve. It creates log files to track client access information. Some of the content that it tracks includes page hit counts, user session activity, user authentication information, and much more. The Access Log valve can be associated with an engine, host, or context container.

The Access Log valve is configured by default in Tomcat 7; you can see its configuration in the Tomcat's server.xml file. Listing 8-3 illustrates an example entry using the AccessLogValve.

Listing 8-3. Access Log Valve Sample Configuration

```
<Valve
    className="org.apache.catalina.valves.AccessLogValve"    #1
    directory="logs"                                          #2
    prefix="localhost_access_log."                            #3
    suffix=".txt"                                             #4
    pattern="%h %l %u %t &quot;%r&quot; %s %b"                #5
/>
```

As expected, we set the AccessLogValve full class name as the className attribute value (#1). Next, we tell Tomcat that the log files will be placed in the <CATALINA_HOME>/logs directory (#2), prepended with the value localhost_access_log. (#3), and appended with the .txt suffix (#4).

Finally, we configure the pattern attribute for the log entries, using the default Apache log pattern configuration. The pattern example from Listing 8-3 will log values, in following order: host name (%h), the remote logical username, if it exists (%l), the request timestamp (%t), the request method followed by request URI (%r), HTTP status code (%s), and bytes sent (%b). If you open the CATALINA_HOME/logs/localhost_access_log.txt file, you will see entries, similar to the console output that follows:

```
127.0.0.1 - - [30/May/2011:17:14:51 +0100] "GET /examples HTTP/1.1" 302 -
127.0.0.1 - - [30/May/2011:17:14:53 +0100] "GET /examples/jsp HTTP/1.1" 302 -
127.0.0.1 - - [30/May/2011:17:14:55 +0100] "GET /examples/jsp/jsp2/el/basic-arithmetic.jsp↵
HTTP/1.1" 200 1583
```

This pattern is known as the common pattern in log file configuration. Table 8-1 shows the log pattern elements you can use to configure the log file output format that best suits your requirements.

Table 8-1. The Available Pattern Attribute Values

Pattern Attribute Parameter	Description
%a	The remote IP address
%A	The local IP address
%b	The number of bytes sent, excluding HTTP headers, or '-' if zero
%B	The number of bytes sent, excluding HTTP headers
%h	The remote host name, or the IP address if resolveHosts is false
%H	The request protocol
%l	The remote logical username from identd
%m	The request method (that is, GET, POST, and so on)
%p	The local port on which this request was received

Pattern Attribute Parameter	Description
%q	The query string prepended with a ?
%r	The first line of the request method and request URI
%s	The HTTP status code of the response sent to the client
%t	The date and time of the request and response
%u	The authenticated remote user, if any; otherwise '-' (hyphen) is logged
%U	The requested URL path
&v	The name of the local server

Our sample configuration used only a handful of attributes to configure the Access Log valve. If you need full control over your log files, `AccessLogValve` leverages a lot of other attributes. Table 8-2 shows all configurable attributes of the `AccessLogValve`.

Table 8-2. Configurable Attributes for the `AccessLogValve`

Attribute	Description
directory	The `directory` attribute references the relative or absolute pathname of the directory into which log files will be created. If an absolute path is not specified, the path is interpreted as relative to `<CATALINA_HOME>`. If no directory is specified, the default value is logs, which creates the log files in the logs directory relative to `<CATALINA_HOME>`.
pattern	The `pattern` attribute defines a formatting layout that identifies the various information fields that will be logged from the request and response. (Table 8-1 contains the possible pattern values.)
prefix	The prefix attribute names the text that will be prepended to the front of each log file name. If not specified, the default value is "access_log."
resolveHosts	The `resolveHosts` attribute determines if the IP address of the remote client should be resolved to its corresponding host name. If not specified, the default value is false, indicating that remote host resolution will not take place. You should consider setting this value to false in a production environment to improve Tomcat performance.
suffix	The `suffix` attribute names the text that will be appended to the end of each log file name. If a value is not specified, no suffix is appended to the file name.

Attribute	Description
timestamp	The timestamp attribute, if set to true, states that log messages will be date/time stamped. The default value is false (log messages will not be date/time stamped). You should consider setting this value to false in a production environment to improve Tomcat performance.
requestAttributesEnabled	If set to true, checks for request attributes that override HttpServletRequest values for remote address, server host and protocol. If false, the original request values are used.
rotatable	Set to true if log file rotation should be performed. If enabled, the rotation period is determined by fileDateFormat attribute.
fileDateFormat	Sets date format to be used for date appended to each log file name. Also determines the rotation period, if rotatable is set to true. For example, value dd-MM-yyyy, will append date in given format to every log file, and rotate the log files daily.
condition	Enables conditional logging. The value of this attribute is the name of the request attribute that will be checked. If such attribute does not exist in the request, the request will be logged. If attribute with configured name does exist, the request will not be logged.
buffered	If set to false, log will be written to the file after every request. If true, in-memory buffering will be enabled, increasing logging performance. Default value is true.

The Remote Address Valve

The Remote Address valve, org.apache.catalina.valves.RemoteAddrValve, allows you to compare the IP address of the requesting client against one or more regular expressions to either allow or prevent the request from continuing, based on the results of this comparison. The Remote Address filter supports additional attributes, as listed in Table 8-3.

Table 8-3. The Remote Address Filter Valve Attributes

Attribute	Description
allow	The allow attribute takes a comma-delimited list of regular expressions used to compare the remote IP address of the client. If this attribute is included, the remote address of the client must match at least one of the patterns to be allowed access. If this attribute is not specified, all requests are allowed, unless the remote address matches a deny pattern.
deny	The deny attribute acts as the inverse of the allow attribute: it denies access based upon a matched pattern of remote IP addresses.

The following code snippet is an example entry using the
`org.apache.catalina.valves.RemoteAddrValve`:

```
<Valve className="org.apache.catalina.valves.RemoteAddrValve" deny="127.*"/>
```

This valve entry denies access to the assigned container for all client IP addresses that begin with
127. If you assign this valve entry to the host container localhost, then all clients with an IP address
beginning with 127 will see a standard error page for HTTP status code 403 – Forbidden.

In addition to the Remote Address valve, Tomcat ships with `RemoteHostValve`. This valve has the
same functionality and syntax as Remote Access valve, except that it checks the remote host name of the
incoming request, instead of the remote IP address.

Crawler Session Manager Valve

The success of many web sites nowadays depends on how they are discovered and indexed by search
engines. Search engines employ special programs, called crawlers or spiders, that browse through the
web and index every web site they encounter. These programs browse the sites automatically,
mimicking users accessing the site from the regular browser. One problem with crawlers is that they run
in great numbers, simultaneously. When hundreds of separate crawler processes access the web site, a
user session will be created for each of them. With hundreds of different search engines out there, this
can quickly lead to thousands of sessions created for crawlers only, affecting the browsing experience of
regular human users of the site.

That's the main reason why Tomcat ships with
`org.apache.catalina.valves.CrawlerSessionManagerValve`. This valve, when configured, ensures that
each unique web crawler is associated with exactly one user session, saving memory and improving
performance of web application. Each crawler is uniquely identified by its user-agent header, which is
the same for every crawler process that accesses the Tomcat server. The user agent of the known web
crawlers can be configured using the `crawlerUserAgents` attribute name. If this attribute is not set, the
default value will recognize the biggest search engines, using value `"*[bB]ot.*|.*Yahoo!
Slurp.*|.*Feedfetcher-Google.*"`.

■ **Note** You can find the list of all currently known user agents at `www.user-agents.org`. The list includes
standard browser, and all crawlers that index the web today, as well.

The following code snippet illustrates simple configuration of the `CrawlerSessionManagerValve` in
the `server.xml` file:

```
<Valve
    className=" org.apache.catalina.valves.CrawlerSessionManagerValve"
    crawlerUserAgents="*[bB]ot.*|.*Yahoo! Slurp.*|.*Feedfetcher-Google.*."
    sessionInactiveInterval="3600"
/>
```

The `sessionInactiveInterval` configures the time in seconds before inactive crawler session will be
marked as inactive.

■ **Note** The `CrawlerSessionManagerValve` is new feature of Apache Tomcat 7, and it's not available in previous versions.

Dead Thread Detection Valve

Each request from a single user is processed by a separate Java thread in Tomcat. Because of programming bugs in web applications, and due to network problems, these threads sometimes get stuck, stopping the request from processing. Users browsing the site experience web site freezes, or lost connections – issues that we, as web application developers and server administrators, would like to avoid. In order to fix the underlying problem that is causing thread deaths, we need to be aware of the problem.

To help with detection of such threads, Tomcat ships with `DeadThreadDetectionValve`, which detects the stuck threads, and logs them as warnings. You can configure the time after which the running thread is considered as stuck, using the threshold attribute. The following code snippet illustrates the configuration of the `DeadThreadDetectionValve` in the `server.xml` file:

```
<Valve
    className=" org.apache.catalina.valves. DeadThreadDetectionValve"
    threshold="300"
/>
```

The `threshold` attribute is set in seconds, and it defaults to 600 if omitted.

This concludes our discussion about valves. Let's now see how we can implement and configure servlet filters to intercept HTTP request and response.

Configuring Servlet Filters

In the previous section, we learned how to use valves, Tomcat's proprietary technology used for HTTP request and response preprocessing. As mentioned previously, at the same time the Apache Tomcat development team worked on the Valve implementation, the Java Servlet specification 2.3 was released. This specification included servlet filters – new servlet technology for request and response preprocessing. While Tomcat Valves configuration applies to a number of web applications deployed on Tomcat server, Servlet Filters must be configured for every single web application separately. However, because servlet filters are part of the Java Servlet specification, they can be reused for web applications deployed to any Java servlet container, while valves will work exclusively on Tomcat server. In this section we're going to learn how to configure servlet filters for web application.

The Java Servlet API defines the contract of the servlet filters via `javax.servlet.Filter` interface. This interface contains three methods that every servlet filter must implement. Table 8-4 describes the methods defined on Filter interface.

Table 8-4. The javax.servlet.Filter Interface Methods

Method	Description
init(javax.servlet.FilterConfig filterConfig)	This method initializes the filter. It is called exactly once, right after the filter is constructed. It is used to set runtime parameters used to configure filter in web.xml.
doFilter(javax.servlet.ServletRequest servletRequest, javax.servlet.ServletResponse servletResponse, javax.servlet.FilterChain filterChain)	This is the main filter method, which is executed for every request that filter intercepts. Filter can access and modify request-and-response objects passed in as method arguments. This method must call filterChain.doFilter(..) method in order to pass control back to servlet container, so that other chained filters, and eventually target servlet, can be executed.
destroy()	This method is called exactly once by the servlet container when the web application is undeployed. Should contain cleanup code required by the filter; for example removing files, closing database connections.

In the next section, we are going to demonstrate how we can implement custom filter, and configure it in the web.xml.

Implementing a Servlet Filter

A web application often has to cater to users in different languages, so it has to be able to render content in different alphabets. We are going to try that, and display some foreign language content in the browser. First, we are going to add some German characters to the index.jsp page. The German pangram sentence (*Victor jagt zwölf Boxkämpfer quer über den Sylter Deich*) is ideal example – it contains all German characters at least once, including special, characters with umlauts (ä, ö and ü). To spice things up a little bit, we are going to display a welcome message in Chinese: (你好 你好吗, which translates to "Hello, how are you"). Let's add these sentences to the index.jsp file. Make sure that the text shows in native alphabet in the JSP. Listing 8-4 shows how the index.jsp file should look.

Listing 8-4. German and Chinese Alphabet Characters Used in the JSP file

```
<%@page contentType="text/html;charset=UTF-8"%>
<html>
  <head>
    <title>Apress Demo</title>
    <meta http-equiv="Content-Type" content="text/html; charset=UTF-8">
  </head>
  <body>
    <div class="content">
```

```
    Chinese: <b>你好.你好吗</b> <br/><br/>
    German: <b>Victor jagt zwölf Boxkämpfer quer über den Sylter Deich</b>
  </div>
 </body>
</html>
```

You will notice that we are using JSP's @page directive at the top of the page, to tell JSP compiler to use UTF-8 encoding so that foreign language characters are interpreted correctly. We also use the standard HTML <*meta*> tag to set the encoding of the generated HTML content to UTF-8. UTF-8 is the standard byte encoding for Unicode standard – the text representation standard for most of the known alphabets.

We will now package the Apress web application to apress.war archive, and deploy it to Tomcat, either by copying the file to CATALINA_HOME/webapps directory, or by using the Manager web application.

Let's access our sample web application, by entering its URL in the browser: http://localhost:8080/apress/jsps/index.jsp. You will see the welcome page, but with some strange characters instead of German umlaut characters and Chinese signs, although we followed all good practices by setting character encoding of the JSP file to UTF-8. Figure 8-1 shows the web page as it appears in the browser.

Figure 8-1. *Web page with non-ISO-8859-1 characters displayed in the browser*

The reason for this behavior is that the Java Servlet specification states that the default content encoding for the servlet response content must be ISO-8859-1. Tomcat 7 complies with the servlet specification, and sets encoding to ISO-8859-1, which overrides our UTF-8 settings in the index.jsp file. Special characters, like German umlauts and Chinese characters, are not interpreted properly with ISO-8859-1 encoding, so they are rendered with question marks, boxes, or as completely incorrect characters in the browser.

In order to make our page appear correctly in the browser, we have to set character encoding for each response from our web application to UTF-8. To do so, we are going to implement a servlet filter that will intercept every request/response to and from our web application, and set character encoding on the ServletResponse object to UTF-8, before the response is sent to the browser. The character encoding value will be configurable as a filter initialization parameter.

Listing 8-5 shows the implementation of CharacterEncodingFilter.

Listing 8-5. *Filter Implemenation for Setting Response Character Encoding*

```
public class CharacterEncodingFilter implements Filter {
    private String encoding;
    public void init(FilterConfig filterConfig)
                    throws ServletException {
```

```
            this.encoding = filterConfig.getInitParameter("encoding");              #1
            System.out.println("Filter initialized.");
        }

    public void doFilter(ServletRequest servletRequest,
                         ServletResponse servletResponse,
                         FilterChain filterChain)
                throws IOException, ServletException {
        HttpServletRequest httpServletRequest =
                        (HttpServletRequest) servletRequest;
        System.out.println("CharacterEncodingFilter.doFilter invoked for requestURI:"+↵
    httpServletRequest.getRequestURI());
            servletResponse.setCharacterEncoding(this.encoding);                    #2
            filterChain.doFilter(servletRequest, servletResponse);                  #3
        }

    public void destroy() {                                                         #4
        System.out.println("Filter destroyed.");
        //NOOP
    }
}
```

The init method reads the initialization parameter encoding, and stores it in private member field with the same name (#1). The doFilter(..) method, simply sets the provided ServletResponse characterEncoding property to the value of encoding field (#2).Finally, we give the control of the request/response processing to the next filter in the chain (#3).

Since this is a simple filter that doesn't use any resources that would require cleanup, the destroy(..) method doesn't do anything (#4).

The next step is to configure this filter to be instantiated, and to be applied to every request to our Apress web application. We configure the filter in the web.xml file for our web application. Listing 8-6 illustrates the filter configuration.

Listing 8-6. *Filter Configuration in* web.xml *file*

```
<filter>                                                                           #1
        <filter-name>characterEncodingFilter</filter-name>                         #2
        <filter-class>
                com.apress.apachetomcat7.chapter8.CharacterEncodingFilter          #3
        </filter-class>
        <init-param>                                                               #4
                <param-name>encoding</param-name>                                  #5
                <param-value>UTF-8</param-value>                                   #6
        </init-param>
</filter>
<filter-mapping>                                                                   #7
        <filter-name>characterEncodingFilter</filter-name>                         #8
        <url-pattern>/*</url-pattern>                                              #9
</filter-mapping>
```

Filter is configured using <filter> XML element (#1). We configure filter name using <filter-name> element (#2). The filter name must be unique within the web.xml file in which it's configured. Then, we set the class where the filter is implemented (#3). The class name should be fully qualified class name of the CharacterEncodingFilter. Finally, we configure the initialization parameters for the filter, using <init-param> element (#4). Our filter has only one parameter, for which we configure name (#5) and value (#6). In this example, we are going to set character encoding for every response to UTF-8.

This concludes <filter> element configuration, which will make sure the servlet container instantiates the filter correctly. The next step is to configure request URLs to which the filter will be applied, using <filter-mapping> element (#7). We need to specify to which filter mapping applies, using the unique name of the filter configured above (#8). Finally, we set the URL pattern for this filter, to all requests served by our web application (#9).

The wild card parameter value (/*) matches every request that resolves to the web application configured in the same context. To match request URLs more strictly, you can specify the subcontext before the wildcard character – for example /test/*.

In addition to the context configuration, you can configure filter mapping based on request extension – for example <url-pattern>*.html</url-pattern> will match any URL in any subcontext that ends with .html.

Let's package an updated web application, and deploy it to Tomcat. Once the application is deployed, access it in the browser, using the same URL we used earlier: http://localhost:8080/apress/jsps/index.jsp. The text on the web page will now be displayed correctly, in German and Chinese, just as we wanted it to be. Figure 8-2 shows the welcome page with the CharacterEncodingFilter configured.

Chinese: 你好.你好吗

German: Victor jagt zwölf Boxkämpfer quer über den Sylter Deich

Figure 8-2. German and Chinese characters are displayed correctly when encoding is set to UTF-8.

Implementing and configuring a servlet filter that sets response encoding correctly is the typical task for any multi-lingual web application. There are a couple of open source implementations that you can use, but we have demonstrated that implementing your own filter is just as easy.

Let's now take a look at some of the filter implementations distributed with Tomcat that you can easily configure and use with your web application deployed on Tomcat.

Request Dumper Filter

The Request Dumper filter is a convenient filter implementation that dumps the entire HttpServletRequest to the Tomcat log. It logs all request attributes and properties, along with all HTTP headers and cookies for the current request. This filter is mainly used for debugging while developing and testing web applications on Tomcat. It is not recommended to use this filter in a production environment, due to performance penalties for the excessive logging.

To enable this filter, all you have to do is configure the filter and its mapping in the web.xml file. Listing 8-7 illustrates RequestDumperFilter configuration.

Listing 8-7. Simple Configuration for the Request Dumper Filter, Mapping all JSP Files

```
<filter>
        <filter-name>dumperFilter</filter-name>
        <filter-class>
                org.apache.catalina.filters.RequestDumperFilter
        </filter-class>
</filter>
<filter-mapping>
        <filter-name>dumperFilter</filter-name>
        <url-pattern>*.jsp</url-pattern>
</filter-mapping>
```

▓ **Note** To use `RequestDumperFilter`, or any other filter distributed with Tomcat, you don't need to add any Tomcat libraries to the classpath. All Tomcat filter classes are already on the Tomcat's classpath at runtime, located in the `CATALINA_HOME/lib/catalina.jar` file.

You deploy the web application with Request Dumper filter configured, and access it from the browser; you will see its output in the Tomcat's log file (catalina.out), similar to the following:

```
Jun 1, 2011 8:04:26 PM org.apache.catalina.filters.RequestDumperFilter doLog
INFO: "http-bio-8080"-exec-1 START TIME       =01-Jun-2011 20:04:26
Jun 1, 2011 8:04:26 PM org.apache.catalina.filters.RequestDumperFilter doLog
INFO: "http-bio-8080"-exec-1          requestURI=/apress/jsps/index.jsp
Jun 1, 2011 8:04:26 PM org.apache.catalina.filters.RequestDumperFilter doLog
INFO: "http-bio-8080"-exec-1   characterEncoding=UTF-8
Jun 1, 2011 8:04:26 PM org.apache.catalina.filters.RequestDumperFilter doLog
INFO: "http-bio-8080"-exec-1          contextPath=/apress
….
Jun 1, 2011 8:04:26 PM org.apache.catalina.filters.RequestDumperFilter doLog
INFO: "http-bio-8080"-exec-1             header=user-agent=Mozilla/5.0 (Macintosh; Intel↵
 Mac OS X 10_6_7) AppleWebKit/534.24 (KHTML, like Gecko) Chrome/11.0.696.71 Safari/534.24
Jun 1, 2011 8:04:26 PM org.apache.catalina.filters.RequestDumperFilter doLog
INFO: "http-bio-8080"-exec-1          servletPath=/jsps/index.jsp
Jun 1, 2011 8:04:26 PM org.apache.catalina.filters.RequestDumperFilter doLog
INFO: "http-bio-8080"-exec-1 -------------=-----------------:------------
```

Request Dumper filter is available in Tomcat since version 7. Earlier Tomcat versions had this functionality available through the valve of the same name.

Expires Filter

Tomcat's Expires filter, implemented in class org.apache.catalina.filters.ExpiresFilter, is the Java version of the popular Apache web server module mod_expires. It controls the HTTP expires header, which tells the client (browser) if the resource it's trying to access has expired since it was last accessed . It is very useful when determining the caching strategy for the web application, as browsers won't fetch non-expired resources from the server, but rather use cached ones. You can, for example, expire dynamically generated pages after shorter time periods, and set the expires header to higher value for resources that are not changed that often – cascading stylesheets or images, for example.

Listing 8-8 shows typical configuration of the ExpiresFilter.

Listing 8-8. The Expires Filter Configured in the web.xml *File for Different Content Types*

```
<filter>
        <filter-name>ExpiresFilter</filter-name>                          #1
        <filter-class>
                org.apache.catalina.filters.ExpiresFilter                 #2
        </filter-class>
        <init-param>
                <param-name>ExpiresByType image</param-name>              #3
                <param-value>access plus 24 hours</param-value>          #4
        </init-param>
        <init-param>
                <param-name>ExpiresByType text/css</param-name>          #5
                <param-value>access plus 6 months</param-value>
        </init-param>
        <init-param>
                <param-name>ExpiresDefault</param-name>                   #6
                <param-value>lastmodified plus 10 minutes</param-value>  #7
        </init-param>
        <init-param>
                <param-name>ExpiresExcludedResponseStatusCodes</param-name>  #8
                <param-value>500, 404, 401</param-value>                 #9
        </init-param>

</filter> ...
<filter-mapping>                                                          #10
        <filter-name>ExpiresFilter</filter-name>
        <url-pattern>/*</url-pattern>
</filter-mapping>
```

After configuring the filter name (#1) and class, referencing the ExpiresFilter class (#2), we can use initialization parameters to configure specific expires header rules per content type.

We are using the ExpiresByType directive with the content type that we want to match as the parameter name. In this example, we match all resources with the content type image using ExpiresByType image as the parameter name (#3). The content type part of the name must match the content type value entirely, or at least the first part of it (value image matches image/jpeg content type, but also image/gif, image/png and any other image). The parameter value has a convenient, easy-to-read syntax – access plus 24 hours – meaning that the image resources for this web application will expire 24 hours after they are last accessed by the client (#4).

We add a similar configuration for cascading stylesheets (css files), with only difference that they expire after 6 months – we don't expect css to change at all, so clients can cache styles for 6 months after accessing them (#5).

For all other content, we configure ExpiresDefault initialization parameter, which matches anything that isn't matched by other parameters (#6). The value of this parameter is slightly different, lastmodified + 10 mins. Lastmodified directive tells ExpiresFilter to check the last-modified HTTP header of the response and set expires header 10 minutes after that (#7). This part of the configuration will make sure that all other HTML content of our web application is not cached more than 10 minutes after each update – making sure that clients always get up-to-date content from Tomcat.

The last parameter we are going to configure is the ExpiresExcludedResponseStatusCodes parameter (#8). Its value is a comma-separated list of all HTTP status codes that, when set on response, ensure that such response don't have the expires header set at all. We set this parameter to known error status codes (#9) – with simple reasoning that clients should never cache any error page.

Finally, we configure the filter mapping, using standard `<filter-mapping>` element (#10).

■ **Note** If you are using Tomcat integrated with Apache web server, you can configure Apache's mod_expires module instead of ExpiresFilter. We will show you how to integrate Tomcat with Apache web server in Chapter 10.

Cross-Site Request Forgery Prevention Filter

The last Tomcat filter we are going to demonstrate is the Cross-Site Request Forgery Prevention filter, implemented in class org.apache.catalina.filters.CsrfPreventionFilter. Cross-site request forgery (commonly known as CSRF, pronounced 'sea-surf') is the hacking technique used to exploit vulnerabilities of web sites by issuing commands to a known web site as a user that the site trusts. The attacker uses the knowledge of the URL that performs some operation using a user's session, and, if the session is still active, it can access the site and perform harmful operations without the user's knowledge. A typical CSRF scenario is embedding known secure URL to HTML image tag, for example `<img src="http://www.mybank/com/myaccount/sendmoney.html?toaccount=122121">`. If the unsuspecting user loads a malicious web page with this URL, and at the same time user has the active session to the www.mybank.com web site, this image tag will be able to transfer money from the user's account without their knowledge.

Tomcat's CSRF filter prevents such attacks by generating a random nonce (random number issued once), which is used to encode the request URL, and is stored in the session as well. On every request, the nonce from the request is compared with the session, and if they don't match, the request will not proceed. This means that a request from the malicious web site will not be able to perform the operation, as it won't have the nonce associated with the current session.

Listing 8-9 illustrates the configuration of the CsrfPreventionFilter.

Listing 8-9. CsrfPreventionFilter Configuration in the web.xml File

```
<filter>
   <filter-name>CSRFPreventionFilter</filter-name>
   <filter-class>
      org.apache.catalina.filters.CsrfPreventionFilter          #1
   </filter-class>
   <init-param>
      <param-name>entryPoints</param-name>                       #2
      <param-value>/secure/index.jsp</param-value>
   </init-param>
</filter>
   <filter-mapping>
       <filter-name>CSRFPreventionFilter</filter-name>
```

```
    <url-pattern>/secure/*</url-pattern>                              #3
</filter-mapping>
```

The filter class must reference the full class name of the `CsrfPreventionFilter` (#1). The `entryPoints` is the only required initialization parameter for the Tomcat's CSFR filter. It specifies the URLs that are mapped to the filter, but that do not require a nonce to be present in the request. These URLs are entry points to the protected part of the web application, and are used to generate nonces for the users who are accessing the application for the first time, and don't have a nonce in the request. There must be at least one entry point present, otherwise the generated nonce would not be sent to the client. The value for `entryPoints` parameter is the comma separated list of the URLs (#2). Since access to URLs configured here will be free (entry points URLs won't be protected by CSFR filter), it is important that those URLs do not perform any security critical operation. In addition, only GET access to `entryPoints` URLs is allowed (POST will be forbidden).

Finally, we set the filter mapping (#3). It is important that the `entryPoints` configured (#2) are matching the filter mapping (#3) – otherwise the nonce value will not be generated as required.

Let's see what this filter does when user tries to access protected URL. A user first must access one of the `entryPoints` URLs; you can consider these as site home pages. A user will be allowed access, but the CSRF filter will intercept the response and generate a random `String` (nonce) for it. This nonce will be cached and stored in the user session. At the same time, the response will encode the URL using the same nonce value. If the user wants to access any protected URL (that is not configured as an entry point), the same nonce value will be required to be present as a request parameter. If the parameter is not present, error page for status code 403 Forbidden will be displayed in the browser.

The URL with the nonce as the required parameter will need to be calculated programmatically before it's rendered as part of HTML on the page. Let's see an example of this based on the configuration from Listing 8-9. The URL `/secure/showAccount.jsp` is protected by a CSFR filter, and is not an entry point. Let's assume that `/secure/showAccount.jsp` displays account information and must be protected from CSRF attack. User must access entry point URL (`/secure/index.jsp`) before going to show account page. If malicious web site tries to access account page directly (via HTML image tag for example), nonce will not be present in the request, and access will be forbidden.

But what if the user types the shown account URL directly in the browser (`/secure/showAccount.jsp`)? The user will still see the forbidden access page! This is because user does not know the nonce value that has been generated, and that must be passed as request parameter. If you are using the CSRF Prevention filter, all pages must be accessed by clicking the links from connected pages, starting from entry point page – you cannot just type the URL in the browser, as you won't have the required nonce to pass back to the server!

Listing 8-10 shows the `/secure/index.jsp` page, and how it links to the protected `/secure/showAccount.jsp` page.

Listing 8-10. *Encoding a URL with Nonce Parameter from JSP page*

```
<%
String url = response.encodeURL("apress/secure/showAccount.jsp");    #1
%>
<a href="<%=url%>">Show Account</a>                                   #2
```

We generate the URL with nonce request parameter, by calling `response.encodeURL(…)` on the response object in the JSP (#1). As we said before, nonce is generated when entry point is accessed the first time. In addition, the URL encoded with the returned response will have same nonce added as request parameter. We use the encoded URL as link in the anchor HTML tag (#2).

If you take a look at the HTML source code of the generated page in the browser, you will see that the Show Account link points to the following URL:

`http://localhost:8080/apress/secure/showAccount.jsp?org.apache.catalina.filters.CSRF_NONCE=CB5`
`C65E1D87A39D5557D6BCBC24E54A9`.

The Show Account URL has been encoded by adding nonce parameter. The nonce parameter name is a constant defined in `CsrfPreventionFilter` - `org.apache.catalina.filters.CSRF_NONCE`. Its long `String` value is the actual random generated nonce. The protected Show Account page will only be rendered if the nonce value passed as parameter matches the one stored in the session cache. If the nonce value is missing, or does not match the session – 403 Forbidden page will be rendered instead.

In addition to the required `entryPoints`, `CsrfPreventionFilter` has two more configurable initialization parameters, `randomClass` and `nonceCacheSize`. Table 8-5 describes these optional parameters.

Table 8-5. Additional Initialization Parameters for CSRF Filter Configuration

Parameter name	Description
`randomClass`	Fully qualified name of the class that generate nonce values. Class specified must be an instance of `java.util.Random`. `java.util.Random` is the default class, if this parameter is not specified.
`nonceCacheSize`	Number of nonce values to be cached for parallel requests, or when back and refresh buttons are used, which may result in nonce being generated twice. The default value is 5.

The CSRF Prevention filter is available from Tomcat version 6.

Summary

In this chapter, we introduced both Tomcat valves and servlet filters, how to use them, and what their similarities and differences are. We implemented a sample valve and described some of the valves included with Tomcat. Next, we demonstrated how you can implement and configure servlet filters. Finally, we described some of the useful filter implementations distributed with Tomcat.

So far, we covered how you can configure Tomcat as a standalone instance, and how you can deploy and access Java web applications deployed on standalone Tomcat. In the next chapter, we will discuss how can we embed Tomcat to standard desktop Java applications, and how we can test web applications by running tests in the embedded Tomcat instance.

CHAPTER 9

Embedding Tomcat

Previously, we learned how to install and use standalone Apache Tomcat server, and discussed some of Tomcat's advanced features. In this chapter, we'll see how we can use all of the Apache Tomcat features in another, independent Java application, by embedding Tomcat.

Testing Tomcat web applications automatically in-container has always been difficult, because the server where the web application is to be deployed must be installed and configured on the machine where the tests are running. When you needed to run a server from your unit and integration tests, usually the Jetty server was the only option – although your application runs in Tomcat in the production environment. With version 7, Tomcat now supports embedding, so you can instantiate Tomcat from your code, deploy the web application, run the tests, and, finally, shut down Tomcat gracefully. Tomcat does not have to be previously installed on the computer where the tests are running – it will be started using the libraries that are supplied with the code.

In another scenario, you may need a servlet container to run within a standalone, desktop GUI Java application – so you can run a web application that should only be available on a user's local machine, and not publicly on the Internet. You don't need to install the servlet container separately from your standalone application – you can embed Tomcat within the Java application instead, and ship it as one integral piece of software.

These are common scenarios for using embedded Apache Tomcat. In this chapter, we will

- discuss the steps to build an embedded Tomcat application;

- create a sample application that contains an embedded version of Tomcat; and

- demonstrate how to use embedded Tomcat in a JUnit test.

Requirements for Embedding Tomcat

To create a Java application that contains an embedded version of the Tomcat server, we will first leverage Tomcat classes that have been developed to ease this type of integration.

Apache Tomcat 7 has a special version for embedding purposes. This can be downloaded from the main Apache Tomcat project downloads page at (http://tomcat.apache.org/download-70.cgi), in the Embedded section. When you download and unpack the file, you will find it contains a number of JAR files that are used as library files for Java projects with embedded Tomcat. Table 9-1 describes the contents these JAR files.

Table 9-1. Embedded Tomcat distribution JAR files

File	Description
tomcat-embed-core.jar	Core Tomcat classes, contains main implementation of the Tomcat server
tomcat-dbcp.jar	Apache DBCP integration classes, used for JDBC integration within embedded Tomcat instance
tomcat-embed-jasper.jar	Tomcat's JSP engine
ecj-3.6.2.jar	Eclipse's JSP compiler, used by the Jasper engine to compile JSP files
tomcat-embed-logging-juli.jar	JULI logging library integration
tomcat-embed-logging-log4j.jar	Log4j logging library integration

The main classes required for embedding Apache Tomcat 7 within your Java application are found in tomcat-embed-core.jar. This is the main library you will need to include in order to use it. It contains implementation of all the architectural concepts of Apache Tomcat that we discussed in Chapter 1, such as Server, Engine, Service, Connector, and Host. The main class we want to use is org.apache.catalina .startup.Tomcat, which provides an embedded server wrapper and can be found in the tomcat-embed-core.jar.

In addition, you will need to include at least one logging integration library, to enable logging of your embedded Tomcat's instance. As with Tomcat's standalone distribution, two options are available: Tomcat's own JULI logging mechanism, or integration with the popular log4j open-source logging project. We will use log4j integration in our example, so log4j library will have to be included in our classpath as well.

Finally, we will want our embedded Tomcat to serve JSP classes, just like standalone Tomcat. For that, we will need to include the Jasper engine in our project. The Jasper engine can be found in the tomcat-embed-jasper.jar library. This jar file contains JSP API interfaces and classes as well, so there is no need to include jsp-api.jar library separately. In addition to JSP API, Tomcat's Jasper engine requires a separate JSP compiler – a library that can compile JSP files (*.jsp) to standard Java binary compiled files (*.class) that can be executed by JVM. Jasper supports two JSP compiler implementations, both of them open source: Eclipse implementation and Apache Ant implementation. The Eclipse implementation is shipped with the Apache Tomcat 7 Embedded distribution (ecj-3.6.2.jar), and we will use that in our example.

We won't be demonstrating JDBC integration with embedded Tomcat, so tomcat-dbcp.jar will not be required for the sample in this chapter. If you are using JDBC code with embedded Tomcat, make sure to include this library to your project's classpath. JDBC integration with Tomcat will be covered in more detail in Chapter 11, where we will go through a full-fledged web application deployed on Tomcat, and in Chapter 13, where we will discuss JDBC in the context of JNDI integration.

> ■ **Note** Table 9-1 lists all the Jar dependencies you may need for any scenario for embedding Tomcat. Make sure the libraries from Table 9-1 are present in your project's classpath.

Embedded Tomcat Java Components

Recall from Chapter 1 that Tomcat can be subdivided into a set of containers, each having their own purpose. These containers are by default configured using the server.xml file. When embedding a version of Tomcat, you won't have this file available, and so you need to assemble instances of these containers programmatically. The Tomcat embedded distribution ships with core interfaces that enable you to build whatever combination of these components you require. Table 9-2 lists the main classes that correspond to Tomcat's architectural components. All these classes can be found in the tomcat-embed-core.jar library of the embedded Tomcat distribution.

Table 9-2. *Tomcat's Classes Corresponding to Tomcat's Main Components*

Interface/Class	Component	Description
Interface org.apache.catalina.Server	Server	Entire Tomcat instance, contains one or more Services
Interface org.apache.catalina.Service	Service	Holder for Engine, which is accessed via Connector
Class org.apache.catalina.Connector	Connector	Defines connections to the Tomcat instance
Interface org.apache.catalina.Engine	Engine	Servlet engine, a key component of Tomcat
Interface org.apache.catalina.Host	Host	Virtual host for one or more web applications deployed to Tomcat instance
Interface org.apache.catalina.Context	Context	Represents individual web applications contained within Host

For all interfaces defined in the Tomcat API in Table 9-2, Tomcat provides one or more implementations that you can use directly to create your own Embedded Tomcat stack. So you have at your disposal classes like org.apache.catalina.core.StandardServer (standard implementation of the Server interface) and org.apache.catalina.core.StandardEngine (standard implementation of Tomcat's servlet engine). These standard classes are used by the standalone version of Apache Tomcat discussed in the previous chapter. By using them, you can be sure that your embedded Tomcat will behave in the same way as the standalone version. However, you are free to customize any of these implementations, or even create your own completely new implementations of the core Tomcat interfaces.

Nevertheless, this is seldom required. Most often you need to embed a single Tomcat instance, with a single Server, single Service, and single Engine to your Java application, and run one or more web applications in it. For that purpose, Tomcat's embedded distribution comes with the convenient class org.apache.catalina.startup.Tomcat, which contains this minimal set up out of the box. All you have to do is instantiate this class, and start using embedded Tomcat server in your Java application.

If we take a look at the source code of this class, you will see that it contains all of Tomcat's main components as properties – exactly one of each component. Listing 9-1 shows a snippet of the org.apache.catalina.startup.Tomcat class.

Listing 9-1. Source Code of the Minimal Embeddable Tomcat Instance

```java
public class Tomcat {
    // Single engine, service, server, connector - few cases need more,
    // they can use server.xml
    protected Server server;
    protected Service service;
    protected Engine engine;
    protected Connector connector;
    protected Host host;
    protected int port = 8080;
    protected String hostname = "localhost";
    protected String basedir;
```

As you can see, there is exactly one server component, one service component, one engine component, one connector, and one host. In addition, the hostname and host are set to the default values "localhost" and 8080.

Implementing a Sample Application with Embedded Tomcat

Let's now implement a sample Java application that will embed Tomcat server. We are going to start Tomcat on port 8080, and deploy an "examples" web application that comes with the standalone Tomcat distribution, but we will deploy it to embedded Tomcat instance without starting the standalone server. The "examples" web application contains both a servlet and JSP sample, so we will be able to test that both features of Tomcat work normally in the embedded instance. Listing 9-2 shows the EmbeddedTomcat class, used to demonstrate embedded Tomcat functionality.

Listing 9-2. Embedding Tomcat in a Sample Java Application

```java
package com.apress.apachetomcat7.chapter9;

import org.apache.catalina.startup.Tomcat;
import org.apache.catalina.core.StandardServer;
import org.apache.catalina.core.AprLifecycleListener;
import org.apache.catalina.LifecycleException;
import javax.servlet.ServletException;

public class EmbeddedTomcat {

    private Tomcat tomcat;

    private void startTomcat() throws ServletException, LifecycleException {

        this.tomcat = new Tomcat();                                    #1
```

```
        this.tomcat.setPort(8080);                                          #2
        this.tomcat.setBaseDir(".");                                        #3

        // Add AprLifecycleListener
        StandardServer server = (StandardServer) this.tomcat.getServer();
        AprLifecycleListener listener = new AprLifecycleListener();
        server.addLifecycleListener(listener);                             #4

        String contextPath = "/myapp";
        String appBase = "/opt/tomcat7/webapps/examples";
        this.tomcat.addWebapp(contextPath, appBase);                       #5

        this.tomcat.start();                                               #6
    }

    private void stopTomcat() throws LifecycleException {
        this.tomcat.stop();                                                #7
    }

    public static void main(String args[]) {
        try {
            EmbeddedTomcat tomcat = new EmbeddedTomcat();                  #8
            tomcat.startTomcat();
            Thread.sleep(100000);
            tomcat.stopTomcat();
        } catch (Exception e) {
            e.printStackTrace();
        }
    }
}
```

We implemented two main server lifecycle operations as two main methods: startTomcat() and stopTomcat().

First, we instantiated the org.apache.catalina.startup.Tomcat class. That will take care of the component structure of embedded Tomcat server (#1). Next, we set port property (#2) and base directory of the embedded Tomcat (#3). Because embedded Tomcat is instantiated in memory, there is no real need for a base directory, as there is with the standalone version (called CATALINA_HOME). However, if you're using JSPs, a temporary directory for storing compiled JSP classes is required, and it's set relative to the base directory configured. We set it to the project's working directory (".").

Next step is to add any required listeners to the Tomcat instance (#4). Any listeners required for any of the Tomcat's components are configured this way programmatically. Tomcat ships with a few implementations of the LifecycleListener interface, such as ServerLifecycleListener (for initialization of MBean for JMX management), GlobalResourcesLifecycleListener (for initialization of global JNDI resources), JasperLifecycleListener (loads the Jasper JPS engine before any web application that requires it), and so forth. A full list of supported listeners and their uses can be found on Apache Tomcat's Listeners web page (http://tomcat.apache.org/tomcat-7.0-doc/config/listeners.html).

In our example, we are adding AprLifecycleListener. Although this listener is not required for the example, we have included it here as an example of a listener configuration with embedded Tomcat. AprLifecycleListener listener checks for the presence of the Apache Portable Library (APR) on the classpath and loads it if present. APR native library is high performance library used by Apache HTTP server and adds better scalability and integration on performance capabilities to the Apache Tomcat server. This library is heavily used in Apache's HTTP server project, and it improves Apache Tomcat's robustness and performance, especially with connection handling and content delivery, so it can be used not only as a servlet container, but also as a capable web server.

Now that we have a configured an embedded Tomcat instance, let's deploy a web application to it (#5). To deploy a web application to embedded Tomcat, we need two pieces of the application: the full path to the expanded web application directory (or the path to the WAR file if we use an unpacked WAR for deployment), and the context path under which our web application will live. As we mentioned before, we are going to deploy the "examples" web application that comes with the standard Tomcat distribution, so we set the application base directory to "/opt/tomcat7/webapps/examples". When we showed the JSP examples in Chapter 1, which we deployed to standalone Tomcat, we accessed the JSP Examples page with the following URL: http://localhost:8080/examples. Therefore, the context for the application was "examples". To make things more interesting, we're going to set a custom context this time, to value "myapp". This means that, once up and running, the application will be available at a new URL: http://localhost:8080/myapp. This will allow you to programmatically change the Context under which the web application can be accessed, regardless of the name of the WAR archive or the application's directory.

Next, we start the Tomcat instance, using Tomcat.start() method (#6).

Now we have embedded Tomcat up and running, and listening for a shutdown command. But it won't shut down itself – that's why we implemented stop() method (#7), which simply invokes Tomcat.stop(), which in turn issues the shutdown command that our server expects (because of previous await()).

The last thing we need to do is to wrap everything into a public static void main(…) method, which we can then run (#8). We simply instantiate our EmbeddedTomcat and start it. Then we wait for 100 seconds so we can test it, and finally we stop the server gracefully. We are using a simple main() method for demonstration only; in reality, you will probably have your main method in the desktop Java application, or even unit test, that starts and stops embedded Tomcat.

Note that you can start Tomcat server and keep it running without pausing the Thread we're running in, like we did in our example. As a last step, after starting the server (#6), we can call the Server.await() method on the Server instance configured for the embedded Tomcat we're using. Calling await() on the server tells Tomcat to keep running, but listen to any shutdown command issued. That way, when the shutdown command is issued (by the same or another process or thread), the server will shut down gracefully. Here is the line of code that can be added after (#6) to achieve this:

```
this.tomcat.getServer().await();
```

After running the main class, you will see familiar output, similar to the output of the started standalone Tomcat server:

```
Apr 10, 2011 10:07:30 PM org.apache.catalina.core.AprLifecycleListener init
INFO: The APR based Apache Tomcat Native library which allows optimal performance in
production environments was not found on the java.library.path: /Applications/IntelliJ IDEA
8.1.3.app/Contents/Resources/Java:/System/Library/PrivateFrameworks/JavaApplicationLauncher.fr
amework/Resources:.:/Library/Java/Extensions:/System/Library/Java/Extensions:/usr/lib/java
Apr 10, 2011 10:07:30 PM org.apache.coyote.AbstractProtocolHandler init
INFO: Initializing ProtocolHandler ["http-bio-8080"]
Apr 10, 2011 10:07:30 PM org.apache.catalina.core.StandardService startInternal
INFO: Starting service Tomcat
Apr 10, 2011 10:07:30 PM org.apache.catalina.core.StandardEngine startInternal
INFO: Starting Servlet Engine: Apache Tomcat/7.0.11
Apr 10, 2011 10:07:30 PM org.apache.catalina.startup.ContextConfig webConfig
INFO: No global web.xml found
Apr 10, 2011 10:07:31 PM org.apache.catalina.core.ApplicationContext log
```

```
INFO: ContextListener: contextInitialized()
Apr 10, 2011 10:07:31 PM org.apache.catalina.core.ApplicationContext log
INFO: SessionListener: contextInitialized()
Apr 10, 2011 10:07:31 PM org.apache.coyote.AbstractProtocolHandler start
INFO: Starting ProtocolHandler ["http-bio-8080"]
```

Now we open the browser and navigate to the "examples" web application, using the configured context "myapp". The application loads in the browser, and you can use all servlet and JSP examples in exactly the same way as we did with standalone server in Chapter 1. Figure 9-1 shows the JSP Examples web application running in the browser, under configured context, using this URL:
http://localhost:8080/myapp.

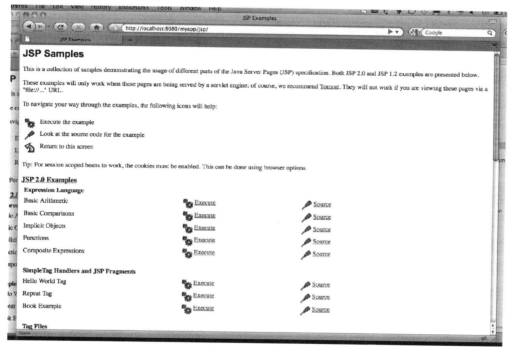

Figure 9-1. JSP Examples web application running in embedded Tomcat server

Once the configure time of 100 seconds expires, the server will shut down. This shows the console output for the embedded Tomcat shutdown process:

```
Apr 11, 2011 11:28:28 AM org.apache.coyote.AbstractProtocolHandler pause
INFO: Pausing ProtocolHandler ["http-bio-8080"]
Apr 11, 2011 11:28:29 AM org.apache.catalina.core.StandardService stopInternal
INFO: Stopping service Tomcat
Apr 11, 2011 11:28:29 AM org.apache.catalina.core.ApplicationContext log
INFO: SessionListener: contextDestroyed()
Apr 11, 2011 11:28:29 AM org.apache.catalina.core.ApplicationContext log
```

```
INFO: ContextListener: contextDestroyed()
Apr 11, 2011 11:28:29 AM org.apache.catalina.loader.WebappClassLoader clearReferencesThreads
Apr 11, 2011 11:28:29 AM org.apache.coyote.AbstractProtocolHandler stop
INFO: Stopping ProtocolHandler ["http-bio-8080"]
```

Testing Servlets with Embedded Tomcat

Testing web applications automatically has always been a challenge in web development. Traditionally, any testing of a web application would involve installing the servlet container, deploying the web application to it, and then manually clicking your way through the web application in order to test a specific scenario. These tests are usually error prone, and involve a lot of manual work – with means that are not easily repeatable and cannot be automated.

However, if you use embedded Tomcat in your tests, you can deploy your applications to Tomcat programmatically, without installing the Tomcat first. The tests implemented this way are repeatable and can be easily scripted to run automatically. In this section we will illustrate how you can use embedded Tomcat to test your servlets.

For this example, we will implement a simple servlet that calculates the square root of the number passed as request parameter, and then write the JUnit test for it, which will run the servlet inside embedded Tomcat server and check the resulting output.

Listing 9-3 shows the implementation of the SimpleServlet.

Listing 9-3. SimpleServlet Implementation That Calculates the Square Root of the Given Number

```
public class SimpleServlet extends HttpServlet{               #1
    @Override
    protected void doGet(
                HttpServletRequest request,
                HttpServletResponse response
                throws ServletException, IOException {        #2
        Double input =
            Double.parseDouble(request.getParameter("number")); #3

        double result = Math.sqrt(input);                     #4
        String message = "The result is " + result;           #5
        response.getOutputStream().write(message.getBytes()); #6
    }
}
```

The SimpleServlet extends the convenient servlet superclass javax.servlet.http.HttpServlet, available as part of the servlet API (#1). To keep things simple, we override only the doGet(…) method (#2), which means that our servlet will only respond to the GET HTTP method. First, we take the required request parameter "number," and parse it to the double value (#3). Because all request parameters are passed as Strings from the browser, we need to create a number from it first, and then calculate the square root of the given number using java.lang.math function (#4). Next, we create the message that will be displayed in the browser, containing the result (#5). And finally, we send the message back to the browser, by writing the message to the HttpServletResponse's output stream (#6). If the user enters the URL in the browser, with the required parameter – for example, www.myhost.com/?number=25 – the result will be displayed on the web page as text: "The result is 5.0."

Traditionally, if we wanted to check that our servlet actually worked as expected, we would need to install a servlet container (such as Tomcat server), configure and deploy the servlet, run the browser, and type the URL with the value we want to test. There are quite a few manual steps involved in that, and it would be very difficult to repeat the steps automatically in order to continually test the servlet.

That's where the embedded Tomcat comes into play. We can write the test that will start embedded Tomcat, deploy our servlet, and then simulate a browser to test the servlet result. All that will be done programmatically, without any manual steps. It will also be possible to run a test manually and automatically, from your favorite IDE or from the command line – you can even automate it as part of the nightly build, for example.

Listing 9-4 shows the JUnit test of the SimpleServlet, using embedded Tomcat.

Listing 9-4. *SimpleServletTest – JUnit Test of the Servlet Using Embedded Tomcat*

```
public class SimpleServletTest {
    private Tomcat tomcat;

    @Before
    public void startTomcat()                                                    #1
            throws ServletException, LifecycleException {

        this.tomcat = new Tomcat();
        this.tomcat.setPort(8080);
        String tmpDirPath = System.getProperty("java.io.tmpdir");
        Context ctxt = this.tomcat.addContext("/sqrt", tmpDirPath);              #2
        this.tomcat.addServlet(ctxt, "simpleServlet",
                                new SimpleServlet());                            #3
        ctxt.addServletMapping("/", "simpleServlet");
        this.tomcat.start();
    }


    @Test
    public void testSuccess()                                                    #4
            throws IOException, SAXException {
        final WebClient webClient = new WebClient();
        final TextPage page = webClient.getPage("http://localhost:8080/sqrt/?number=49");  #5
        String responseText = page.getContent();                                #6
        Assert.assertEquals("Incorrect result", "The result is 7.0", responseText);  #7
    }


    @After
    public void stopTomcat()                                                     #8
            throws LifecycleException {
        this.tomcat.stop();
    }
}
```

The first step is to start embedded Tomcat before the test, which is done in the startTomcat() method (#1). Note that this method is annotated with @Before annotation – this is JUnit annotation, and it marks the method that should be invoked before the test. Similar to the standalone embedded Tomcat example from the previous section, we create the Tomcat instance and set based properties, such as port number. This time, we are creating Context node manually (#2). Our servlet will be in the context path /sqrt. Next we add our servlet to the created context, with name simpleServlet (#4). And that's it. Note that we didn't have to write any web.xml file or any configuration whatsoever – everything is done programmatically. Of course, if you want to use ready web.xml configuration, you can, using the same syntax as the standalone example from the previous section.

Now that the embedded Tomcat is up and running and our servlet is deployed, we can write the actual test (#4). The test is annotated with standard JUnit @Test annotation.

We are using HtmlUnit library to access our servlet. HtmlUnit is a lightweight library for accessing web applications programmatically, without the browser. It emulates the browser and its common features, including GET requests using URLs, POST form submissions, JavaScript engine, and even AJAX functionality. It is often used as an extension to the JUnit testing framework for testing web applications. You can learn more about this helpful library and download it here: http://sourceforge.net/projects/htmlunit/.

■ **Note** In order to use HtmlUnit with these samples, make sure you have the htmlunit.jar file on your classpath.

Using HtmlUnit is very simple. Just call the getPage(…) method passing the URL you want to access (#5). Because our SimpleServlet writes the output as text, we are loading the response as text (#6), and checking if the text is coming as expected using simple assertion (#7).

Finally, we have to stop the Tomcat instance after the test is finished (#8). We are simply using the Tomcat.stop() command, as we did in the earlier example. The method that stops the Tomcat instance is annotated with the @After JUnit annotation, marking the method to be executed after the test and shutting down the Tomcat server gracefully when it is no longer needed.

Now you can run the test from your IDE, like Eclipse (right-click on the class and select Run as JUnit test). You will see Tomcat starting in the logs, and the test executing. If everything goes as expected, the test will pass – which means that the servlet worked as expected. If the test fails, you can find out why and fix the code. Then you can run it again, until it passes – in the true test-drive development fashion.

If this test is a part of the bigger build script, it can be run automatically as part of test suite – just like any other test. And you don't need to install Tomcat or anything else before the test can be run – all you need is the actual test code, and it will work.

Summary

In this chapter, we discussed the required steps of embedding Tomcat into a Java application and the dependencies required to do that. Next, we created our own example application, embedded Tomcat in it, and ran a Java web application from the embedded Tomcat instance. Finally, we illustrated how you can use embedded Tomcat for testing servlets using JUnit.

In the next chapter, we will discuss how to store state with Tomcat using HttpSession.

CHAPTER 10

Integrating Apache Web Server

We have discussed how to use Apache Tomcat as a server for both static and dynamic pages of a web application. Apache Foundation, however, owns Apache Httpd Server Project – a high-performance, scalable HTTP server. As its name suggests, Apache Httpd Server (or Apache Web Server, or just Apache, as its mostly known) is optimized for high-performance content serving over the HTTP protocol. It does not know anything about Servlets or JSPs, though. It is possible to closely integrate Apache Web Server and Apache Tomcat so we can benefit from Tomcat's servlet container, but at the same time serve static content via the high-performance Apache Web Server, and possibly use some of its great load balancing capabilities as well.

In this chapter we will

- Describe Apache Web Server

- Learn how to use Apache proxy module to integrate with Apache Tomcat

- Learn how to use AJP protocol for Apache Web Server – Apache Tomcat integration

- Implement a simple load balancer using Apache Web Server and AJP protocol

What Is the Apache Web Server?

It is fair to say that the Apache Web Server is the de-facto standard http web server available today. Apache Web Server is an open-source project (just like Apache Tomcat) hosted by the Apache Foundation. With its popularity, it has become a synonym for the Apache Foundation, widely known simply as Apache. Rob McCool is the original author of the HTTP daemon at the National Center for Supercomputing Applications, University of Illinois. After the development of the HTTP daemon at NCSA stalled, a group of webmasters came together and continued to develop it – eventually forming the Apache Foundation. The Apache Httpd Server as its main project.

The latest stable release of the Apache Web Server at the time of writing is 2.2.X, and it can be downloaded at http://httpd.apache.org/.

Before continuing with this chapter, you will have to download the version for your operating system, and complete installation as per the instructions available on the Apache Web Server site.

After a successful installation, you should see the test page shown in Figure 10-1 in your browser when you go to http://localhost. The default port for Apache Web Server is port 80, which is also the default port for the most browsers, so you don't have to include port in the test URL. The same page will be available if the port is set – http://localhost:80/.

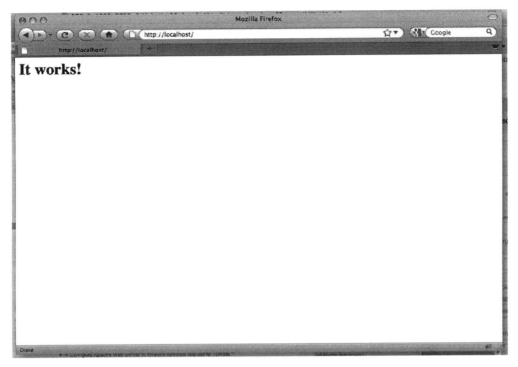

Figure 10-1. Test page for Apache Web Server, confirming successful installation

Integrating Tomcat and Apache Web Server

There are several reasons why you would consider integrating Tomcat with Apache, instead of using standalone Apache Tomcat as both a servlet container and HTTP server.

Historically, the first reason has been performance. Apache is a high-performance web server that served static content — such as html files, images, and videos — faster than Tomcat. However, with recent Tomcat releases, especially with Tomcat 7, its performance as a web server has improved significantly, and the performance gains of the integration protocol have diminished in single-server instances.

The second reason is the configurability of Apache Web Server. With Apache Web Server's 15-year lifespan, huge popularity, and large developer community across different programming languages, Tomcat simply cannot match it for all its configuration possibilities. Hundreds of modules are currently available as extensions for Apache Web Servers. Modules range from language-specific extensions (for PHP, Perl, Python, and so on) and security features (SSL and authentication). Then there is the proxying module, mod_proxy, a powerful URL rewriting module, mod_rewrite, support for custom logging and request filtering, and so on. Most websites require some of these functionalities, and even if using Apache Tomcat as servlet container, Apache Web Server will most likely be public facing web server for your new website.

Finally, the Apache Web Server is very robust, highly scalable piece of software, which is a must for any production-grade web server of choice. Apache Web Server has good resource handing, minimal memory leaks, and graceful startup and shutdown. It's not uncommon to see Apache Web Server instances happily running for months without a restart.

As a general rule of thumb, when deciding whether to run Tomcat standalone or integrate it with Apache Web Server, consider the requirements of your web application and deployment infrastructure. If you are likely to use some non-Java scripting for parts of your application – like PHP or Perl – Apache Web Server integration would be the best option, with its rich support for scripting languages. If your web application is expecting to serve a great number of users concurrently, or it needs to perform some heavy processing, consider load balancing multiple Tomcat instances behind Apache Web Server. Because Apache Web Server has become the industry standard – and a very popular web server – you are more likely to find experienced network administrators with in-depth knowledge of Apache Web Server administration and find running Tomcat behind Apache Web Server more efficient option for maintenance. Apache Web Server has a lot of modules that can extend its functionality quickly and easily, so you can perform various search engine optimization tasks, modify headers, and introduce friendly URLs using URL rewriting with Apache. Finally, Apache Web Server's startup time is much shorter then Tomcat's, and with its robustness it can run for months without a restart. You can potentially perform Tomcat maintenance and upgrades while Apache is still running and redirect your users to the "Site under maintenance" page.

On the other hand, if you're deploying an internal application that is accessible only from within your company's network, for example, then a standalone Tomcat server would be sufficient. Any low-traffic web applications can also happily run on standalone Tomcat without any performance loss. More to the point, if the performance of serving static content is the only reason you're considering running Apache Web Server in from of Tomcat, then you should probably think twice. With Tomcat 7 connectors, the performance of static content rendering matches that of Apache Web Server.

When it comes to Apache-Tomcat integration, here are the issues we need to cover in order to make Tomcat and Apache Web Server work together:

- Configure Apache Web Server to forward selected request to Tomcat.

- Configure Apache Web Server and Tomcat to communicate with one another, using a well-known protocol.

- Configure Tomcat to understand the requests coming from Apache Web Server, and process them accordingly.

We will cover two ways of achieving all of these points. In the next, section we'll use Apache's mod_proxy module to simply forward selected requests from Apache to Tomcat's Http connector. After that, we'll take a look at more advanced integration over AJP protocol using mod_jk module.

Using mod_proxy

As its name suggests, mod_proxy is an Apache extension module for proxying web traffic. By configuring the mod_proxy, you can forward specific requests to the backend Tomcat server.

Mod_proxy comes in few flavors: mod_proxy_http is used for proxying traffic over HTTP protocol, while mod_proxy_ajp (as its name suggests) uses AJP protocol to proxy requests between Apache and Tomcat. The configuration for both of these flavors is very similar, and in this chapter we will be using mod_proxy_http to demonstrate the Apache/Tomcat integration using proxy.

■ **Note** Although mod_proxy_http and mod_proxy_ajp both work well, in our experience mod_proxy_http implementation is more robust and has fewer bugs. Therefore, if you're deciding which proxying flavor to use with your new application, mod_proxy_http is probably a safer bet. However, if you require load balancing over AJP protocol, mod_proxy_ajp is the only flavor that supports that.

The first step is to enable mod_proxy_http in your Apache Web Server installation. The easiest way to do that is to load the http proxy module dynamically. All you need to do is edit the main Apache configuration file (http.conf, located in the home directory of the Apache Web Server installation). The path to the Apache's configuration file, depending on the Apache version, is usually /etc/apache2/http.conf, /etc/httpd/http.conf or /usr/local/apache2/http.conf (on Linux-based operating systems), or C:/Program Files/Apache/http.conf (on Windows). Depending of the Apache Web Server version you are using, sometimes the name of the file is apache2.conf.

Add the following lines to the apache configuration file:

```
LoadModule proxy_module modules/mod_proxy.so
LoadModule proxy_http_module modules/mod_proxy_http.so
```

■ **Note** The *.so extension is typical for UNIX-flavored operating systems (UNIX, Linux-es, OSX, and so on). If you are using a Windows distribution, the library extension is *.dll. For simplicity and consistency, we will be using the .so extension when referring to module libraries throughout this chapter.

LoadModule directive from previous code snippet loads the precompiled apache module "proxy_http_module", from the library file mod_proxy_httpd.so, found in the module subdirectory of the Apache home installation directory. Apache Web Server distribution comes bundled with a number of modules included in the distribution. All you have to do is make sure you load the required module dynamically (using LoadModule directive). Proxy module itself is modular, so you'll need to load the common functionality for all mod_proxy flavors, which are contained in mod_proxy.so library file.

Alternatively, you can compile the required module directly in the Apache Web Server, so it's loaded automatically whenever Apache Web Server starts. This will give you some performance improvement when loading the module. However, you will lose flexibility if you want to disable the module at any given time, because recompilation of Apache would be required in that case. So, you should use the precompiled module loading *only* if you're certain to need the module in question all the time. To check which modules are precompiled with your version of Apache, you can run the following command:

```
httpd -l
```

The results will list the modules precompiled, as you can see on Listing 10-1.

Listing 10-1. Checking the List of Precompiled Modules for Apache Web Server

```
aleksav@aleksa-vukotics-macbook-pro:~$ httpd -l
Compiled in modules:
  core.c
```

```
prefork.c
http_core.c
mod_so.c
```

Finally, after the proxy module is enabled, you'll need to restart Apache for the changes to take effect. You can use the following command to restart Apache Web Server on Linux:

```
sudo apachectl restart
```

With Windows, you can just restart your Apache Web Server, or use Apache start/stop shortcuts in the Start menu.

If you made any typos or any other errors in your configuration files, the Apache Web Server will not start, and you will receive an error message. If no messages are displayed, that generally means that no problems were encountered, and the server restarted successfully. Go to http://localhost/ to confirm you can still see the Apache test page, as shown in Figure 10-1.

Now we have proxy module loaded, and we can proceed with configuring Apache Web Server to forward specific requests to the Tomcat servlet container. First, let's add a new VirtualHost directive to the Apache Web Server configuration. We are going to create a specific virtual host, so that any changes we make are applied only to the specific virtual host that will communicate with the Tomcat backend. Next, we are going to add a ProxyPass directive to forward all requests coming to Apache on the /examples path to the same path, but on the Tomcat server listening to port 8080. In addition to this, we will add a ProxyPassReverse directive to set information flow in the opposite direction – more details about ProxyPassReverse will be coming shortly.

■ **Note** Both the ProxyPass and ProxyPassReverse directives are part of the mod_proxy module, and are only available if mod_proxy is loaded, as per instructions we discussed previously.

Listing 10-2 shows the VirtualHost section of the Apache configuration after all required changes are made.

Listing 10-2. Proxy Configuration Within VirtualHost Directive

```
<VirtualHost *:80>                                              #1
        ServerAdmin webmaster@localhost
        ServerName localhost
        DocumentRoot /var/www                                  #2
        ProxyPass /examples http://localhost:8080/examples     #3
        ProxyPassReverse /examples http://localhost:8080/examples  #4
</VirtualHost>
```

In our example, we first configured a virtual host for all requests coming on port 80 (#1), and set a few general properties for this virtual host – admin's email address, name of the server as it will be accessed from the browser, and the root directory where all static content will be loaded from (#2). All the directives used so far (VirtualHost, ServerAdmin ServerName, and DocumentRoot) are part of the common Apache configuration, and not of major interest for our topic. If you want to learn more about Apache Web Server configuration, visit http://httpd.apache.org/.

Now comes the interesting part. In order for Apache Web Server proxy requests to be made to the backend Tomcat server, we must first invoke a ProxyPass directive (#3). What we are saying to Apache with this directive is the following: if a request comes that matches /examples URL (or any other URL that starts with examples, like /examples/index.html), forward the request to http://localhost:8080/examples (and append any additional URL parts from the original request). This will make any request to Apache on port 80 be forwarded to Tomcat – regardless if it's a servlet or static content that needs to be served.

Finally, we invoke ProxyPassDirective, using exactly the same parameters as we did for the ProxyPass (#4). ProxyPassReverse takes care of any internal redirects that happen within a web application deployed on Tomcat. When such a redirect happens, the Location HTTP header will contain the redirect URL as it's used on Tomcat (something like http://localhost:8080/example/index.html). Because Tomcat itself is not available publicly on port 8080, when such a redirect occurs, it will result in a URL with the 8080 port appearing in the browser – which is something we're trying to avoid when using Apache Web Server. That's where ProxyPassReverse kicks in. For any such redirects, this directive modifies the Location header, using the rule specified in the directive parameters (so it will change any http://localhost:8080/examples redirects to /examples path on localhost).

Let's now restart Apache (sudo apachectl restart) and open the JSP examples URL in the browser, but without the 8080 port: http://localhost/examples. Figure 10-2 shows the familiar screen, under a different URL.

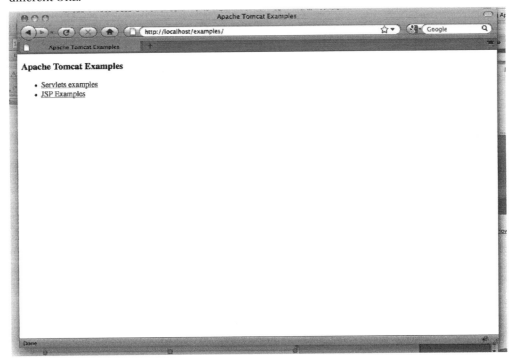

Figure 10-2. JSP examples web application page proxied by Apache Web Server

What just happened? We typed http://localhost/examples URL in our browser. Invoked on default port (80), the request came to Apache Web Server, which recognized it as a proxied request (because it matched `ProxyPass` directive). The request was then forwarded to Tomcat, and served as part of the JSP examples web application we used before. All this time Tomcat is invisible to the user – the browser URL was always showing without the usual 8080 port.

The sample shows the simple but effective way to integrate Apache Web Server with Tomcat. Apache's `mod_proxy` includes a lot more useful features that can be used for advanced tuning of Tomcat integration. For example, you don't have to proxy Tomcat requests on the same path as they come in. If you have your servlet web application deployed on Tomcat under /example servlet context path (`http://localhost:8080/examples`), you may want it to be accessible in `ROOT` context of your web server (`www.examples.com/` or `http://localhost/` for local Apache testing – note no examples path). This can easily be achieved using `ProxyPass` directive as follows:

```
ProxyPass / http://localhost:8080/examples
```

If you now go to `http:/localhost/`, you will again see the familiar JSP examples home page. If you follow the links, you'll see that the functionality works as expected from a Java web application deployed on Tomcat – but the URL in the browser address field will stay in root context. The user will be unaware that the application actually has the /examples path on backend Tomcat server. Figure 10-3 illustrates this (note the address bar of the browser).

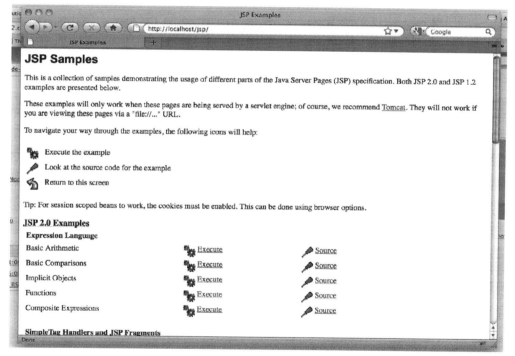

Figure 10-3. *Changing context path of Java*

You may notice that `ProxyPass` and `ProxyPassReverse` work on the entire paths of the web applications (so the /examples path used in the `ProxyPass` directive applies to all URLs that start with that given path). Apache 2.2+ versions of mod_proxy include the advanced directives ProxyPassMatch and ProxyPassReverseMatch, which take regular expressions of matching URLs as parameters. For more details on these directives, you can take a look at mod_proxy, version 2.2, documentation at http://httpd.apache.org/docs/2.2/mod/mod_proxy.html.

We have seen how to use mod_proxy for integration of Tomcat with Apache Web Server. In the next section, we'll explore how can we perform the same task using the mod_jk Apache module.

Using mod_jk

The http proxy mechanism, which we discussed in the preceding section, used the HTTP protocol for communicating between the web server (Apache Web Server) and the application server (Apache Tomcat). Another protocol used for this communication is Apache JServ Protocol (AJP). AJP protocol carries the same data as HTTP, but in an optimized, binary format. Apache provides an implementation of AJP protocol as part of its Tomcat Connectors subproject (or mod_jk), which is a collection of libraries containing AJP protocol implementation for integration between its popular Apache Web Server and the Tomcat application server. The current development and latest release of mod_jk is JK 1.2. Although other versions are available for download (such as the newer but now deprecated mod_jk2 and the older mod_jserv and mod_webapp), we recommend working with JK 1.2, as it is the latest and only currently supported version available. The examples in this book will be using the mod_jk 1.2.X version only.

▪ **Note** The latest version of AJP protocol is AJP 1.3. Earlier AJP 1.2 is deprecated from Tomcat 3.3, and has not been supported by Tomcat since version 4.

First step in using mod_jk is to download the library binaries, which can be found here: http://tomcat.apache.org/download-connectors.cgi. Next, you need to load this Apache module with your Apache Web Server. You can download a ready-to-install compiled version for your operating system. However, if a version for your system is not available, you'll have to download the source code and compile the mod_jk.so file yourself. For download and building instructions, you can visit the how-to page for Tomcat Connectors project (http://tomcat.apache.org/connectors-doc/webserver_howto/apache.html). Once you have the mod_jk.so file ready, copy it to Apache's modules directory, which is usually the /modules subdirectory of Apache's home directory.

▪ **Note** The modules libraries directory varies across operating systems and Apache Web Server versions. Depending on your combination, you should check the following paths: APACHE_HOME/modules, /etc/apache2/modules, /usr/libexec/apache2, /usr/lib/apache2/modules.

Similar to the mod_proxy configuration, the next step is to add the LoadModule directive to Apache's main configuration file (http.conf):

```
LoadModule jk_module modules/mod_jk.so
```

Now restart Apache, If everything goes smoothly, no messages will be visible in the console, and `http://localhost/` URL will load Apache's test page in your browser.

We have `mod_jk` module loaded, so we can now proceed with the configuration of AJP connector to our Tomcat instance.

AJP integration requires one additional configuration file to be included with Apache: workers.properties. This file will contain the entire required configuration for the Tomcat instance that Apache will talk to. Tomcat's processes in the language of JK are called workers; hence the name of the file workers.properties. As the name suggests, you can configure multiple Tomcat instances to integrate with a single Apache Web Server. For the examples in this section, we will use a single Tomcat server – but multiple Tomcats will be covered later in this chapter.

Listing 10-3 shows the minimal workers.properties file configuration, for a single Tomcat instance.

Listing 10-3. *Tomcat Process Defined in workers.properties File*

```
worker.list=mytomcat                  #1
worker.mytomcat.port=8009             #2
worker.mytomcat.host=127.0.0.1        #3
worker.mytomcat.type=ajp13            #4
```

First, we list the Tomcat instances we wish to configure (#1). In our example, we are going to use a single Tomcat instance, and call it mytomcat. Next, we set the port of the Tomcat's AJP connector, as defined in `server.xml` file, in our case 8009 (#2). The host is the IP address of the Tomcat server (#3). We are running everything locally, so we have set host to localhost's IP - `127.0.0.1`. Finally, we set the protocol we're going to use – we default to standard AJP 1.3 protocol (#4).

The settings in this configuration match the AJP connecter of our Tomcat installation that can be found in the `CATALINA_HOME/conf/server.xml` file. Listing 10-4 shows a snippet of `server.xml` that contains the AJP connector configuration.

Listing 10-4. *AJP Connector Configuration in Tomcat's server.xml File*

```
...
<!-- Define an AJP 1.3 Connector on port 8009 -->
 <Connector port="8009" protocol="AJP/1.3" redirectPort="8443" />
...
```

Now that we have Tomcat workers configured, we have to configure Apache Web Server to use mod_jk and read the workers.properties configuration. As with the mod_proxy configuration from the previous section, we will add the required configuration within virtual host directive, as Listing 10-5 shows.

Listing 10-5. *Simple Apache Configuration for mod_jk Integration*

```
<VirtualHost *:80>
        ServerAdmin webmaster@localhost
        ServerName localhost
        DocumentRoot /var/www
        JkWorkersFile /etc/httpd/conf/workers.properties     #1
        JkMount   /examples/*.jsp mytomcat                    #2
        JkUnMount   /examples/servlet/* mytomcat              #3
</VirtualHost>
```

First, using JsWorkersFile directive, we specify where Apache can find the workers.properties file (#1). After that, we "mount" the URLs that we want mod_jk to forward to Tomcat (#2). The URL specified as first parameter allows the use of the wildcard character (*) for matching extensions (*.jsp in our example), or for matching entire sub-paths (for example, /examples/*). The second parameter is the name of the Tomcat worker we want to forward requests to, as specified in the workers.properties file.

Finally, we "unmount" the /examples/servlet/* previously mounted (#3). Again, we specify the URL to be unmounted with the wildcard as first parameter and the worker's name as second parameter. When using JkMount and JkUnMount at the same time, you have to take care of the order, as directives will be executed in the order they appear in the configuration file.

When everything is ready, you'll have to restart Apache Web Server. Point your browser to http://localhost/examples and, again, the familiar JSP examples page will be displayed – handled by Tomcat, but without port 8080 part in the address bar, as in Figure 10-2. If, however, you click on the Servlet examples link, the error page will be displayed, as shown in Figure 10-4.

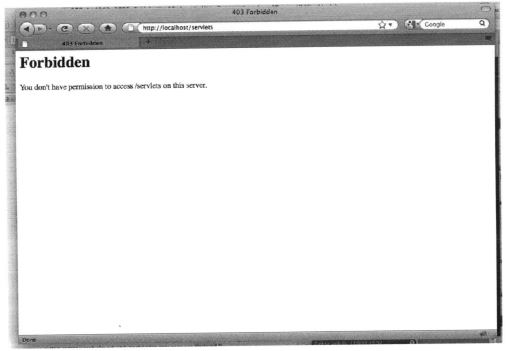

Figure 10-4. An error page after trying to access the unmounted servlet examples page

What happened here? Apache Web Server responded to request at http://localhost/servlets/, but because of the JkUnMount directive (#3 in Listing 10-5), the request wasn't forwarded to the Tomcat instance. Instead, Apache tried to resolve the request itself, but because file system access wasn't allowed, the 403 Forbidden error page was received.

Which Approach to Use

Let's discuss some of the pros and cons for both the mod_proxy and mod_jk approaches.

The most notable differences between http proxy and AJP protocol exist in the security and encryption areas.

You can easily encrypt the traffic between Apache and Tomcat using mod_http_proxy. All you have to do is specify https as the protocol for the Tomcat target instance, and it will just work. On the other hand, AJP protocol does not support encryption. To have encrypted communication between Apache Web Server and Tomcat backend using mod_jk, you'll have to configure that separately, using IPSec (Internet Protocol Security) or SSH tunneling, for example.

If, however, you need to have HTTPS connection details (SSL certificate details, for example) exposed to backend Tomcat instance, then mod_jk has an advantage. If you configure your Apache Web Server to expose SSL details, the mod_jk will make these available to Tomcat. Mod_proxy_http does not pass the HTTPS connection details to Tomcat.

Finally, the style of configuration is quite different for each of the modules. Although mod_jk configuration style feels natural to Tomcat users, developers, and administrators, it seems a bit weird to the experienced Apache Web Server administrator. On the other hand, mod_proxy_http configuration looks very similar to standard Apache configuration.

■ **Note** We have mentioned before that the mod_proxy_ajp flavor of mod_proxy allows proxying using AJP protocol. Although using this module is an option, in our opinion it fares worse than the two approaches described in this chapter – mainly because of some stability issues. That is the reason we haven't included it in our comparison.

When it comes to selecting Apache integration technology, there are many opinions. After considering the points discussed in this section, it is up to you and your requirements to pick one. But, in the end, both approaches are capable of accomplishing the job of stable integration between Tomcat application server and Apache Web Server.

Load Balancing

So far, we have demonstrated how to integrate Apache Tomcat with Apache Web Server using mod_proxy_http and mod_jk modules. We used one instance of Tomcat server for all examples so far. But in the production environment, the amount of requests and users requires multiple application servers running so that all requests can be handled in timely manner, and to have a safety option if one of the servers crashes. One of the common approaches in situations like that is to use Apache Web Server as a load balancer for the web traffic targeted to multiple Tomcat application servers. Because Apache Web Server is quick and has only one responsibility – to forward requests to Tomcat servers, which do the actual work, such as loading data from the database and returning it to the user – it makes sense to use it as a load balancer to easily relieve the pressure on hard-worked Tomcat instances.

We will use mod_jk to demonstrate load-balancing configuration. Let's assume we have two Tomcat instances, on IPs 192.168.1.101 and 192.168.1.102, respectively, and let's call these workers tomcat1 and tomcat2. We will configure both tomcat1 and tomcat2 as workers, but we'll add another, third worker – let's call it tomcat-load-balancer. The tomcat-load-balancer worker won't have its own backed Tomcat instance, but will be solely responsible for splitting traffic and forwarding one set of requests to tomcat1 and another set of requests to tomcat2. Listing 10-6 shows the configuration required in the worker.properties file.

Listing 10-6. *Load Balancer Workers Configuration*

```
worker.list=mytomcat                                              #1

worker. tomcat1.port=8009
worker. tomcat1.host=192.168.1.101
worker. tomcat1.type=ajp13
worker.tomcat1.lbfactor=5                                         #2

worker.tomcat2.port=8009
worker. tomcat2.host=192.168.1.102
worker. tomcat2.type=ajp13
worker.tomcat2.lbfactor=5                                         #3

worker.tomcat-load-balancer.type=lb                              #4
worker.tomcat-load-balancer.balance_workers=tomcat1,tomcat2     #5
worker.tomcat-load-balancer.sticky_session=True                 #6
# Load balancing method can be [R]equest, [S]ession, [T]raffic, or [B]usiness
worker.tomcat-load-balancer.method=R                             #7
```

First, we set the list of Tomcat workers (#1). Note that we only list tomcat-load-balancer (our load balancer) as the worker – the tomcat1 and tomcat2 will be configured as part of load balancer, as you will see shortly.

Next, we configure our two physical Tomcat instances (#2 and #3). The configuration is very similar as before, with the addition of the lbfactor property. This property specifies the relative proportion of the requests that should be handled by each instance. In our example, both instances are configured to handle the same proportion of the requests (lbfactor has the same value, 5). The higher the value of the lbfactor for Tomcat instance, the more work the server will do, and vice versa. In a case of two different servers, where one has better characteristics (better CPU or more memory), it makes sense to tweak the lbfactor so that the more powerful instance handles more requests.

Let's now configure the load balancer itself – or the tomcat-load-balancer worker, as we named it. The first and most important step is to set the type of the tomcat-load-balancer worker as load balancer, by setting the type property to value lb (#4). This will tell mod_jk to treat tomcat-load-balancer worker not as any worker, but as special one: load-balancer. Next, we list the physical workers that are going to be used for load balancing – tomcat1 and tomcat2 – using the balance_workers property (#5). And our load balancer is almost ready to go.

Before we restart Tomcat and try our load balancer, we're going to set and explain few advanced properties.

The first of these is sticky_session property, which can be set to True or False (#6). The sticky session property tells load balancer to keep requests belonging to the same session (which means the same user) forwarded to the same worker. This is particularly important if your user session contains the information that is used by Tomcat on subsequent requests. If one request of the session goes to tomcat1 and the next one goes to tomcat2, tomcat2 won't have the required session information previously set on the tomcat1 instance. There is a complex solution for this problem, called session replication, where Tomcat instances are configured to send the session information to each other. However, for the simplicity of the configuration, we'll use sticky sessions here.

> ≋ **Note** Sticky session and session replication are two main strategies for dealing with user sessions across load-balanced servers. Because the discussion about these strategies is beyond the scope of this book, we won't cover it in any great detail. If you wish to know more about Tomcat clustering and session replication, you can find online resources on Tomcat's website at `http://tomcat.apache.org/tomcat-7.0-doc/cluster-howto.html`

The `method` property (#7) specifies what method should load balancer use to determine what is the best worker to use for each request. Table 10-1 lists the allowed values for method property.

Table 10-1. Permitted values for method load balancing property

Property Value	Description
[R]equest	Number of request is used to determine the best worker – the requests will be distributed as per lbfactor for each worker. This is the default value.
[S]ession	Number of session will be determined to distribute requests. Should be used when session resources (memory) are scarce.
[T]raffic	Load balancer will monitor network traffic between workers; the one with highest bandwidth available will be used.
[B]usiness	This method will check how many requests each worker is currently serving, and pick the one with lowest load. Should be used for applications that have long request processing times.

If you restart Apache, you can see your load balancer at work, by monitoring Tomcat logs, for example. You'll see that requests will be distributed between configured Tomcat instances. In addition, if any of the workers stop responding (if you experience server crashes or network problems), the load balancer will be smart enough not to use it until it's back online. Because other workers will still be available, all traffic will be redirected to the working ones – giving you time to address the failing worker problem without any downtime for your users.

Summary

In this chapter, we discussed how Tomcat can be integrated with Apache Web Server in production environments. We have demonstrated the integration using the `mod_proxy_http` and `mod_jk` modules, and discussed some of the reasons for using one approach over the other. Finally, we have shown you how to use Apache Web Server as a load balancer by demonstrating load-balancing configuration to split the load of a high-usage application between multiple independent Tomcat instances.

In the next chapter, we'll see how we can use Spring MVC, one of the most popular web development frameworks, to develop professional web application for Tomcat.

Integrating Spring MVC Framework

Java Servlet API provides a rich and customizable framework for the development of web applications. However, in the professional Java development world, that is often not enough. While Java Servlet API provides low-level interfaces and classes for interaction with web requests, efficient programming often requires an abstraction layer on top of the core servlet components. We are going to take a look at one such framework in this chapter: Spring MVC. In this chapter we are going to

- Describe the Model-View-Controller pattern, which is the core part of Spring MVC

- Discuss the Front Controller pattern that Spring MVC also implements

- Introduce the Spring framework, of which Spring MVC is part

- Implement and configure a sample Spring MVC application, by adding model, view, and controller components

Introducing Spring MVC

Spring MVC is a Java framework for the development of Java web applications using servlets. It uses the MVC design pattern to organize the structure of web applications. It also implements the Front Controller design pattern to create configurable and easy-to-implement web components. Spring MVC is a part of the Spring framework—a popular, multi-purpose, open source Java framework.

In this section, we will discuss each of the design patterns implemented by the Spring MVC framework, and introduce the core principles of Spring framework, to which Spring MVC belongs.

Spring Framework Overview

Spring framework is a lightweight, open source Java application framework designed to enable application developers to concentrate on the functional problems at hand by providing the infrastructure, or glue-code, for Java enterprise applications. Spring is the brainchild of Rod Johnson, who first introduced in it his book *Expert One-on-One J2EE Design and Development* (Wrox, 2002) In the book, Johnson takes a critical look at what was, at the time, standard Java enterprise application design and development, and gives his views about how it can be improved. The framework he implements for the book was then released as the open source Spring framework, and with scores of Java professionals sharing his views, it quickly grew in popularity. Today, Spring is the Java framework of choice for enterprise application development, has had proven success in complex production environments, and is more popular and more frequently used than official Java EE components.

The core part of the Spring framework is the dependency injection container, which is the implementation of the Inversion of Control design pattern. It is designed to help developers and architects compose the complex applications from its contributing parts, or components. Using Spring, you can split your application into loosely coupled components and wire them together using Spring's dependency-injection container, which manages all your components' lifecycles. The application components in Spring are called *beans*, and they are configured using XML or Java annotations. All configured beans are instantiated and managed in the Spring container, typically called the Spring application context. When creating beans from the configuration, Spring can pass (or inject) each bean to other beans, providing dependency injection functionality.

In addition to this core functionality, Spring ships with many other components, built with the purpose of helping developers follow best-practices in architecture and implementation of Java applications; for example, database access and integration with popular Java data access frameworks, aspect-oriented programming support, Java Messaging Service (JMS) integration, the development and design of web applications using servlets and portlets, scheduling, and the like.

Spring is non-invasive, so application components managed by Spring don't have any dependency on the Spring framework itself. Non-invasiveness is an important characteristic of the Spring framework; your Java classes do not depend on Spring-specific classes and interfaces at all. That is, if you don't want them to—Spring has a lot of very useful and convenient components that you will actually want to use in your code, so the choice is all yours.

Spring MVC represents the part of the Spring framework that is designed to make the development of Java web applications easier. In the next section, we're going to explore the Spring MVC framework for the development of a web application deployed on Tomcat.

MVC Pattern

At the beginning of user-oriented architecture and development, the major challenge was how to model the user-interface part of the system architecturally. The requirements were to decouple the presentation part of the application's user-interface and the data it displays to the user. For example, different user interface components sometimes display different views of the same data (for example, HTML web pages and PDF files). In addition, the user interface is typically platform dependent, whether you consider desktop applications that are often completely different on Windows and Linux, for example, or web applications with different visual representations in a desktop browser and on a mobile device. Finally, the development of the look-and-feel aspects of the user interface is usually related to completely different skill sets from the back-end, data-centric functionalities.

MVC came to life in 1979 by Trygve Reenskaug, a computer scientist at the Oslo University in Norway. It defines three collaborating aspects of the application from the user interface perspective: model, view, and controller.

- Model represents the data and the behavior of the application's domain model. It contains the information presented to the user. It also serves as the container for data additions or updates performed via the user interface (for example, data submitted using HTML forms in web applications).

- View component is responsible for visual display of the data. It transforms the information contained in the model to the chosen visual representation, and usually does not contain any logic. Examples of view technologies in web application development are HTML, CSS, and JavaScript. Java Server Pages can be considered view technology if they are used with MVC principles, so that they don't have any business logic, and are used only for data display and retrieval.

- Controller is the component responsible for responding to user actions and, based on the input, manipulates and queries the model, and renders the view with data from the model. In a Java web application sense, servlets can be considered as controller components: when a user clicks on a link or presses the submit button, the action invokes the servlet, which performs the operation on the model (loads or updates data in the database, for example), and renders the HTML view in the user's browser.

■ **Note** It is important to follow good practices when implementing the MVC pattern in your web applications. The business logic should be encapsulated within the controller (or, to be more precise, delegated to the transactional service layer from the controller), the model should only contain data, and the view should only have visual markup, without any logic. In Java web application development, this means that JSP pages should only be used for data rendering and collection, without any embedded Java code. All logic, such as database queries and updates, should be invoked from the servlet (Controller) code or its delegating components.

Figure 11-1 illustrates the architecture of the MVC pattern.

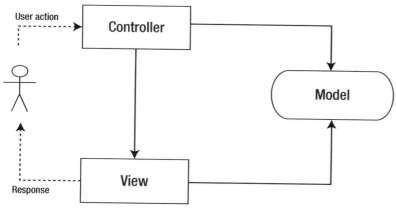

Figure 11-1. Model-View-Controller pattern

There are two main benefits of using the MVC pattern in user-interface development:

- With the view decoupled from the model, it becomes easy to maintain multiple views while keeping the model unchanged. In web application design, for example, using the MVC pattern, you are able to develop web applications that can be accessed on standard desktop browsers as well as multiple mobile devices.

- Adapting to change in application design is easy with MVC. You can change the presentation of the data to the user without changing the way your application responds to user actions or the data itself (for example, you can change the complete look and feel of the web page by changing HTML and CSS code, without making any changes to servlets or to the database schema). In addition, you can make the changes to the model and controller components without affecting the application visibility to the user.

In the Spring MVC framework, the controller component is represented with the `Controller` interface, the model is represented as a Java `Map` containing the collection of key-value pairs, where values are objects that are stored in the model, which are then accessed in the view using keys. Finally, views can be configured to be any web technology you like—HTML, JSP, Freemarker, and so on.

In addition to the MVC pattern, Spring MVC employs another important architectural software pattern: the Front Controller pattern.

Front Controller Pattern

The Front Controller pattern is a popular pattern in web applications architecture. In addition to Spring MVC, many other web frameworks implement this pattern, including Ruby on Rails and PHP frameworks such as Cake PHP and Drupal. Servlet filters are implementations of the Front Controller pattern as well.

The main principle of the Front Controller pattern is that all web requests to web applications are handled by a single entry point. This central entry point is called the front controller, and its role is to route requests to the specific web application component that should handle it. After a specific handler has completed processing the request, the control is returned to the front controller, which is responsible for sending the web response back to the calling client. In addition to routing requests to specialized handlers, front controller is responsible for all common web application functionalities: session handling, caching, and filtering the requests for example.

Figure 11-2 illustrates the Front Controller pattern architecture.

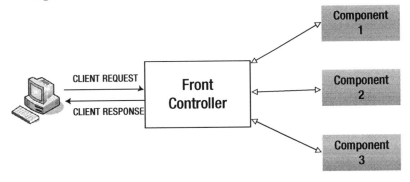

Figure 11-2. Architecture of the Front Controller pattern

In the case of Spring MVC framework, this central entry point is the Java servlet implemented in class `org.springframework.web.servlet.DispatcherServlet`.

In the next section, we are going to use the Spring MVC framework to develop and configure a sample web application.

Spring MVC Web Applications

Spring MVC framework uses proven MVC and Front Controller patterns to guide developers to use best practices in web application development. Spring MVC contains many components that are configured to work together in order to create a working web applications. Figure 11-3 illustrates the inner workings of the Spring MVC application.

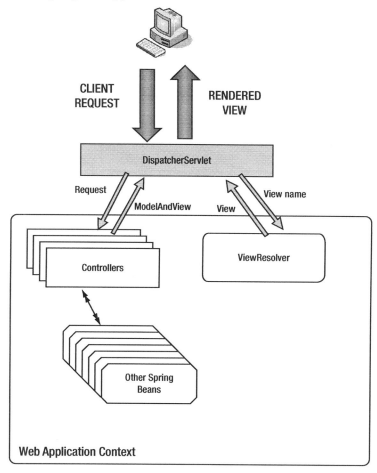

Figure 11-3. Spring MVC application architecture

DispatcherServlet (the front controller in Spring MVC implementation) processes all incoming client requests. It then delegates each request for handling by the Spring's Controller component (or handler, as it's sometimes called), based on the handler mapping. During request processing, a controller can collaborate with any of the configured Spring beans. After finishing with request processing, a controller returns an instance of `ModelAndView` to the `DispatcherServlet`. `ModelAndView` is the spring abstraction of the model and view components in the MVC pattern, which contains the data (model) and the view template. `DispatcherServlet` then uses `ViewResolver` Spring component to load the view template and render it using the model data—the rendered view is finally sent to the client (as an HTML page in the browser, for example). In this section, we are going to learn how to use each of these Spring components.

Most of the components are readily available in Spring MVC, and all we need to do in order to use them is to add configuration to our web application. The key parts that need to be implemented by developers are views and controllers. Spring MVC supports almost all view technologies available in Java: JSP, Freemarker, Velocity, and Flex. In this section, we are going to use JSPs as our view technology. The controllers in Spring MVC are implemented as Plain Old Java Objects (POJOs), with Spring-specific annotations.

In the following sections, we are going to guide you through configuration and basic implementation of a Spring MVC web application. Let's start by configuring the `DispatcherServlet`.

Configuring DispatcherServlet

The `DispatcherServlet` is the only servlet we are going to configure for the Spring MVC web application. It's configured like any other servlet, in `web.xml` file. Listing 11-1 shows the example configuration of `DispatcherServlet`.

Listing 11-1. Spring MVC's DispatcherServlet Is Configured as Front Controller in `web.xml`

```xml
<?xml version="1.0" encoding="ISO-8859-1"?>
<web-app xmlns="http://java.sun.com/xml/ns/javaee"
         xmlns:xsi="http://www.w3.org/2001/XMLSchema-instance"
         xsi:schemaLocation="http://java.sun.com/xml/ns/javaee
                   http://java.sun.com/xml/ns/javaee/web-app_3_0.xsd" version="3.0">

    <display-name>Chapter 11</display-name>
    <description>Spring MVC Demo</description>


    <servlet>
        <servlet-name>chapter11</servlet-name>
        <servlet-class>
            org.springframework.web.servlet.DispatcherServlet          #1
        </servlet-class>
        <load-on-startup>1</load-on-startup>
    </servlet>

    <servlet-mapping>
        <servlet-name>chapter11</servlet-name>
        <url-pattern>*.html</url-pattern>                               #2
    </servlet-mapping>

</web-app>
```

There is nothing new in this configuration: we configured the servlet with the name chapter11 using the `<servlet>` element, specifying the `org.springframework.web.servlet.DispatcherServlet` as servlet class (#1). We then mapped this servlet to all URLs with .html extensions (#2).

Let's now implement and configure all the components used in the MVC pattern: model, view, and controller. We're going to start with the view and its model representation.

Adding Views

Let's start by adding a view component to our Spring MVC example. We will use a standard JSP file as a view in our application, which will display the message to the user. The message itself will be our model from the Model-View-Controller pattern. The message is the information that is displayed in the view—it's not hard-coded in the view itself, but rather passed to the view from the controller component. Listing 11-2 shows the JSP file implementation.

Listing 11-2. View Implementation Using JSP

```
<html>
  <head>
   <title>Spring MVC Demo</title>
   <meta http-equiv="Content-Type" content="text/html; charset=UTF-8">
  </head>
  <body>
    <div class="content">
      <b>
          ${message}                              #1
      </b>
    </div>
  </body>
</html>
```

We are displaying the message in a JSP file using JSP Expression Language (EL), which we introduced in Chapter 3. We used the key message to reference the message object from the model (#1); this object will need to be added to the model by the controller.

We are going to save this JSP file as index.jsp in the /WEB-INF/views/ directory.

Now that we have the view to display the data from the model, we need to implement the controller component.

Implementing Controllers

The controller component from the MVC pattern is called just like that in the Spring MVC: controller. It's a POJO implementation, which does not extend any other class or implement any interface from the framework. To mark the Java class as controller, all we have to do is annotate it with Spring's @Controller annotation. Let's take a look at our HelloWorldController implementation in Listing 11-3.

Listing 11-3. Controller Implementation That Connects Model and View Components

```
package com.appress.apachetomcat7.chapter11;

import org.springframework.stereotype.Controller;
import org.springframework.web.bind.annotation.RequestMapping;
import org.springframework.web.servlet.ModelAndView;

import javax.servlet.http.HttpServlet;
import java.util.HashMap;
```

```
import java.util.Map;

@Controller                                                            #1
public class HelloWorldController{                                     #2

    @RequestMapping(value = "/helloWorld.html",
                    method = RequestMethod.GET                         #3
    public ModelAndView hello(){                                       #4
        Map<String, Object> model = new HashMap<String, Object>();    #5
        model.put("message", "Hello, Spring-MVC World");              #6

        return new ModelAndView("index", model);                      #7
    }

}
```

The class itself is annotated with @Controller annotation, which will tell the Spring MVC framework to treat it as a controller component (#1). The class is just a POJO, without any super class or implementing interface (#2). This approach enables easy out-of-container testing of your controllers, as they don't have any dependency on the Servlet API at all—for example, we don't have to extend HttpServlet like we did in earlier servlet examples in this book.

Each implemented method in the controller class acts as a separate web handler. We use @RequestMapping annotation on the method level to configure mapping for the particular handler: the URL pattern it will be mapped to and the HTTP method it accepts. In our example, we mapped our method hello() to /helloWorld.html URL, using GET HTTP method (#3).

The handler method itself does not have any arguments, and has a return parameter of type ModelAndView (#4). ModelAndView class is the Spring's abstraction of the view MVC component and the model that is used in the view. Each Spring MVC handler returns the instance of ModelAndView to the front controller (DispatcherServlet), which in turn sends the response of the view with model to the calling client (browser in our case).

Model itself is nothing more than a Java Map instance—a collection of String keys with Object values (#5). In our sample controller, we are adding the message object to the model using key message (#6), the same key used in the JSP view to display the message in Listing 11-2.

Finally we return the constructed instance of ModelAndView (#7). We pass two arguments to the ModelAndView constructor: the name of the view ("index") and the instance of the model. Spring will translate the view name to the actual view (JSP file) using the view resolver, which we will cover in the next section.

So far, we have implemented the view that displays the model information, and the controller that populates the model and passes it to the view for rendering. Let's now wire all these components together in the Spring application context.

Wiring Spring Application Context

Spring application context is configured using XML in the Spring configuration files. In Spring MVC, the DispatcherServlet configured in the web.xml file will automatically load its Spring context from the /WEB-INF/{servlet-name}-servlet.xml file packaged in the web application, where the {servlet-name} is the configured <servlet-name> element used in the web.xml. Because we specified the servlet name chapter11 in the web.xml (Listing 11-1), the Spring configuration file will be /WEB-INF/chapter11-servlet.xml, and we are going to put Spring MVC XML configuration in that file. Listing 11-4 shows the configuration we are going to use for our Spring MVC example.

Listing 11-4. Configuration of Spring Application Context in `chapter11-servlet.xml` *file*

```
<?xml version="1.0" encoding="UTF-8"?>
<beans xmlns="http://www.springframework.org/schema/beans"
       xmlns:xsi="http://www.w3.org/2001/XMLSchema-instance"
       xmlns:mvc="http://www.springframework.org/schema/mvc"
       xsi:schemaLocation="http://www.springframework.org/schema/beans
       http://www.springframework.org/schema/beans/spring-beans-3.0.xsd
       http://www.springframework.org/schema/mvc
       http://www.springframework.org/schema/mvc/spring-mvc.xsd">       #1


    <mvc:annotation-driven/>                                            #2

    <bean name="helloWorldController"
          class="com.appress.apachetomcat7.chapter11.HelloWorldController"/>  #3

    <bean id="viewResolver"
          class="org.springframework.web.servlet.view.InternalResourceViewResolver">  #4
        <property name="viewClass" value="org.springframework.web.servlet.view.JstlView"/> #5
        <property name="prefix" value="/WEB-INF/views/"/>              #6
        <property name="suffix" value=".jsp"/>                         #7
    </bean>

</beans>
```

Spring application context is configured in XML format, using XML schemas defined in the Spring framework. To configure Spring MVC application context, we are using two XML schemas: beans schema to configure Spring components (beans), and mvc schema for Spring MVC specific configuration (#1).

We used @Controller annotation to mark Java class used as controller component. Annotations in Java are only used for code markup; the application itself must understand Java annotations at runtime. That's why we have to configure Spring runtime to understand the @Controller annotation, and configure classes annotated with it as controller components in MVC architecture. Spring comes with the convenient XML configuration element <mvc:annotation-driven/> that enables us to do just that (#2). In addition to @Controller annotation, this XML element enables all other class-level, method-level, and method-argument-level annotation used in the Spring MVC framework. We will see examples of other Spring MVC annotations in the next section.

All spring-managed components must be defined as beans in the Spring framework. So our next step is to configure HelloWorldController as a spring-managed bean (#3).

The final step is to configure Spring to recognize and use view names referenced in the controller, and map them to the JSP files we created. To do this we configured view resolver (#4). Spring comes with few view resolver implementations, and we are using InternalResourceViewResolver, which is convenient to use with JSP files. We specify three properties for view resolver bean:

- viewClass (#5) is set to org.springframework.web.servlet.view.JstlView, which is the Spring's implementation of JSP view with support of JSP Standard Tag Library (JSTL).

- prefix (#6) is set to "/WEB-INF/views" and specifies the prefix path where all our JSP files are located.

- suffix (#7) is set to ".jsp", and is appended to prefix and view name in order to complete the path of the JSP file that represents the view.

If you take a look at our controller implementation in Listing 11-3, you will remember that we referenced our view using its name only ("index"). Now we can understand how Spring uses this view name to reference the actual view: the JSP file that we saved to /WEB-INF/views/index.jsp location. Spring uses a configured view resolver bean to transform the view name to the fully qualified path of JSP view file using prefix and suffix. Starting from the configured prefix ("/WEB-INF/views/"), Spring appends view name reference in controller implementation ("index"), and finally appends the configured suffix (".jsp") to complete the full path tour JSP file, relative to the web application root - /WEB-INF/views/index.jsp.

■ **Note** Make sure you have the view resolver bean defined in your web application context, as it's responsible for translating view names you use in your controller code to actual views (JSP files for example). If you see error messages in your browser stating that Tomcat cannot find a JSP file, make sure your view resolver is configured correctly, as it's a typical cause of such errors.

And that completes the configuration of the Spring MVC web application. If you package the web application, and deploy it to Tomcat, you can navigate to http://localhost:8080/chapter11/helloWorld.html URL in your browser to see Spring MVC in action. Figure 11-4 shows the how the page looks in the browser.

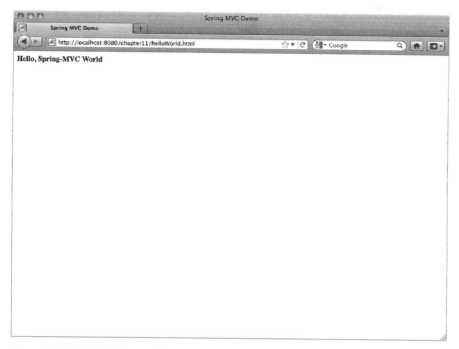

Figure 11-4. Model, view, and controller are combined to display the "Hello, Spring MVC World" message in the browser.

And that's it: we now have a Spring MVC web application deployed and running in Tomcat.

Spring framework's vision is to enable developers to write lightweight Java Enterprise applications that are capable of delivering enterprise functionality without the heavy infrastructure usually related to it. Being lightweight as it is, with rich application server functionality, Tomcat has been a good match for Spring application since the beginning of Spring. Using Tomcat and Spring enables organizations to develop and deploy high-level enterprise Java applications at a low cost (as both Tomcat and Spring are open source), and with rich functionality and high performance.

Summary

In this chapter we introduced the Spring MVC framework used for web application design and development. We started by introducing Spring framework itself, following with the description of two core design patterns that Spring MVC implements: the Model-View-Controller pattern and the Front Controller pattern.

In the second part of the chapter we implemented a sample web application using Spring MVC. We discussed the architecture of Spring MVC framework. Next, we implemented model, view, and controller components, and using Spring MVC. Finally, we configured the web application so it can be deployed and run on Apache Tomcat server.

In the next chapter, we are going to take a look at logging mechanisms in Tomcat.

CHAPTER 12

Logging in Tomcat

Logging relevant application details at runtime is a practice that has been followed since the early days of programming. Before debuggers were available, reading log statements was the only way to find out what was going on with an application at runtime. Even with all the debugging tools available today, log statements are still an invaluable tool for monitoring production systems and diagnosing any problems that occur on the deployed application.

In this chapter, we are going to take a look at the logging options available in Tomcat, for both Tomcat internal logging and logging in individual web application. We will cover following topics:

- Introduce the Java Logging framework and its Tomcat version JULI

- Demonstrate how to use JULI to configure logging in Tomcat

- Introduce Log4j logging framework, its API, and configuration options

- Demonstrate switching to Log4j as Tomcat logging mechanism

- Discuss the usage of the Slf4j framework for web application logging

Using Tomcat's JULI Logging Library

Since version 1.4, Java itself comes with the capable logging package, java.util.logging (Java Logging framework), which enables JVM-wide logging configuration shared by all applications running in the JVM. While it is simple-to-use, customizable, and extensible API, there is one problem with using plain java.util.logging: it's designed to have a single configuration within the JVM, making it impossible to configure specific logging per-class-loader for separate web applications on Tomcat. In order to get around this issue, Tomcat developers extended the functionality of the standard Java logging framework. The new implementation is known as JULI, and is part of Tomcat's standard distribution. The package structure has been changed to avoid class-loading issues with JVM-wide logging, and the new code is packaged in tomcat-juli.jar, located in the CATALINA_HOME/bin directory.

■ **Note** The access log contains information about all requests handled by Apache Tomcat server. Access logging is handled by Tomcat's AccessLogValve, and is configured in CATALINA_HOME/conf/server.xml file. Access logging is not related to the Tomcat logging described in this chapter, and we describe valves and AccessLogValve configuration details in Chapter 8.

Introduction to Java Logging and JULI libraries

The main abstractions of the Java Logging framework are loggers—objects that log messages to configured destinations. Loggers are referenced by their configured names. For example, you would typically have one logger per class or package, so that all logging from the given class or package would be performed by a single logger instance; you can use a logger name to reference an existing logger. To instantiate a logger instance in your Java code, you will use static factory method, and construct a logger with the selected name:

```
Logger logger = Logger.getLogger("com.apress.mypackage");
```

Each logger accepts messages with different logging levels, based on their importance. Using a properties file (as we will demonstrate in the next section), you can configure the level of log output at runtime, decide which logging levels should be written to the destination, and determine which should be discarded. When using Java Logging API, you will invoke different logging method based on the selected level.

Table 12-1 shows the logging levels defined by the Java Logging framework and the API methods used to invoke logging for each level.

Table 12-1. Logging Levels Defined by Standard the Java Logging Framework

Level	Description	API method
SEVERE	Used to log exceptions, errors, and other unexpected system failures.	`Logger.severe(String message)`
WARNING	Used to log warning messages.	`Logger.warning(String message)`
INFO	Used to log information messages, usually in the important steps in the code execution.	`Logger.info(String message)`
CONFIG	Logs configuration messages; for example, initialization of objects based on properties files.	`Logger.config(String message)`
FINE	Used to log more detailed information; useful for debugging purposes.	`Logger.fine(String message)`
FINER	Logs more detailed information than FINE.	`Logger.finer(String message)`
FINEST	Logs all messages, to the low-level details.	`Logger.finest(String message)`

The levels described are ordered hierarchically, so FINEST is the lowest logging level and it includes all levels above it. For example, if your logging configuration is set to log at FINEST level, it will output all messages logged using `Logger.finest()` method, but also all messages logged using `Logger.finer()`, `Logger.fine()`, `Logger.info()`... At the same time, if you configure your logging to SEVERE level, only messages logged using `Logger.severe()` will actually be sent to the output. All other logging calls will be discarded.

Levels below INFO are usually producing huge amount of log information, so it's not recommended to use them in production. However, they can be very useful during development and testing, or when diagnosing problems in production.

■ **Note** You can specify two more generic options when configuring logging level with JULI: ALL and OFF. ALL has the same meaning as FINEST; all logging levels will be written to the output. OFF disables logging altogether—no logging level will be output.

Handlers

Each logger has a list of handlers associated with it (represented by abstract class java.util.logging.Handler), which are responsible for writing log messages to its destination. There are three main handlers available in Java Logging framework:

- java.util.logging.ConsoleHandler simply outputs the logged messages to the JVM System.err output stream.

- java.util.logging.FileHandler writes the message to the file on disk, supporting file rotation.

- java.util.logging.SocketHandler writes messages to the network socket connection.

Typically, FileHandler is used for most production systems. It's natural to think of logs as "log-files," and with a numerous file processing tools available (file editors and log file analyzer) for all platforms, logging to a file has become a standard in application monitoring. While Tomcat's JULI logging implementation still uses java.util.logging.ConsoleHandler and java.util.logging.SocketHandler from Java Logging framework, JULI also provides its own org.apache.juli.FileHandler, with improved log buffering capabilities, and has simplified configuration comparing to the one available in JDK as default. We will use JULI implementation of FileHandler in the configuration examples in this chapter.

Formatters

The last component of the Java Logging framework that we're going to discuss is the formatter. There is always one formatter configured for each handler, and its responsibility is to format the log messages before they are sent to output destination. You would typically configure the formatter to include timestamp of the log event, as well as class name and line number where the logging occurred, along with the actual log message. Java Logging library (and Tomcat's version JULI) comes with the two following formatters: SimpleFormatter and XMLFormatter.

SimpleFormatter formats log message with brief log summary, including date and time of the log and the logger information. This is the default output format. It writes every log as two lines in the log file:

```
Jul 23, 2011 11:23:05 AM org.apache.catalina.core.ApplicationContext log
INFO: SessionListener: contextInitialized()
```

XMLFormatter writes the log message in XML format (the XML schema for the output format is available on Oracle's web site http://download.oracle.com/javase/1.4.2/docs/guide/util/logging/overview.html#3.0) The following log snippet illustrates an example of an XML formatted log message:

```
<record>
  <date>2011-07-23T11:21:14</date>
  <millis>1311416474822</millis>
  <sequence>41</sequence>
  <logger>org.apache.catalina.core.ContainerBase.[Catalina].[localhost].[/examples]</logger>
  <level>INFO</level>
  <class>org.apache.catalina.core.ApplicationContext</class>
  <method>log</method>
  <thread>11</thread>
  <message>SessionListener: contextInitialized()</message>
</record>
```

In addition to these two, JULI logging implementation adds three convenient formatters (located in the org.apache.juli package):

- OneLineFormatter has the same format as the default SimpleFormatter, but written in a single line, so it's easier to process.

- VerbatimFormatter writes the log message only, without any additional information.

- JdkLoggerFormatter uses a compact output format, with a timestamp in the millisecond format and abbreviated log level:

```
1311416945846  I [/examples]ContextListener: contextInitialized()
```

The human-readable SimpleFormatter is usually sufficient for most scenarios. If you require searching and processing of log messages, OneLineFormatter can be a good alternative, as it's easier to grep log files if they contain end-of-line separator after each message.

Logging Configuration

The logging configuration is typically specified in the file logging.properties. Listing 12-1 shows the simple logging configuration.

Listing 12-1. Java Logging Configuration Is Provided in the logging.properties Configuration File

```
handlers = 1myhandler.org.apache.juli.FileHandler, ↵          #1
2anotherhandler.org.apache.juli.FileHandler

.handlers = 1myhandler.org.apache.juli.FileHandler            #2

1myhandler.org.apache.juli.FileHandler.level = FINE           #3
1myhandler.org.apache.juli.FileHandler.directory = ${catalina.base}/logs   #4
1myhandler.org.apache.juli.FileHandler.prefix = foo.          #5
1myhandler.org.apache.juli.FileHandler.formatter = org.apache.juli.OneLineFormatter   #6

2anotherhandler.org.apache.juli.FileHandler.level = FINE
```

```
2anotherhandler.org.apache.juli.FileHandler.directory = /var/logs          #7
2anotherhandler.org.apache.juli.FileHandler.prefix = bar.

com.mycompany.app1.MyClass.handlers=2anotherhandler                        #8
com.mycompany.app1.MyClass.level=INFO                                      #9
```

The first line of configuration defines all handlers that we are going to use (#1). In the standard Java Logging framework, each handler is specified by its class name, as there is only one instance of each handler in JVM. As we mentioned before, Tomcat's JULI implementation supports handler-per-class-loader configuration, and that is reflected in the configuration by adding a prefix to each handler type. A handler prefix starts with a number, then has an arbitrary string, and ends with a period (.). In our sample, we define two file handlers, prefixed with 1myhandler and 2anotherhandler, respectively.

Next, we specify the default handlers using .handlers property (#2). The default handlers will be used for loggers that do not have a specific handler configured. We specify 1myhandler as default handler.

Now we need to configure properties for each of the handlers:

- Default logging level for handler is specified using level property (#3). When you configure loggers, you can override this property for each logger, but you cannot set it to lower level than specified here. In our example, we set the default level to FINE, which means we can logger configuration can override it to CONFIG or INFO, but not to FINER or FINEST level.

- Next, we set the director where the log files should be stored (#4). You can use Tomcat's environment properties in logging configuration: we configured the logs directory relative to CATALINA_HOME.

- The prefix property sets the filename prefix to use when creation log files (#5). Similarly to prefix, you can set the file suffix, but if you don't it will default to .log.

- Finally, we set the formatter for 1myhandler handler to already described OneLineFormatter (#6).

The same configuration is required for the second handler. In this case we used the absolute directory path (#7), and omitted the formatter configuration, which means the default SimpleFormatter will be used.

Finally, we need to configure loggers for the defined handlers:

- The 1myhandler is defined as default one, so we don't need to specify logger for it—all logs to non-existing loggers will go to this handler.

- We define one logger, com.mycompany.app1.MyClass, and set its handler property to 2anotherhandler (#8).

- We also override its log level to INFO (#9). We can do this, as INFO is higher in the hierarchy of levels then the default handler level FINE.

We configured the loggers, but how can we use them? In the following paragraphs, we are going to explain a few example code snippets demonstrating the Java Logging API.

To instantiate a logger with given name, you can use factory method in the java.util.logging.Logger class:

```
Logger logger = Logger.getLogger("com.mycompany.app1.MyClass");
```

You can now log messages to the logger.

Example 1:

```
logger.info("INFO MESSAGE");
```

In the previous example, Java Logging framework will match the logger name to already configured logger ("com.mycompany.app1.MyClass"). Because it's configured to accept INFO logging level, 2anotherhandler will write the log message to the /var/logs/bar.log file.

Example 2:

```
logger.warning("WARNING MESSAGE");
```

This message will also be written to the /var/logs/bar.log file, because WARNING log level is higher in the level hierarchy then the level configured for this logger (INFO).

Example 3:

```
logger.fine("TRACE MESSAGE");
```

Although 2anotherhandler will accept logging on FINE level, this message will not be visible in the log. This is because the "com.mycompany.app1.MyClass" logger overrides the logging level to INFO, and since the FINE level is lower than configured level, the log will not be written.

Let's take a look at another logger:

```
Logger logger2 = Logger.getLogger("testlogger");
```

There is no logger configured with name "testlogger," so the root logger will be used, with default handler (1myhandler).

Example 4:

```
logger2.info("INFO MESSAGE");
```

This message will be written to the CATALINA_HOME/logs/foo.log file, as configured for 1myhandler.

Example 5:

```
logger2.fine("TRACE MESSAGE");
```

This message will be written to the CATALINA_HOME/logs/foo.log file, as configured for 1myhandler. Because the logger with given name does not exists, the level configure on the default handler will be used.

Example 6:

```
Logger2.finer("DETAILED TRACE MESSAGE");
```

The level FINER is lower than the FINE level configured for default handler, so this message won't be written to the log file

Rotating Logs

You can use Tomcat JULI logging framework to rotate log files daily. The format of the log files is {prefix}{date}{suffix}. The new file is created at midnight every day, and used for logging until end of that day.

The log file rotation is enabled by default, but you can control it using the rotatable property in your handler configuration:

```
1myhandler.org.apache.juli.FileHandler.rotatable = false
```

The rotation can only rotate files daily, and you don't have any options about the filename format used. If you need richer rotating options (rotating by maximum file size, weekly, or monthly, for example), use java.util.logging.FileHandler or some of the specialized logging frameworks, like Log4j, which we will discuss in the second part of this chapter.

Servlet API Logging

The Java Servlet specification defines the logging API to be used when logging messages from servlet-related classes. The logging based on Servlet API is performed by calls to ServletContext.log(String message) method, passing in the message to be written to the log.

This logging method has become obsolete with emergence of more powerful, customizable logging frameworks for Java, such are java.util.logging or log4j. Developers tend to prefer these logging frameworks to Servlet API logging.

In Tomcat, all messages logged to Servlet log are intercepted and handled by internal Tomcat logging. Tomcat provides handlers for ServletContext logs, for each engine, host, and context combination. The names of such loggers follow the convention:

```
org.apache.catalina.core.ContainerBase.[ENGINE].[HOST].[CONTEXT]
```

All ServletContext loggers' names start with org.apache.catalina.core.ContainerBase, followed by the engine name, host name, and context name in square brackets, separated by dots (.). The following code snippet illustrates the logger configuration:

```
org.apache.catalina.core.ContainerBase.[Catalina].[localhost].[/manager].level = INFO
org.apache.catalina.core.ContainerBase.[Catalina].[localhost].[/manager].handlers =↩
 3manager.org.apache.juli.FileHandler
```

Now that we covered the basic concepts of Java Logging framework and Tomcat-specific improvements in JULI, we can have a look at how to configure Tomcat to use it. In the next two sections, we cover the configuration of internal Tomcat logging and logging in web applications deployed to Tomcat.

Configuring Internal Tomcat Logging with JULI

The server-wide logging configuration is located in the CATALINA_HOME/conf/logging.properties file. We're going to explain the internal Tomcat logging configuration using the default logging.properties file, which is part of the Tomcat distribution. Listing 12-2 shows the contents of the default logging.properties file.

Listing 12-2. Default JULI Logging Configuration in the logging.properties file

```
handlers = 1catalina.org.apache.juli.FileHandler, 2localhost.org.apache.juli.FileHandler,↩
 3manager.org.apache.juli.FileHandler, 4host-manager.org.apache.juli.FileHandler,↩
 java.util.logging.ConsoleHandler                                                    #1

.handlers = 1catalina.org.apache.juli.FileHandler, java.util.logging.ConsoleHandler   #2

1catalina.org.apache.juli.FileHandler.level = FINE                                   #3
1catalina.org.apache.juli.FileHandler.directory = ${catalina.base}/logs             #4
1catalina.org.apache.juli.FileHandler.prefix = catalina.                            #5
```

```
2localhost.org.apache.juli.FileHandler.level = FINE
2localhost.org.apache.juli.FileHandler.directory = ${catalina.base}/logs
2localhost.org.apache.juli.FileHandler.prefix = localhost.

#Similar configuration is available for manager and host-manager web application.
#which is omitted here for clarity

java.util.logging.ConsoleHandler.level = FINE
java.util.logging.ConsoleHandler.formatter = java.util.logging.SimpleFormatter

org.apache.catalina.core.ContainerBase.[Catalina].[localhost].level = INFO
org.apache.catalina.core.ContainerBase.[Catalina].[localhost].handlers =↵
 2localhost.org.apache.juli.FileHandler

org.apache.catalina.core.ContainerBase.[Catalina].[localhost].[/manager].level = INFO
org.apache.catalina.core.ContainerBase.[Catalina].[localhost].[/manager].handlers =↵
 3manager.org.apache.juli.FileHandler

org.apache.catalina.core.ContainerBase.[Catalina].[localhost].[/host-manager].level = INFO
org.apache.catalina.core.ContainerBase.[Catalina].[localhost].[/host-manager].handlers =↵
 4host-manager.org.apache.juli.FileHandler
```

Tomcat by default defines five log handlers: one system wide ConsoleHandler and four FileHandlers (#1). Both the 1catalina FileHandler and the ConsoleHandler are configured as default handlers (#2); all messages logged to non-configured loggers will go to both of these handlers.

Each of the five handlers is configured separately. Log level is set to FINE for all of them by default, so no messages logged at FINER or FINEST level will appear in any tomcat logs (#3). All FileHandlers are storing log files to CATALINA_HOME/logs directory by default (#4).

There are four different file handlers configured. Handler 1catalina is configured to write log messages to CATALINA_HOME/logs/catalina.log file (#5). Because of the file rotation, which is enabled by default, the file name will actually contain the date as well—for example, catalina.2011-07-21.log.

Similar configuration (with different filename prefixes only) is defined for other three file handlers.

Because ConsoleHandler and 1catalina FileHandler are configured as default log handlers, there are no loggers configured for them.

The remaining three file handlers each have one logger configured. These loggers are

- org.apache.catalina.core.ContainerBase.[Catalina].[localhost] logs all ServletContext.log() messages for all web applications deployed to host with name "localhost", which is the default host available in Tomcat. The handler for this logger is 2localhost, which writes to CATALINA_HOME/log/localhost.log.

- org.apache.catalina.core.ContainerBase.[Catalina].[localhost].[/manager] logs all ServletContext.log() messages for the Tomcat's Manager web application. The handler for this logger is 3manager, which writes to CATALINA_HOME/log/manager.log.

- org.apache.catalina.core.ContainerBase.[Catalina].[localhost].[/host-manager] logs all ServletContext.log() messages for the Tomcat's Manager web application. The handler for this logger is 4host-manager, which writes to the CATALINA_HOME/log/host-manager.log file.

Console Logging

The console output in Tomcat contains all messages sent to System.out and System.err output streams, and all exception stack traces. On Linux systems, and when running Tomcat as a windows service, Tomcat intercepts all console output and logs it to the file configured by CATALINA_OUT environment variable. By default, the location of this file is CATALINA_HOME/logs/catalina.out on Linux-based systems. If you're running Tomcat as a Windows service, console output will be appended to files CATALINA_HOME/logs/stdout.log and CATALINA_OUT/logs/stderr.out instead.

> ▓ **Note** If you're running Tomcat using startup.bat file on Windows, the console output will be redirected to the current Windows prompt window, and won't be written to a file.

While it is useful to have console output in a file, there are few pitfalls that you should be aware of. On Linux, the console output file (catalina.out) cannot be rotated without stopping Tomcat. If you have a lot of System.out output in your applications, these files can grow huge, and affect the Tomcat performance and stability.

For production environments, it's advisable not to use console output at all, but to log everything using chosen logging framework. You can disable console logging in Tomcat by removing ConsoleHandler from logging configuration. If you want to disable console logging for selected web applications only, you can set the swallowOutput attribute to true in the <Context> element configuration for desired web application:

```
<Context path="/manager" swallowOutput="true">
```

But make sure you have proper logging configured before you do this. If the console output is the only logging you have configured, you will not see any logging from your web application.

Configuring Web Application Logging with JULI

To configure JULI for each web application, all you need to do is create web-application specific logging.properties file and package it in WEB-INF/classes directory of your web application. Listing 12-3 illustrates a simple web application logging configuration.

Listing 12-3. Single Web Application Logging Configuration

```
handlers=1chapter12.org.apache.juli.FileHandler, 2chapter12.org.apache.juli.FileHandler   #1

.handlers=1chapter12.org.apache.juli.FileHandler                                            #2


1chapter12.org.apache.juli.FileHandler.level=FINE
1chapter12.org.apache.juli.FileHandler.directory=${catalina.base}/logs
1chapter12.org.apache.juli.FileHandler.prefix=chapter12-default.                            #3

2chapter12.org.apache.juli.FileHandler.level=FINE
2chapter12.org.apache.juli.FileHandler.directory=${catalina.base}/logs
2chapter12.org.apache.juli.FileHandler.prefix=chapter12-special.                            #4
```

```
com.apress.apachetomcat7.chapter12.level=INFO
com.apress.apachetomcat7.chapter12.handlers=
2chapter12.org.apache.juli.FileHandler                                    #5
```

If the Tomcat's class loader detects the logging.properties file located in the WEB-INF/classes directory of the web application, it will use it to configure logging for that web application—ignoring the configuration in CATALINA_HOME/conf/logging.properties. This means that no default handlers from Tomcat's main logging configuration will be defined, and you should take care to add default handlers in your web application's configuration, or you risk losing logged messages.

We defined two file logging handlers, 1chapter12 and 2chapter12 (#1). We are going to use the 1chapter12 as default handler (#2), so any loggers not explicitly defined will write output to this handler. We configured 1chapter12 handler to log to file chapter12-default.log, located in the CATALINA_HOME/logs directory (#3).

We will use 2chapter12 handler for "special" web application logging, and it will log messages to the chapter12-special.log file (#4).

Finally, we created a single logger, which uses 2chapter12 handler, and gave it a name to match our web application's root package: com.apress.apachetomcat7.chapter12.

Now in the servlet Java code we implemented, we can simply log to the configured logger:

```
Logger logger = Logger.getLogger("com.apress.apachetomcat7.chapter12");
logger.warning("test message");
```

And the message will appear in the CATALINA_HOME/logs/chapter12-special.log file:

```
Jul 23, 2011 5:04:45 PM com.apress.apachetomcat7.chapter12.HelloWorldServlet doGet
WARNING: test message
```

If you log your message to a logger that isn't configured in the logging.properties file, the message will be appended to the file configured as the default handler:

```
Logger logger2 = Logger.getLogger("unknown logger");
logger2.info("This message will go to console");
```

The message will not be present in the chapter12-special.log, but instead you can see it in the chapter12-default.log file:

```
Jul 23, 2011 5:35:22 PM com.apress.apachetomcat7.chapter12.HelloWorldServlet doGet
INFO: This message will go to the console output
```

Using this approach, you can configure as many loggers as you need for your web application. Common strategy is to have different layers of the web application log to separate files (so you can have web.log, services.log, dataaccess.log). Or, for smaller web applications, you can have a single file handler defined as default handler, and log all messages to a single file.

■ **Note** You will see no output in the Tomcat console in case you handle all logging using Java logging properties. You will have to check the configured log file in order to see output from your application. But you won't lose any messages, so that can only be a good thing.

By using a logging library, such as Java logging or its JULI version, you will get consistent log handling throughout your web application, without fear that some messages will be lost.

Although JULI logging can address all your application's needs for logging, there are other logging frameworks that gained popularity before Sun included Java Logging framework with Java 1.4. One of the most popular logging frameworks is Apache's Log4j, and open source logging implementation providing easy-to-use API, rich configuration options, and high performance. In the next section, we are going to see how we can use Log4j instead of JULI framework for Tomcat logging.

Using Log4j Library for Web Application Logging

Sun has introduced Java Logging framework from Java version 1.4. However, the need for a powerful logging framework in Java was present long before that. In addition, the Java Logging framework was only available for Java SDK 1.4 and later, so applications running on Java 1.3 and earlier could not use it.

Ceki Gulcu originally wrote Log4j, and it quickly gained popularity, becoming an open source project as part of the Apache Software Foundation. With a large user base, Log4j is still one of the most widely used logging frameworks, and a lot of the features in Java Logging framework features were inspired by Log4j.

Just like with the Java Logging framework, logger is a central abstraction in Log4j. However, the logger in Log4j is defined as class `org.apache.log4j.Logger` (as opposed to `java.util.logging.Logger` in Java Logging). Log messages are handled by appenders, which have the same role as `java.util.logging` handlers. Finally, messages are formatted using layouts in Log4j, which have the same role as formatters in Java Logging framework. Table 12-2 shows the comparison between corresponding elements from Java Logging framework and Log4j.

Table 12-2. Main Components of Java Logging Framework and Log4J

Java Logging	Log4j
`java.util.logging.Logger`	`org.apache.log4j.Logger`
`java.util.logging.Handler`	`org.apache.log4j.Appender`
`java.util.logging.Formatter`	`org.apache.log4j.Layout`

Log4j uses slightly different logging levels than Java Logging framework. Because Log4j was started before Sun's Java Logging, developers are usually more familiar with logging levels from Log4j. Tomcat's JULI implementation even offers abstraction of `java.util.logging.Logger` that uses the Log4j levels instead of Java Logging standard levels. Table 12-3 lists the logging levels in Log4j.

Table 12-3. Logging Levels and Their API Log Calls in Log4J

Level	Description	API Method
FATAL	Used to log fatal errors, when an application cannot recover and continue.	Logger.fatal(String message)
ERROR	Used to log error messages; for example, handled exceptions.	Logger.error(String message)
WARN	Used to log warnings.	Logger.warning(String message)

Level	Description	API Method
INFO	Logs information messages.	Logger.info(String message)
DEBUG	Logs developer debug information, usually used during development and diagnostics.	Logger.debug(String message)
TRACE	Traces information about application execution.	Logger.trace(String message)

▪ **Note** DEBUG and TRACE logging levels log huge amounts of information, and they should be turned off in production systems. They are analogous to FINE, FINER, and FINEST log levels in JULI.

In order to use Log4j, you have to place log4j-{version}.jar file on your application classpath. The configuration can be provided using the properties file (log4j.properties) or as XML file (log4j.xml). In this chapter we will be using properties file for Log4j configuration. The configuration file needs to be located on the application classpath as well. Listing 12-4 illustrates the simple Log4j configuration file.

Listing 12-4. Simple Log4j Configuration File

```
log4j.rootLogger=DEBUG, FOO                                        #1
log4j.appender.FOO =org.apache.log4j.ConsoleAppender              #2
log4j.appender.FOO.layout=org.apache.log4j.PatternLayout         #3
log4j.appender.FOO.layout.ConversionPattern=%d [%t] %-5p %c - %m%n  #4
log4j.logger.com.foo=WARN                                         #5
```

All configuration elements must start with string log4j.

In Log4j, it's mandatory to configure root logger (#1), which will take over the logging for all loggers that are not explicitly configured (similar to default handlers in Java Logging). The name of the logger is the property name (log4j.logger), and the value contains logging level (DEBUG) and the name of the appender to use (FOO).

Next, we configure the appender, using Log4j's ConsoleAppender (#2), which appends all log messages to console output (similar as Java Logging's ConsoleHandler). We set the name of the appender to FOO.

The next part is the log layout (#3). We are using PatternLayout, a powerful pattern formatter from Log4j. The pattern to be used with PatternLayout is specified as separate configuration property, ConversionPattern (#4).

▪ **Note** Although Log4j supports a few other layouts, with the power of PatternLayout you will probably not need any other. The configuration options of PatternLayout itself are a good reason to start using Log4j for logging. We will discuss features of PatternLayout in the separate section.

Finally, we specify another logger, called com.foo, and set its logging level to WARN (#5). Note that we haven't specified the appender for com.foo logger—Log4j will inherit the appender from root logger in this case.

Logger inheritance is mandatory in Log4j and is a very convenient mechanism for logging configuration. Logger com.foo will accept log messages from loggers com.foo, but also com.foo.bar, com.foo.bar.MyClass, com.foo.bar.MyClass$Test... Using logger inheritance mechanism, you can easily configure specific loggers on package levels in your application, and use class name to reference underlying logger:

```
package com.foo.bar
import org.apache.log4j.Logger;
public class MyClass{
    Logger logger = Logger.getLogger(MyClass.class.getName());
...
    logger.warn ("Warning message");
...
}
```

The logger instantiation in the previous code snippet is the same as Logger.getLogger("com.foo.bar.MyClass"), and in Log4j this logger will inherit configuration of logger com.foo from Listing 12-4.

PatternLayout

PatternLayout is a flexible and powerful class designed to transform logging events to text in Log4j, based on the supplied conversion pattern. The conversion pattern options are largely inspired by the printf function in C programming language. Table 12-4 lists some of the commonly used pattern configuration options.

Table 12-4. Common Pattern Configuration Elements for Log4j's PatternLayout

Pattern Syntax	Description	Pattern Syntax	Description
%d	Logging date. You can specify date pattern in curly brackets (%d{HH:mm:ss,SSS})	%c	Fully qualified class name (use %c{1} to print only simple class name)
%t	Name of the thread where logging occurred	%F	Filename of the logging event
%p	Logging level	%L	Line number of the logging event
%m	The actual logging message	%n	Line separator (add this to the end of the pattern to force new line)

You can specify text width and justification for every pattern element:

- %20m: Specify minimum width of 20 characters.

- %20.50m: Specify minimum and maximum width to 20 and 50 characters, respectively.

- %-20m: Specify minimum width of 20 characters, left justified.

Here are some of the pattern examples and the log entries they generated:

```
%d [%t] %-5p %c - %m%n
2000-09-07 14:07:41,508 [main] INFO  MyClass - Executing...

%5p [%t] (%F:%L) - %m%n
INFO [main] (MyClass.java:12) - Executing...
```

Now that we covered basic functionality and configuration of Log4j, let's take a look how we can configure Tomcat and web applications to use Log4j logging instead of JULI.

Using Log4j for Tomcat Internal Logging

When you download Tomcat, JULI logging library and configuration are available out of the box. In order to use Log4j for Tomcat internal logging instead, you will need to replace the existing JULI library with the Log4j-JULI integration. You can achieve that by following these six steps:

1. Delete existing JULI library (CATALINA_HOME/bin/tomcat-juli.jar file) and the existing Tomcat Java Logging configuration file (CATALINA_HOME/conf/logging.properties).

2. Download JULI Log4j Tomcat library (tomcat-juli.jar) from the Tomcat downloads' Extras section (http://tomcat.apache.org/download-70.cgi). Place the downloaded file to CATALINA_HOME/bin directory.

3. Download Tomcat JULI adapters library (tomcat-juli-adapters.jar) from the Tomcat downloads' Extras section. Place this file in the CATALINA_HOME/lib directory.

4. Download Log4j (version 1.2 or later), and place the downloaded library file to CATALINA_HOME/lib directory.

5. Create the Log4j configuration file at the following location: CATALINA_HOME/lib/log4j.properties. Listing 12-5 illustrates the log4j configuration matching the default Java Logging configuration.

6. Restart Tomcat.

Listing 12-5. The Contents of the Log4j configuration File Matching the Default Tomcat Logging Settings

```
log4j.rootLogger=INFO, CATALINA

# Define all the appenders log4j.appender.CATALINA=org.apache.log4j.DailyRollingFileAppender
log4j.appender.CATALINA.File=${catalina.base}/logs/catalina.
log4j.appender.CATALINA.Append=true log4j.appender.CATALINA.Encoding=UTF-8

# Roll-over the log once per day
log4j.appender.CATALINA.DatePattern='.'yyyy-MM-dd'.log'
log4j.appender.CATALINA.layout = org.apache.log4j.PatternLayout
```

```
log4j.appender.CATALINA.layout.ConversionPattern = %d [%t] %-5p %c- %m%n

log4j.appender.LOCALHOST=org.apache.log4j.DailyRollingFileAppender
log4j.appender.LOCALHOST.File=${catalina.base}/logs/localhost.
log4j.appender.LOCALHOST.Append=true log4j.appender.LOCALHOST.Encoding=UTF-8
log4j.appender.LOCALHOST.DatePattern='.'yyyy-MM-dd'.log'
log4j.appender.LOCALHOST.layout = org.apache.log4j.PatternLayout
log4j.appender.LOCALHOST.layout.ConversionPattern = %d [%t] %-5p %c- %m%n

log4j.appender.MANAGER=org.apache.log4j.DailyRollingFileAppender
log4j.appender.MANAGER.File=${catalina.base}/logs/manager.
log4j.appender.MANAGER.Append=true log4j.appender.MANAGER.Encoding=UTF-8
log4j.appender.MANAGER.DatePattern='.'yyyy-MM-dd'.log'
log4j.appender.MANAGER.layout = org.apache.log4j.PatternLayout
log4j.appender.MANAGER.layout.ConversionPattern = %d [%t] %-5p %c- %m%n

log4j.appender.HOST-MANAGER=org.apache.log4j.DailyRollingFileAppender
log4j.appender.HOST-MANAGER.File=${catalina.base}/logs/host-manager.
log4j.appender.HOST-MANAGER.Append=true log4j.appender.HOST-MANAGER.Encoding=UTF-8
log4j.appender.HOST-MANAGER.DatePattern='.'yyyy-MM-dd'.log'
log4j.appender.HOST-MANAGER.layout = org.apache.log4j.PatternLayout
log4j.appender.HOST-MANAGER.layout.ConversionPattern = %d [%t] %-5p %c- %m%n

log4j.appender.CONSOLE=org.apache.log4j.ConsoleAppender
log4j.appender.CONSOLE.Encoding=UTF-8
log4j.appender.CONSOLE.layout=org.apache.log4j.PatternLayout
log4j.appender.CONSOLE.layout.ConversionPattern = %d [%t] %-5p %c- %m%n

# Configure which loggers log to which appenders
log4j.logger.org.apache.catalina.core.ContainerBase.[Catalina].[localhost]=INFO, LOCALHOST
log4j.logger.org.apache.catalina.core.ContainerBase.[Catalina].[localhost].[/manager]=INFO,↩
MANAGER
log4j.logger.org.apache.catalina.core.ContainerBase.[Catalina].[localhost].↩
[/host-manager]= INFO, HOST-MANAGER
```

And that's it: your Tomcat will now use Log4j for all internal logging. For additional information and details about the Log4j configuration, take a look at the Log4j project home page http://logging.apache .org/log4j/index.html.

Using Log4j for Web Application Logging

In order to have your application use Log4j for logging, you'll have to make to add log4j.jar library to the web application classpath (in the WEB-INF/lib directory of your web application). Then, you'll have to place Log4j configuration file, log4j.properties, into the web application classpath as well (in the WEB-INF/classes directory). Listing 12-6 shows sample log4j.properties file you can use.

Listing 12-6. Sample Log4j Configuration for a Web Application Using RollingFileAppender

```
log4j.rootLogger=WARN, rolling                                              #1

log4j.appender.rolling=org.apache.log4j.RollingFileAppender                 #2
```

```
log4j.appender.rolling.File=/var/log/default.log                              #3
log4j.appender.rolling.MaxFileSize=10MB                                       #4
log4j.appender.rolling.MaxBackupIndex=5                                       #5

log4j.appender.rolling.layout=org.apache.log4j.PatternLayout                  #6
log4j.appender.rolling.layout.ConversionPattern=%p [%t] %C{1}.%M(%L) | %m%n

log4j.logger.com.apress.apachetomcat7.chapter12=DEBUG                         #7
log4j.logger.javax.servlet=INFO                                              #8
```

The root logger is configured to log WARN logging level, and use appender with name rolling (#1). Next, we configure the rolling appender—we're using Log4j's RollingFileAppender in this example (#2). RollingFileAppender writes output to a file configured using File property (#3). When the log file size reaches size specified using MaxFileSize property—10MB, in our example (#4)—the RollingFileAppender will create a new file and continue logging to it. We specify the number of old log file to keep as backup using MaxBackupIndex property (#5).

Finally, we configure layout for the rolling appender—we're using familiar PatternLayout (#6), with ConversionPattern set.

We added two additional loggers, extending the root logger. First we added a logger for the classes in the main package of our web application, overriding logging level to DEBUG (#7). Second logger we added logs any messages from javax.servlet package with INFO level (#8).

You can use this sample configuration, and the earlier Log4j configuration examples to create Log4j configuration for most common usage scenarios. For more information about Log4j, consult Log4j documentation (http://logging.apache.org/log4j/1.2/publications.html).

Web Application Logging Using Slf4j Library

Both Log4j and Java Logging framework provide logging functionality that can be used in any Java project. The biggest issue in choosing one or another is that you cannot switch easily. Not only that these frameworks use different libraries and configuration, but they have incompatible APIs (java.util.logging.Logger vs. org.apache.log4j.Logger), so you would have to replace every logging call in your code from one framework to another. This can be a tedious job, and most of the times developers stick to the first choice logging library for the entire life of the project.

This is unfortunate, as the differences between frameworks aren't that big after all. How good would it be to have a bridging library, with unified API that can pick any logging implementation that is available on the classpath? Welcome Simple Logging Façade for Java (commonly called Slf4j), Java logging bridge library designed exactly for that reason.

■ **Note** Apache commons-logging library was designed with the same goal, as a universal logging API that delegates logging to the discoverable underlying logging framework. However, due to class-loading issues with the commons-logging discovery mechanism, it is recommended to avoid it and use Slf4j instead.

Using Slf4j

To start using Slf4j, you will need slf4j-api.jar library, which contains the Slf4j API classes and interfaces.

▓ **Note** You can download slf4j-api.jar and all other slf4j libraries from the project's download page: www.slf4j.org/download.html.

Once you have `slf4j-api.jar` on your project's class path, you can use its API to log statements in your Java code. Listing 12-7 demonstrates its usage.

Listing 12-7. Using Slf4j API for Logging in Java

```
import org.slf4j.Logger;                                      #1
import org.slf4j.LoggerFactory;                               #2
…
Logger logger = LoggerFactory.getLogger(HelloWorld.class);    #3
logger.info("Hello World");                                   #4
logger.warn("Warning message");                               #5
```

Note that we imported the Slf4j classes in this case (#1, #2), instead of logging-framework specific ones. We will use `org.slf4j.Logger` for all logging (instead of `java.util.logging.Logger` or `org.apache.log4j.Logger`, which we used before). The `Logger` instance is created using `LoggerFactory` static factory method (#3). You can use the Slf4j `Logger` in the familiar manner, to log message on INFO level (#4), WARN level (#5), or any other logging level available.

▓ **Note** You will notice that the Slf4j API is more similar to Log4j than to Java Logging, and that it uses Log4j logging levels as well. This is understandable as the creators of Log4j started the Slf4j project.

You can use the previously mentioned API calls in your code regardless of which underlying logging framework you decide to use—Slf4j will bridge these calls to the native API of logging library used. Slf4j achieves this by using bindings, the Java library that bridges the Slf4j API calls to the native logging calls. Slf4j has bindings for all popular logging frameworks, including Java Logging framework and Log4j, which we used throughout this chapter. All you have to do is download the binding for your logging library, and add it to the application classpath. Of course, you will have to include the logging library itself and its configuration as well.

Let's see how would this work with Java Logging library, for example. You would include Java Logging library on your classpath, including its configuration in `logging.properties` file—just like we described in the first part of this chapter. You will also include `slf4j-api.jar` on your library with the Java Logging binding (`slf4j-jdk14.jar`), which can be downloaded from the Slf4j download page. To actually log messages in your code, you will use slf4j API (`org.slf4j.Logger` and `org.slf4j.LoggerFactory` classes). When you deploy your application to Tomcat, the logging will work just the same as before. Invisible to you, the `org.slf4j.Logger` calls will be bridged to the `java.util.logging.Logger` class, using the binding library supplied on classpath.

Let's say that you decide to switch to Log4j a few months later. You will have to remove Java Logging configuration from your application classpath, and include Log4j library and `log4j.properties` configuration file instead. You will also have to remove the Java Logging Slf4j binding (slf4j-jdk14.jar), and replace it with the binding for Log4j (slf4j-log4j.jar).

And that's it! There is no need to change any of the API calls, as Slf4j API you used will still work. Only this time it will find the log4j binding on the classpath, and it will bridge all calls to org.slf4j.Logger class to the Log4j's org.apache.log4j.Logger, as expected!

In case you tried to switch logging framework without using Slf4j in the first place, you would need to change all source files where you used java.util.logging classes, replace it with log4j API, recompile, repackage and redeploy the application—a time consuming, error-prone exercise.

Slf4j enables you to choose logging framework at deployment time, and change it as often as you like, using only classpath changes (adding and removing jar files and configuration). It supports all major logging frameworks, and it has rich API and excellent performance. If you're starting new project, you should consider using Slf4j as a bridge to your selected logging framework

Summary

In this chapter we discussed the logging options available in Apache Tomcat. We configured default JULI logging for Tomcat internal logging and for logging in individual web applications deployed in Tomcat.

We then introduced Log4j, a popular logging library, and explained how you can switch to Log4j for Tomcat internal logging. We also demonstrated how you can use Log4j for web application logging.

Finally, we demonstrated how you can use Slf4j API and bindings to abstract the concrete logging library in use, and enable easy switching between logging frameworks at deployment time.

In the next chapter, we are going to take a look at JNDI resources in Tomcat and use JNDI to configure database connections and mail sessions.

CHAPTER 13

Configuring JNDI in Tomcat

Most real-world web applications store data or process data stored in the relational databases and send e-mails to users. Efficient configuration of these resources is required for the development of web applications, but also for server administration and maintenance. JNDI-configured resources are commonly used to configure such resources in production, mainly for its portability and easy configuration. In this chapter, we will discuss JNDI configuration, and look at how to configure database connectivity and mail sending servers using JNDI resources.

In this chapter, we will

- Introduce JNDI technology and its role and usage in Java applications

- Explain the principles of JDBC usage and configuration in web applications

- Demonstrate database configuration using JNDI

- Introduce the JavaMail API for sending e-mail from Java applications

- Demonstrate mail server configuration using JNDI

Introduction to JNDI

Java Naming Directory Interface (JNDI) is the standard Java API for directory and naming services. You can think of a naming service as a library catalogue. In a library, all books are organized hierarchically by subject, author, and title—so if you're looking for a particular book, you can locate the catalogue for the particular topic, then find the drawer for the author, and finally find the book you want. In programming, such catalogues contain objects, and are called naming and directory services.

Large enterprise applications can be very complex, and require many services from different providers to work together in order to achieve their goal. A robust, portable way to find resources is very important for such applications.

JNDI is a Java API for accessing and manipulating named resources. It is designed as an interface to the standard naming and directory services, such as Light Directory Access Protocol (LDAP) and Domain Name Server (DNS). However, the naming service can contain objects of any type that can be looked up by name using JNDI.

Naming services store a number of bindings, which bind the unique name to an object. Objects represent services available on the server that clients can look up and use. Clients need to know only the name of a service to look it up. When clients obtain the service by name, they can start using it. A service object usually defines an interface, so that clients can invoke its methods without any knowledge of the internal workings of the service—all clients need to know is the service name and the interface it implements. Figure 13-1 illustrates the naming service and its relationship to a client.

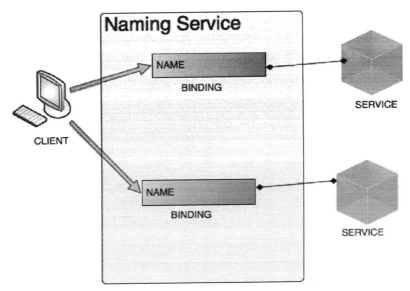

Figure 13-1. Naming service structure, with bindings between JNDI names and objects (services)

Let's take a look at some of the classes and interfaces defined in the JNDI API.

JNDI API Overview

The main interface in the JNDI API is javax.naming.Context, which represents the abstraction of the naming context in Java. It defines method to create, update, and examine the bindings stored in the naming context by their name. The main implementation of the Context interface is the javax.naming.InitialContext class, which is instantiated based on the environment configuration of the naming service, and is used as a starting point for any resource lookup.

JNDI resources are organized in a hierarchical tree, where lookup is performed relative to the current context. Listing 13-1 shows typical access to JNDI Context from Java code.

Listing 13-1. Looking Up Resources by Name from JNDI Context

```
Context initContext = new InitialContext();                          #1
Context rootContext  = (Context)initContext.lookup("java:/comp/env"); #2
Object myService = rootContext.lookup("apress/myservice");           #3
```

In the first line, we instantiate InitialContext (#1). You can provide additional settings for the naming service you are using. Tomcat's naming service does not require any special configuration parameters.

Next, we perform the lookup by name, but the lookup that returns another Context, the sub-context of the initial naming context. The name we use for this Context is "java:/comp/env" (#2), which is the standard convention used for naming a context that stores java components. Finally, we look up the Object (service) from the JNDI context, using the name "apress/myservice" (#3). Because we are performing a lookup operation on the sub-context, the name we look up is relative to the Context we're

using. That means that the full JNDI name for the myService object is
"java:/comp/env/apress/myservice". We could have used a single lookup to get the myService object
directly, without going via sub-context:

```
Object myService = initContext.lookup("java:/comp/env/apress/myservice");
```

Note that we performed lookup on the initContext object in this case.

■ **Note** Due to the hierarchical nature of the JNDI naming context, you will get the same result whether you look up the object directly from the initial naming context or by looking up the sub-context first, and then using the relative name to look up the actual object.

Tomcat JNDI Configuration

The JNDI resource in Tomcat is configured using the <Resource> XML element. Table 13-1 describes the attributes available for JNDI resource configuration element.

Table 13-1. The Valid Atttributes for <Resource> Configuration Element in Tomcat

Attribute Name	Description
Name	The name of the resource, relative to the root Java context, java:comp/env.
Description	The human readable description of the JNDI resource.
Type	The fully qualified class name for the type of object that will be returned for any JNDI lookup of this resource.
Auth	Specifies if the authentication for the resource access is container-managed or application-managed. Allowed values are Container and Application.
Scope	Specifies whether the object looked up using this resource can be shared. Allowed values are Shareable and Unshareable. The default value is Shareable.
Singleton	Specifies whether multiple lookups of the resource will return a new Object every time (when set to false), or whether the same Object will be reused (when set to true). Default is true.
closeMethod	Name of the method used to perform cleanup after the singleton resource is no longer required. Method specified must not accept any arguments.

JNDI resources in Tomcat can be defined as global resources, when the configured resource is available to all contexts deployed on the Tomcat instance, or as <Context> elements, when the resource is available to the web application defined in that context only.

If the JNDI resource is configured as global, the <Resource> element needs to be placed within the <GlobalNamingResources> in the server.xml configuration file.

Once the JNDI resource is configured using the <Resource> element, you have to configure the resource reference in the web deployment descriptor of your web application using the <env-ref>, <resource-ref>, or <resource-env-ref> element. Using the <env-entry>, you can specify a custom JNDI environment property for the given web application. The elements <resource-ref> and <resource-env-ref> are defining the reference to the resource factory defined using the <Resource> element in the Tomcat configuration files.

Tomcat will use the information in the web.xml configuration and main <Resource> configuration to create the resource used within the web application. In case the JNDI resource factory is not found (if the settings configured in the web.xml file do not match the <Resource> configuration), Tomcat will throw an exception and the application will fail to start.

Strictly speaking, adding a resource reference to the web.xml configuration is not required when <Resource> is configured in the <Context> element for a single web application. However, it is recommended to include for verification and documentation purposes, so that developers working on the web application know which JNDI resources are required.

Let's now take a look at some practical examples of JNDI resource configuration, and configure JDBC DataSource as JNDI resource.

Configuring the Database Connection

Accessing a relational database is a must for almost all non-trivial web applications. Relational databases store data in the tables and columns, which are accessed programmatically using SQL language. To connect to the database and issue SQL statements to it, Java provides JDBC. Using the JDBC API, developers can access relational databases using a high-level Java API, which contains a set of classes and interfaces abstracting database connectivity. In addition, the JDBC library requires the database-specific driver, which understands the particular database server used by the application. The JDBC driver is part of the database distribution, and can usually be downloaded from the database vendor's web site (for example, MySQL JDBC driver, or Oracle JDBC driver).

Introducing JDBC

The main abstraction of a relational database in JDBC is the java.sql.Connection interface, which encapsulates the connection to the database server, through which you can create tables and columns and run select, delete, and update SQL queries.

Let's take a look at how the database Connections are obtained and used in a typical Java application. For this example, we are going to use a MySQL database of users, which we used for the examples in Chapter 6. If you have already followed the steps for creating the database as outlined in Chapter 6, you can just continue to use the same database. In case you haven't created the database, Listing 13-2 shows the SQL script required to create the users database and populate it with several rows of data.

Listing 13-2. SQL Script for Creating a Database of Users and Insterting Sample User Data

```
create user 'test'@'localhost' identified by test;
grant all privileges on tomcatusers.* to test@localhost
create database tomcatusers;
use tomcatusers;
create table users
(
user_name varchar(12) not null primary key,
user_pass varchar(12) not null
);
create table users_roles
(
user_name varchar(12) not null,
role_name varchar(12) not null,
primary key(user_name, role_name)
);

insert into users values("tomcat", "tomcat");
insert into users values("role1", "tomcat");
insert into users values("both", "tomcat");
insert into users values("bob", "password");
insert into user_roles values("tomcat", "tomcat");
insert into user_roles values("role1", "role1");
insert into user_roles values("both", "tomcat");
insert into user_roles values("both", "role1");
insert into user_roles values("bob", "apressuser");
```

We are going to implement the servlet that will display all users and their roles on the web pages. Listing 13-3 shows the servlet implementation, using the JDBC API to access database.

Listing 13-3. Accessing the Tomcatusers Database from the Servle Using the JDBC API

```
@WebServlet(urlPatterns = {"/displayUsers.html"})
public class DisplayUsersServlet extends HttpServlet {

    protected void doGet(HttpServletRequest request, HttpServletResponse response)
            throws ServletException, IOException {
        Connection conn = null;
        StringBuffer sb = new StringBuffer("<HTML><BODY>");
        sb.append("<TABLE>");
        sb.append("<TR><TH>USER NAME</TH></TR>");
        try {
            conn = getDbConnection();                              #1
            Statement statement = conn.createStatement();          #2
            ResultSet users =
                statement.executeQuery("select * from users");     #3
            while (users.next()){                                  #4
                sb.append("<TR><TD>");
                String username = users.getString("user_name");
                sb.append(username);
```

```
                        sb.append("</TD></TR>");
                    }
                } catch (Exception e) {
                    System.err.println("Error connecting to database server");
                } finally {
                    if (conn != null) {
                        try {
                            conn.close();
                            System.out.println("Database connection terminated");
                        }
                        catch (Exception e) {
                            System.err.println("Error closing database connection");
                        }
                    }
                }
                sb.append("</TABLE>");
                sb.append("</BODY></HTML>");
                response.getOutputStream().write(sb.toString().getBytes());        #5


    }

    private Connection getDbConnection(){
//obtains connection to the database,
//using database URL, username and password
    }
}
```

The most important part of the code is obtaining the database connection (#1), which is done in the getDbConnection(..) method, which we haven't implemented in Listing 13-3. We will explain that part in a moment, but let's skip it for the time being. Once we have the database connection, we prepare the SQL statement (#2). Using the statement, we execute the SQL query (#3). We are loading all rows in the tomcatusers table, using the simple SQL query select * from tomcatusers. The result of the executeQuery(..) method is the ResultSet object, which contains all rows returned by the executed statement. We iterate through the ResultSet (#4) and prepare the HTML table row with each username contained in the database. Finally, we write the generated HTML to the HttpServletResponse's OutputStream, to be displayed in the browser (#5).

Obtaining a database connection involves loading the JDBC driver for the selected database (in our case, MySQL), and then creating a connection using the database URL, username, and password. Listing 13-4 shows a typical implementation.

Listing 13-4. Obtaining a Database Connection Using DriverManager

```
    private Connection getDbConnection()
            throws SQLException,
                ClassNotFoundException,
                IllegalAccessException,
                InstantiationException {
        String userName = "test";                                    #1
        String password = "test";                                    #2
        String url = "jdbc:mysql://localhost:3306/tomcatusers";      #3
```

```
Class.forName("com.mysql.jdbc.Driver").newInstance();          #4
return DriverManager.getConnection(url, userName, password);   #5
}
```

First, we specify the username (#1), password (#2), and URL (#3) for the database we are using. The username and password represent the user that has permission to connect to the database, and we specify these details in the database creation script (see Listing 13-2). The database connection URL is effectively specifying the server where the database is installed, as well as the type of the database. You can see that our database connection URL contains text "mysql" (as we're using MySQL database), and specifies localhost as the database server, as we're running this code on the same PC where the database is installed.

The next step is to load the MySQL driver class (#4). The driver class is vendor specific, and the jar library containing the driver class is distributed with the database itself. You have to make sure that the jar file containing this class is on your project classpath, and that it gets copied to the WEB-INF/lib directory of your WAR-packaged web application. The class name is different for each database, so consult the vendor documentation to find out the correct class name for your database. The fully qualified driver class name for MySQL database we use is com.mysql.jdbc.Driver.

Finally we create the connection using DriverManager factory class, which creates the Connection instance using the database connection URL, username, and password passed as method arguments (#5).

The database access code implemented like this will undoubtedly work. However, it has some flaws—it's difficult to change the database configuration easily based on the runtime environment, and it doesn't support scaling very well.

For example, if you want to connect to a different database server on a development, testing, and production environment, it's not such an easy thing to do. In order to switch, you have to change the source code, specify a different URL, username, and password, recompile and repackage the web application for different environments—each time you want to deploy to a different environment. At the same time, if you want to change the database setting on a production server, you will have to go through the same steps, which means making any changes will be very time consuming, inefficient, and most important, error prone.

In addition, the code in Listing 13-4 will obtain a new JDBC connection every time it's executed—for every request in case of web application. If you're expecting multiple users to access your web application at the same time, this approach won't scale; the more users access the database, the more connection objects get created, increasing memory usage and lowering performance. The solution to this problem is using connection pooling—a defined number of database connections that is managed by the application server, which is then reused by the application.

Considering all of this, it seems that database connection configuration naturally belongs to the deployment environment configuration, so you can have different database settings on different servers, and exactly the same web application code running on all of them. In addition, we could change the database configuration on the server directly, and apply any changes with simple server restart, without any web application code changes. All of that is available when using JNDI to configure database connectivity. Finally, production JNDI database configuration includes a connection pooling mechanism, so your application uses expensive database connection more efficiently, improving the scaling.

Configuring Data Source as a JNDI Resource

A JNDI resource for a database connection can be configured as part of the <Context> element in the Tomcat configuration, making the resource available only to the web application in the specified context. However, we are going to configure JNDI resource in the <GlobalNamingResources> section in the server.xml file. Resources configured in this way will be available to all web applications deployed on the Tomcat instance—very useful if multiple web applications share the same database for storing data.

Listing 13-5 shows the simple JNDI resource configuration for database connection.

Listing 13-5. JNDI Resource for MySQL Data Source

```
<Resource
    name="jdbc/testDataSource"                              #1
    auth="Container"                                        #2
    type="javax.sql.DataSource"                             #3
    driverClassName="com.mysql.jdbc.Driver"                 #4
    url="jdbc:mysql://localhost:3306/tomcatusers"           #5
    username="test" password="test"                         #6
    validationQuery="select count (*) from users"           #7
/>
```

The name of the resource will be used to reference the same resource in the web application later, and it must be unique in the server's naming context (#1). The name specified is actually relative to the root naming context, which is defined as java:/comp/env, meaning that the full JNDI name of the resource will be java/comp/env/jdbc/testDataSource. The name specified can be selected freely, but by Java convention, it should start with the jdbc/ namespace in case of a JNDI data source.

The auth attribute specifies whether the signon to the resource manager to access the resource is done by the server container itself (in which case, it's set to value "Container"), or by the application that uses the resource (in which case, it's set to value "Application"). We are using container-managed authorization (#2).

The next step is to specify the type of resource created by the resource factory, which is set to javax.sql.DataSource (#3). DataSource is a JDBC API factory interface for creating physical connections to the database. It is somewhat similar to DriverManager, and it's the preferred alternative to creating connections using the DriverManager, due to its richer API, and its support for naming lookup. A vendor-specific database driver implements the DataSource interface, and that concrete implementation is used to create Connection objects. The database vendor driver is specified using driverClassName attribute (#4). The jar library containing this class must be available to Tomcat's class loader, which is achieved by copying it to the CATALINA_HOME/lib directory. We will discuss the classpath issue in a bit more detail in the "Classpath Dependencies" section later in this chapter.

To specify the actual database we want to connect to, we specify the database connection URL (#5), username and password (#6).

We also specify the attribute validationQuery (#7). The server executes this query each time just before it passes the Connection to the application, in order to check the accessibility of the database. Although it adds slight overhead to the process of obtaining Connection, it's very useful to check the Connection for validity before it's handed to the application—any problems are easier to diagnose that way. For example if we made a syntax error in the configuration, or if the database crashes during execution. The query specified should be quick to execute, and it must return exactly one row—counting SQL queries are therefore good candidates.

And that's it. After Tomcat restarts, this DataSource JNDI resource will be available to all web applications to look up in the server's naming context.

Using Connection Pool

To be in line with the J2EE specification for enterprise applications, Tomcat's resource factory for JDBC JNDI resources is using connection pool for JDBC Connections.

The process of logging in to the database server and obtaining a Connection object is the most expensive part of Java JDBC code. It's therefore very inefficient to create a new Connection object every time your application needs to access the database. That's where connection pooling comes in. Connection pool creates and caches a number of database Connection objects. When an application requires database access, connection pool simply assigns one of the cached Connections to the applications. Once the application finishes with the database operation, it closes the Connection, and the Connection object is then returned to the connection pool to be reused again when another application thread requires it. Because there is a limited number of Connections that are created upfront, the process of obtaining Connection is very quick and memory efficient. And the database login is performed only on the initial Connection creation, so it doesn't affect the performance of running application.

Tomcat uses Apache Commons DBCP for connection pooling. Apache Commons DBCP is an open source project hosted by the Apache foundation, which has a primary goal to provide vendor-independent, easy to use and high-performing connection pools. The subset of Apache DBCP library is distributed with Tomcat, and can be found in file CATALINA_HOME/lib/tomcat-dbcp.jar.

The JNDI resource configuration therefore provides a number of attributes to configure the connection pool properties. Listing 13-6 shows the typical JNDI DataSource configuration, using connection pooling.

Listing 13-6. JNDI DataSource Configuration with Connection Pooling

```
<Resource
    name="jdbc/testDataSource"
    auth="Container" type="javax.sql.DataSource"
    initialSize="5"                                        #1
    maxActive="20"                                         #2
    minIdle="2"                                            #3
    maxIdle="10"                                           #4
    maxWait="15000"                                        #5
    username="test" password="test"
    driverClassName="com.mysql.jdbc.Driver"
    url="jdbc:mysql://localhost:3306/tomcatusers"
    validationQuery="select count (*) from users"
/>
```

Let's discuss the details of the connection pooling configuration.

The attribute initialSize specifies the number of Connection instances that will be created on server startup (#1). If you expect certain database activity on the server straight after startup, you should set this attribute to a reasonable value, to speed up the application's data access from the start, at the expense of slower server startup time and a higher memory footprint. The default is 0, so the first Connection object will be created when it's required. For example, if your web application has an initialization phase where data is loaded from the database on application startup, you should set initialSize value to match the number of connections you're expecting. If you'd like to keep the memory footprint and startup of your application to a minimum, then set it to lower value, or zero.

Next, we configure the maximum number of active Connections (#2). The default value is 8, and you should set this value based on the number of concurrent database operations expected and available memory and number of processors on the server.

Attribute minIdle specifies the minimum number of idle Connections (#3). When the usage goes up, and there is less idle Connection then specified here, Tomcat would create more (until the maxActive value is exceeded). The default value is 0.

Similarly, you can specify the maxIdle attribute, setting the maximum number of Connections that can be idle (#4). If the number of idle Connection exceeds this value, some idle Connections will be destroyed. The default value is 8.

Finally, you can specify maxWait attribute, setting maximum amount of time to wait to get new Connection if none is available in the pool (#5). The default value is -1, which means indefinite time to wait. If the time waiting for the new Connection is exceeded, connection pool will throw an exception.

Classpath Dependencies

In order to use the JNDI configured DataSource, the driver class needs to be available to Tomcat's class loader. As we mentioned before, the CATALINA_HOME/lib is by default on Tomcat's classpath, so by simply copying the driver jar file to this directory the classes contained in the jar library will be available to Tomcat class loader.

In the first example of this chapter, we copied the MySQL driver jar file to the WEB-INF/lib directory so it can be found on the web application's classpath. It is important to remove this jar dependency now, as having two copies of the same class on the classpath can have undesired consequences for the Tomcat's class loader. In case you encounter ClassNotFoundException or ClassCastException errors when using JNDI configured DataSource, check if the driver library is available in the CATALINA_HOM/lib directory, and NOT in the web application's WEB-INF/lib directory – as that is the common cause of such problems.

Accessing the JNDI DataSource

We have the JNDI DataSource resource available in Tomcat, what we need to do now is change our web application so it uses the configured resource.

The first step is to create reference to the configured JNDI resource in the web deployment descriptor file (web.xml). Listing 13-7 illustrates the XML code snipped that you should add to the web.xml file for your web application.

Listing 13-7. JNDI Resource Reference Configuration in the web.xml File

```
<resource-ref>
    <description>
        Sample JNDI DataSource resource reference
    </description>
    <res-ref-name>jdbc/testDataSource</res-ref-name>             #1
    <res-type>java.sql.DatSource</res-type>                      #2
    <res-auth>Container</res-auth>                               #3
</resource-ref>
```

The <res-ref-name> element specifies the name of the JNDI resource configured in Tomcat configuration files, which we illustrated in the previous sections (#1). Element <res-type> contains the type of the resource instance returned to the web application (#2). Finally, <res-auth> specifies the type of authentication configured for the resource, in our case container-managed (#3).

When a web application starts up, the resource reference verifies its configuration with the underlying resource. If the resource cannot be found, or the type/authentication does not match, an exception will be thrown, and the application will fail to start.

As for the servlet Java code, most of it will stay the same as in Listing 13-3. The only part that will change is the getDbConnection(..) method, which will use the JNDI naming context to obtain the

Connection object. Listing 13-8 shows the code that obtains the Connection using the configured JNDI resource.

Listing 13-8. Obtaining Connection from JNDI DataSource in a Java Application

```
private Connection getDbConnection() throws NamingException {
        Context initialContext = new InitialContext();                #1
        Context envContext =
            (Context) initialContext.lookup("java:/comp/env");        #2
        Connection connection =
            (Connection) envContext.lookup("jdbc/testDataSource");     #3
        return connection;
}
```

After instantiating InitialContext, which is the starting context for naming operation (#1), we lookup the root java environment context, stored under java:/comp/env name (#2). Once we have the root-naming context, we can look up the JNDI DataSource resource, using the configured resource name, jdbc/testDataSource (#3). Because the Context.lookup(...) method returns instances on java.lang.Object, we have to cast it to the java.sql.Connection class. However, this casting is safe at this point, as the type check has been performed on application start-up, based on the resource reference configuration in the web.xml file.

The returned Connection object is exactly the same as the Connection returned by DriverManager in the initial servlet implementation, so the rest of the code can remain the same.

The functionality application is therefore the same, but we have a more robust and portable database configuration. If we want to use different databases for test and production Tomcat servers, all we have to do is configure separate JNDI DataSources with required settings—the web application deployed on all server would be the same. At the same time, if we need to change the production database at any point in time, all we need to do is to change the production Tomcat JNDI configuration, and restart server—no code changes or redeployment of web application are necessary. The changes made this way will be available to all web application using the configured JNDI resource on server startup.

Configuring the Oracle JNDI DataSource

Oracle database is known for its high stability and performance, and it's often chosen as the first choice for data-intensive and mission-critical applications. The JNDI resource for Oracle DataSource isn't much different from the MySQL configuration we used earlier in the chapter, apart from different values for driver name, connection URL, username, and password. Listing 13-9 illustrates simple a Oracle DataSource JNDI resource configuration.

Listing 13-9. Oracle JNDI DataSource Configuration

```
<Resource
    name="jdbc/testDataSourceOracle"
    auth="Container" type="javax.sql.DataSource"
    initialSize="5"
    maxActive="20"
    minIdle="2"
    username="test" password="test"
    driverClassName="oracle.jdbc.OracleDriver"            #1
```

```
    url="jdbc:oracle:thin:@oracle.mydevserver.com/INTL"    #2
/>
```

The driver class name for Oracle database is oracle.jdbc.OracleDriver (#1). This class, along with other Oracle-specific JDBC classes, can be found in the Oracle JDBC library, distributed with Oracle database, or downloadable from Oracle web site. This library should be, just the same as MySQL driver jar file, and copied to CATALINA_HOME/lib directory in order to be available to Tomcat's class loader.

One thing to note here, is that Tomcat only scans *.jar files in the CATALINA_HOME/lib directory, so the driver's library file must have a .jar extension. Older Oracle drivers, for example (version 1.4 or older), are commonly distributed as zip archive, named classes14.zip (or classes12.zip, depending on the version). So if you simply copy the zip archive to the lib directory, the Tomcat wouldn't be able to find the required driver class, and it would throw an exception. The simplest solution for this problem is renaming the library file from classes14.zip to classes14.jar. Because jar file format is exactly the same as zip, no other action is required, and a simple extension change will make the driver class discoverable to Tomcat class loader. The latest Oracle drivers are distributed, however, as jar files (ojdbc5.jar and ojdbc6.jar), so you won't experience this issue if you're using later versions.

This concludes the JNDI DataSource configuration. You can find all code samples in the code that accompanies this book.

Let's now take a look at another typical usage on JNDI with Tomcat—configuring mail server for sending e-mail from your web application.

Configuring Mail Session

Whether it's sending a registration confirmation e-mail, or a newsletter filled with useful content, sending e-mails is a common functionality requirement for most web applications nowadays. The JavaMail API provides an easy to configure and use framework for sending e-mails from Java applications. However, the JavaMail API only enables you to create and manipulate e-mail messages. The actual e-mail sending is the responsibility of an independent SMTP mail server. SMTP (which stands for Simple Mail Transfer Protocol) is the widely used protocol for outgoing mail traffic. The e-mail clients, such as Outlook and Java applications that send e-mail, use SMTP protocol for sending e-mail only. For receiving e-mail, other protocols are used, such as Post Office Protocol (POP), Internet Message Access Protocol (IMAP), or commercial products like Lotus Notes or Microsoft Exchange. In this section, we will demonstrate using SMTP server configured to send e-mail from a Java web application deployed on Tomcat. We will also see an example of accessing a mail inbox from a Java application.

Introducing JavaMail

JavaMail API defines javax.mail.Session class, which represents the mail session in Java code. Using Session instance, which is configured to communicate to the specific SMTP server, Java application can actually send e-mails.

■ **Note** To use the JavaMail API in your web application, its library, the mail-api.jar file, must be on your project's classpath. In addition, you will have to make sure activation.jar library is on the classpath, too. If you're using Java 6 or later, activation.jar is already part of the Java classpath. For Java 5 and earlier, make sure to add activation.jar to your project's classpath.

You can get the instance of the JavaMail Session programmatically, and use it to send e-mail. Let's first demonstrate how you can use JavaMail API programmatically to send e-mail from your servlet code. Listing 13-10 shows the servlet that sends an e-mail to the recipient whose e-mail address is passed as a request parameter.

Listing 13-10. Servlet Implementation of E-mail Sending Using JavaMail API

```
@WebServlet(urlPatterns = {"/sendemail.html"})
public class MailSendingServlet extends HttpServlet {
  private Session session;

  public void init() throws ServletException {
    try {
        Properties props = System.getProperties();
        props.put("mail.smtp.host", "mailserver.mycompany.com");
        props.put("mail.smtp.user", "emailAdmin");
        props.put("password", "Sw4nLake!389");                      #1
        this.session = Session.getDefaultInstance(props, null);     #2
    }catch (Exception ex) {
        ex.printStackTrace();
    }
  }
  protected void doPost(HttpServletRequest request, HttpServletResponse response)↵
  throws ServletException, IOException {
      String emailRecipient = request.getParameter("sendTo");       #3
      try {
          Message msg = new MimeMessage(this.session);              #4
          msg.setFrom(new InternetAddress("no-reply@tomcat7.apress.com"));   #5
          msg.setRecipients(Message.RecipientType.TO, InternetAddress.parse(emailRecipient,↵
  false));
                                                                     #6
          msg.setSubject("Test email");                             #7
          msg.setText("Hello and welcome to apress mailing list!"); #8
          msg.setSentDate(new Date());
          Transport.send(msg);                                      #9
          System.out.println("Message sent OK.");
      }catch (Exception ex) {
          ex.printStackTrace();
      }
  }
}
```

In order to configure the javax.mail.Session object, you have to prepare Properties with the details of the SMTP server to use. In this example, we set the host name of the SMTP mail server, and the username and password required to authenticate before sending any e-mail (#1). In the next step, we instantiate Session, using its factory method, passing the prepared properties as argument, and store it to the class field session (#2).

Now that we have mail session ready, we can create an e-mail message and send it.

We are going to send an e-mail to the recipient whose e-mail address has been entered in the web form, and is available in our servlet as a request parameter (#3).

We are using MimeMessage, which is part of the JavaMail API (#4). We set the From field to the standard no-reply e-mail address for our server (#5), and the recipient to whom we're sending e-mail to the value received as request parameter before (#6). We also set other standard e-mail parameters, like subject line (#7) and the body of the message (#8).

Finally, we send message using JavaMail API's standard `Transport.send(..)` static method (#9).

This example shows standard implementation e-mail sending code for Java application, and there is nothing wrong with it as such. However, let's consider some pitfalls.

What would happen if you wanted to use different SMTP servers for development, testing, and in production? Or even just use a different account (username and password) for each environment? Our SMTP configuration (#1 and #2 in Listing 13-10) is part of the source code, and for any change we would need to recompile and repackage the application, which can easily become cumbersome to manage. Similarly, if you wanted to change your server, or login details, in production environment, you would have to recompile the code, build and redeploy application—which may take even few hours depending on the environment.

E-mail session configuration, similarly to JDBC Data Sources from previous sections, is naturally part of the deployment environment the application runs on. If the mail session properties are configured on the server, you can easily manage different settings on different environments, or change the configuration (server's IP or login credentials) directly to the server—without any changes to the code or the deployed web applications. In addition, in case you have multiple web applications running on the same server, you can share the same configuration between them.

This is where JNDI configuration comes into place, promoting reusability and loose coupling between the code and the external services it uses, such as SMTP server.

Configuring Mail Session as a JNDI Resource

Let's make the changes to our web application and configure JavaMail Session as a JNDI resource.

The first step is to add JNDI resource for mail session to the Tomcat's configuration, using the `<Resource>` XML element. If you place the XML configuration within the web application's `<Context>` element, the configured JNDI resource will be available for that web application only. You can also configure JNDI resource in the server.xml file, within the `<GlobalNamingResources>` element, in which case the JNDI resource will be shared between all web applications deployed on the same Tomcat instance.

Listing 13-11 shows the typical JNDI resource configuration for a JavaMail Session.

Listing 13-11. JNDI Resources Configuration of a JavaMail Session

```
<Resource name="mail/testEmailSession"          #1
              auth="Container"                  #2
              type="javax.mail.Session"         #3
              mail.smtp.host="localhost"        #4
              mail.smtp.user="emailAdmin"       #5
```

```
        password="sw4nLake1389"          #6
        mail.debug="true"                #7
/>
```

We set the name of the resource to `"mail/testEmailSession"` (#1), and this is the name our web application will look for when loading the resource. You can use whatever name you want, but using `"mail"` sub-context is a convention for JavaMail Session JNDI resources, so it's a good practice to keep to the convention for better code readability and easier maintenance. This name is relative to the standard root JNDI context `java:/comp/env`, so the full absolute name of this JNDI resource will be `java:/comp/env/mail/testEmailSession`.

We want Tomcat container to manage this resource for us and sign on to the resource manager, so we set authentication attribute to value "Container" (#2). The type attribute specifies the Java type that the instances created by the resource will have—for JavaMail session JNDI resource, we set this to fully qualified class name `javax.mail.Session` (#3). The SMTP server properties are set as attributes: host (#4), user (#5) and password (#6).

We are also setting optional attribute `mail.debug` to `true` (#7), so that all communication between Tomcat and SMTP server will be logged to the Tomcats log file (`catalina.out`). Setting mail debug output to true can be very useful during troubleshooting and diagnosing e-mail sending problems.

Tomcat is shipped with the resource factory that creates `javax.mail.Session` instances ready to be used, based on the configuration provided. When using JNDI for mail configuration, object factories configured and managed in Tomcat will be responsible for creating the Session objects, so we won't have to worry about mail server configuration in the code anymore. If we want to change any part of the configuration (using different server, change login detail, or turn the debugging on or off), we can make the change directly on the server, and after restart, new settings will be applied, without any changes to the code.

Classpath Dependencies

Because Tomcat will be responsible for instantiating `javax.mail.Session` objects, the JavaMail API library must be available to the Tomcat's mail class loader. So, if you are using JNDI mail configuration, you will have to move `mail.jar` and `activation.jar` to the Tomcat's classpath (`CATALINA_HOME/lib` directory). We say move on purpose, because you will have to remove those libraries from your web application's classpath. In case mail.jar and activation.jar are found in both Tomcat's classpath (`CATALINA_HOME/lib` directory) and the web application's classpath (`WEB-INF/lib` directory of your WAR file), class loading errors will occur as there is no guarantee which version of the class will be loaded at any time. If you are using Java 6 or later, you have to move only `mail.jar` library, as `actication.jar` will be already available on the global Java classpath.

Accessing JNDI Mail Session

So far, we have configured JNDI resource in Tomcat. Now we have to make changes to our web application to use the `Session` JNDI resource for sending e-mail.

First we need to set reference to the configured mail session resources in the web deployment descriptor (`web.xml` file). Listing 13-12 illustrates the references configuration, which you should add to your web.xml file.

Listing 13-12. JavaMail Session Resource Reference in web.xml

```
<resource-ref>
    <description>
        Sample JNDI javamail session resource reference
    </description>
    <res-ref-name>mail/testEmailSession</res-ref-name>      #1
    <res-type>javax.mail.Session</res-type>                  #2
    <res-auth>Container</res-auth>                           #3
</resource-ref>
```

The resource reference name must match the name of the configured JNDI resource mail/testEmailSession in our example (#1). The other properties must match the configured JNDI resource: type is set to javax.mail.Session (#2) and authentication mechanism is set to container (#3).

The resource reference has a role to verify that we are using the correct JNDI configuration, and also as a useful reference to the developer about JNDI resource available to be used. In a case in which the underlying JNDI resource type is not matching the class defined in the resource reference, or if the authentication attribute does not match the authentication of the configured resource, our application would fail to start with javax.naming.NamingException.

Next, we need to change the code of our MailSendingServlet – instead of configuring and instantiating Session programmatically (lines marked with #1 and #2 in Listing 13-10); we will look up the configured resource from JNDI. Listing 13-13 shows the improved implementation of the MailSendingServlet.

Listing 13-13. Sending E-mail Using Session Looked Up as a JNDI Resource

```
public class MailSendingServlet extends HttpServlet {
    private Session session;

    public void init() throws ServletException {
        try {
            Context initContext = new InitialContext();                       #1
            Context envContext  =
                (Context)initContext.lookup("java:/comp/env");                #2
            this.session =
                (Session)envContext.lookup("mail/testEmailSession");          #3
        }catch (Exception ex) {
            ex.printStackTrace();
        }
    }

    protected void doPost(HttpServletRequest request, HttpServletResponse response)↵
    throws ServletException, IOException {
        String emailRecipient = request.getParameter("sendTo");
        try {
            Message msg = new MimeMessage(this.session);
            msg.setFrom(new InternetAddress("no-reply@tomcat7.apress.com"));
            msg.setRecipients(Message.RecipientType.TO, InternetAddress.parse↵
(emailRecipient, false));
            msg.setSubject("Test email");
            msg.setText("Hello and welcome to apress mailing list!");
```

```
                    msg.setSentDate(new Date());
                    Transport.send(msg);
                    System.out.println("Message sent OK.");
            } catch (Exception ex) {
                    ex.printStackTrace();
            }
        }
}
```

There are only three line changes to the code in Listing 13-10, and they are marked with #1, #2, and #3 in the previous sample. First, we instantiate initial JNDI context, using `InitialContext` class, which is available from standard Java SDK (#1). Next, we look up the root JNDI java environment context, using prefix `java:/comp/env` (#2). All JNDI resources configured in Tomcat are relative to the root context, and can be looked up using their configured name. Finally, we look up our JavaMail Session object from the root context, using the name we configured before (#3). Because `Context.lookup(..)` method returns `Object` instance, we need to cast the result to the `javax.mail.Session` here. But because we know the JNDI name belongs to the `Session` resource (as defined in the JNDI configuration and in the resource reference in the web.xml), and that type verification is made on application start-up, no problem is expected here.

The rest of the code looks exactly the same: we use `Session` object to create e-mail message and send it using JavaMail API's Transport abstraction.

Using JNDI resource for e-mail configuration, we can now deploy our web application on any application server with the configured JNDI resource, and it will just work. We don't need to make any changes to the code if we switch hosting provider, and start using different SMTP server—as long as the JavaMail `Session` is configured on the server (Tomcat, or any other), with the name we specified, the e-mails will be sent successfully.

Configuring Secure SMTP Server

The sample configuration we illustrated is usable in most scenarios. SMTP servers are usually configured so they are not publicly available, but only from a firewall-protected internal network. Such servers required only one property to the configured: server host. If the server requires username and password for authentication, they can be configured as server properties, as our examples show.

However, with popularity of cloud-based services, a lot of SMTP servers can be used as a service over the Internet. These servers, in addition to a username and password, require secure SSL protocol for communication. In addition, they are usually configured on a different port, then the default port 25, commonly used for mail servers. One typical example is Google's SMTP server (Gmail), which you can use to send e-mail from your Gmail account.

Listing 13-14 shows the typical JNDI mail `Session` configuration if you want to use your Google's SMTP server and your Gmail account to send e-mails from the web application.

Listing 13-14. Google SMTP Server JNDI Configuration

```
<Resource name="mail/gmailSession"
    auth="Container"
    type="javax.mail.Session"
    mail.smtp.host="smtp.gmail.com"                       #1
    mail.smtp.port="465"                                   #2
    mail.smtp.auth="true"
    mail.smtp.user="mygoogleaccount@gmail.com"             #3
```

```
    password="mypassword"
    mail.smtp.starttls.enable="true"                                    #4
    mail.smtp.socketFactory.class="javax.net.ssl.SSLSocketFactory"      #5
/>
```

In order to send e-mails using our Gmail account, we have to specify Google's SMTP server, `smtp.gmail.com` (#1), and port 465 (#2). The username and password we set for authentication are valid Gmail account credentials (#3).

Because the Gmail's SMTP server is only accessible over SSL protocol, we need to enable STARTTLS command of the mail protocol, using `mail.smtp.starttls.enable` property (#4). If `mail.smtp.starttls.enable` is set to true, any communication with the mail server will start with STARTTLS command, which will switch the communication to secure SSL protocol before issuing any login or mail sending command to the server. Finally we configure the java class that should be used to create secure SMTP sockets (#5).

And that's it—if you configure you web application to use this JNDI resource for JavaMail Session, you can easily send e-mail from your Gmail account.

Summary

In this chapter we introduced JNDI and how it is used to write portable Java applications. Next, we illustrated JNDI configuration of JDBC data sources with connection pooling. Examples include MySQL and Oracle databases. Finally, we demonstrated how you can use JavaMail API configured using JNDI to send e-mail from your web application deployed on Tomcat.

The Server.xml File

In this appendix, we discuss the configuration of Tomcat containers and connectors in the server.xml configuration. This file is located in the CATALINA_HOME/conf directory and can be considered the heart of Tomcat. It allows you to completely configure Tomcat using XML configuration elements. Tomcat loads the configuration from server.xml file at startup, and any changes to this file require server restart. However, you can configure Tomcat is such way that it allows runtime changes to the deployed web applications.

Containers

Tomcat containers are objects that can contribute to the request-response communication between clients (e.g. browsers) and the targeted servlets. There are several types of Tomcat containers, each of which is configured within the server.xml based upon its type. We introduced Tomcat's containers when we discussed Tomcat's architecture in Chapter 1. In this section, we discuss the containers that are configured in the default server.xml file.

The Server Container

Let's first take a look at the top level server container, which is configured using the <Server> XML element. It is used as a top-level element for a single Tomcat instance; it is a simple singleton element that represents the entire Tomcat JVM. It may contain one or more Service containers. The server container is defined by the org.apache.catalina.Server interface. Table A-1 defines the possible attributes that can be set for the <Server> element.

Table A-1. The Configurable Attributes for <Server> XML Element

Attribute	Description
className	Names the fully qualified Java name of the class that implements the `org.apache.catalina.Server` interface. If no class name is specified, the default implementation is used, which is the `org.apache.catalina.core.StandardServer`.
address	This attribute specifies the TCP/IP address on which this server listens for the shutdown command. The default value is `localhost`, which means that the server can be shut down from the same machine where it is installed (i.e., remote shutdown is disabled).
port	Names the TCP/IP port number on which the server listens for a shutdown command. If you're running Tomcat as daemon (i.e.,as Windows service), you can disable shutdown port by setting this value to `-1`. This attribute is required.
shutdown	Defines the command string that must be received by the server on the configured address and port to shut down Tomcat. This attribute is required.

The default `server.xml` distributed with Tomcat uses following code snippet to configure the server container:

```
<Server port="8005" shutdown="SHUTDOWN">
...
</Server>
```

The `<Server>` element must be the root XML element in server.xml file, and cannot be configured as the child of any element. However, it can be configured as the parent of other XML elements. The allowed nested child XML elements for `<Server>` component are

- `<Service>` element, which we discuss in the next section, and
- `<GlobalNamingResources>` element, used for configuration of global JNDI resources, which are described in Chapter 13.

The Service Container

The next Tomcat container we're going to discuss is the service container. The service container is configured using the `<Service>` XML element in the `server.xml`. The service container holds a collection of one or more connectors, and a single engine container. The service container is configured as a nested XML element within the `<Server>` element. Multiple service containers can be configured within the same server container. The service container element is defined by the `org.apache.catalina.Service` Java interface. Table A-2 describes the `<Service>` element's attributes.

Table A-2. *The Configurable Attributes of the <Service> XML Element*

Attribute	Description
className	Names the fully qualified Java name of the class that implements the org.apache.catalina. Service interface. If no class name is specified, the implementation will be used, which is the org.apache.catalina.core.StandardService.
name	Defines the display name of the defined service. The service name must be unique within the enclosing server container. This value is used in all Tomcat log messages. This attribute is required.

The only <Service> definition that can be found in the default server.xml file is the Catalina service:

```
<Service name="Catalina">
...
</Service>
```

The <Service> XML element is configured as a child of the <Server> element. As we mentioned before, multiple connectors and a single engine container can be configured for each service container. Allowed nested XML elements within <Service> element are:

- the <Connector> element, which we describe in the "Connectors" section later in this Appendix, and

- the <Engine> element, which we will discuss in the following section.

The Engine Container

Engine container represents the heart of the request-processing mechanism in Tomcat. It is responsible for processing all incoming requests from configured connectors, and returns the processed response back to the connector for dispatching to the calling client. Engine container is configured in the server.xml file using the <Engine> XML element. Each defined service container can have one and only one engine container, and this single engine receives all requests received by all of the defined connectors. The <Engine> element must be nested after the <Connector> elements, inside its owning <Service> element.

The <Engine> element is defined by the org.apache.catalina.Engine interface. Table A-3 describes the possible <Engine> element attributes.

249

Table A-3. *The Attributes of the <Engine> Element*

Attribute	Description
className	Names the fully qualified Java name of the class that implements the org.apache.catalina.Engine interface. If no class name is specified, the implementation is used, which is the org.apache.catalina.core.StandardEngine.
defaultHost	Names the host name to which all requests are defaulted if not otherwise named. The name specified must reference a host defined by a child <Host> element. This attribute is required.
Name	Defines the logical name of this engine. The name defined is used in log messages, and must be unique within the server component that this engine belongs to. This attribute is required.
backgroundProcessorDelay	Defines the delay time in seconds before the child containers' background processes will be invoked, in case they are executing in the same thread. This background processing thread is responsible for live web application deployment tasks. The default value is 10.
jvmRoute	String identifier appended to every session in load balancing scenarios. It's used to enable the front-end load balancer to send requests with the same session identifier to same Tomcat instances. If configured, the value of jvmRoute must be unique among all servers in a cluster.

The following code snippet contains the <Engine> element defined in the default server.xml file:

```
<Engine name="Catalina" defaultHost="localhost">
```

The <Engine> element is configured as a child of the <Service> element, and as a parent to the following elements:

- <Host>: Used to configure host container, which is discussed in the next section.

- <Realm>: Used to configure Tomcat's security realm, which is covered in Chapter 6.

- <Valve>: Used to configure Tomcat's valve, covered in Chapter 8.

- <Listener>: Used to configure Tomcat's listener, which is used to react on events occurring internally in the Tomcat engine.

The Host Container

The host container links the server machine where the Tomcat is running to the network name (for example, www.apress.com or 174.17.0.204). The host container is configured using the <Host> XML element within the <Engine> element. Each <Host> can be a parent to one or more web applications, represented by a context container (which is described in the next section).

You must define at least one <Host> for each <Engine> element, and the name of one defined host must match the defaultHost attribute of the parent engine container. The default <Host> element is usually named localhost. The possible attributes for the <Host> element are described in Table A-4.

Table A-4. *The Attributes of the <Host> Element*

Attribute	Description
className	Names the fully qualified Java name of the class that implements the org.apache.catalina.Host interface. If no class name is specified, the implementation is used, which is the org.apache.catalina.core.StandardHost. This attribute is required.
Name	Defines the hostname of this virtual host. This attribute is required and must be unique among the virtual hosts running in this servlet container. This attribute is required.
appBase	Defines the directory for this virtual host. This directory is the pathname of the web applications to be executed in this virtual host. This value can be either an absolute path or a path that is relative to the CATALINA_HOME directory. If this value is not specified, the relative value webapps is used.
xmlBase	The directory location of the XML deployment descriptors that are deployed to this host. If not specified, the path [engine_name]/[host_name] is specified.
createDirs	Specifies whether the directories specified in appBase and xmlBase attributes should be created on Tomcat startup. The default value is true.
autoDeploy	Specifies whether Tomcat should check for new or updated web applications to be deployed to this host. The default is true.
backgroundProcessorDelay	The delay time in seconds between the background process method invocation on this container and any child containers. This background process is responsible for webapp deployment tasks. The default value is -1, which means that this host will rely on the delay setting of its parent engine.
deployIgnore	The regular expression pattern that specifies directories to skip when performing auto deployment, for example *.svn* will skip deployment of the SVN files in case your web applications are deployed directory from an SV version control system.
deployOnStartup	Specifies if the web applications found in appBase and xmlBase directories should be deployed on server startup. The default value is true.

If you're using the Tomcat's default StandardHost implementation, you can use the additional attributes listed in the Table A-5.

Table A-5. The Additional Attributes for Configuration of StandardHost Implementation

Attribute	Description
unpackWARs	Determines if WAR files should be unpacked or run directly from the WAR file. If not specified, the default value is true.
workDir	Specifies the work directory for all web applications deployed to this host. If not specified, the default value is CATALINA_HOME/work.
copyXML	If set to true, the context configuration file specified within the web application (/META-INF/context.xml) should be copied to the xmlBase directory. The default value is false.
deployXML	Specifies whether the context configuration supplied with web application (/META-INF/context.xml) should be parsed during web application deployment. Default value is true.
errorReportValveClass	Configures the valve responsible for rendering the Tomcat error pages. By default, the host will use org.apache.catalina.valves.ErrorReportValve.

The default server.xml configuration has one host configured for the Catalina engine:

```
<Host name="localhost"  appBase="webapps"
     unpackWARs="true" autoDeploy="true">
```

This host definition defines a Tomcat virtual host named localhost that can be accessed by opening the following URL (with default Tomcat port 8080):

```
http://localhost:8080/
```

The <Host> element is configured as a child of the <Engine> element, and can have the following nested XML elements:

- <Context>: Context container, described in the next section.
- <Realm>: Used to configure Tomcat's security realm, which is covered in Chapter 6.
- <Valve>: Used to configure Tomcat's valve, covered in Chapter 8.
- <Listener>: Used to configure Tomcat's listener, which is used to react on events occurring internally in the Tomcat engine.

The Context Container

The context container represents a single web application deployed to Tomcat. It is configured using the <Context> XML element, and is the most commonly used container in the server.xml file. Any number of contexts can be defined within a <Host>, but each <Context> definition must have a unique context path, which is defined using the path attribute. There are over 50 different attributes that you can configure for the <Context> element. Table A-6 lists the most important configuration attributes and attributes that are most commonly used for production Tomcat configuration.

Table A-6. *The Main Attributes of the <Context> XML Element*

Attribute	Description
className	Names the fully qualified Java name of the class that implements the org.apache.catalina.Context interface. If no class name is specified, the implementation is used, which is the org.apache.catalina.core.StandardContext.
cookies	Determines if you want cookies to be used for a session identifier. The default value is true.
crossContext	If set to true, allows the ServletContext.getContext() method to successfully return the ServletContext for other web applications running in the same host. The default value is false, which prevents the access of cross context access.
docBase	Defines the directory for the web application associated with this <Context>. This is the pathname of a directory that contains the resources for the web application. This attribute is required.
path	Defines the context path for this web application. This value must be unique for each <Context> defined in a given <Host>.
reloadable	If set to true, causes Tomcat to check for class changes in the /WEB-INF/classes/ and /WEB-INF/lib directories. If these classes have changed, the application owning these classes is automatically reloaded. This feature should be used only during development. Setting this attribute to true causes severe performance degradation and therefore should be set to false in a production environment.
wrapperClass	Defines the Java name of the org.apache.catalina.Wrapper implementation class that is used to wrap servlets managed by this context. If not specified, the standard value org.apache.catalina.core.StandardWrapper is used.
sessionCookieName	Overrides any session cookie name specified by individual web applications. If not specified, and no web application specific value is defined, JSESSIONID name will be used. You can configure other session cookie attributes using the sessionCookiePath and sessionCookieDomain attributes.
override	Should be set to true, if you wish to override the configuration settings inherited from parent <Host> or <Engine> elements. The default value is true.
swallowOutput	If set to true, all System.out and System.err output will be redirected to the web application logging engine, instead if being written to catalina.out file. The default value is false.

If you're using the Tomcat's default StandardContext implementation, you can use the additional attributes. Table A-7 describes some of the available attributes.

Table A-7. The Additional Attributes for Configuration of StandardContext Implementation

Attribute	Description
unpackWar	Determines if the WAR file for this web application should be unpacked or the web application should be executed directly from the WAR file. If not specified, the default value is true.
workDir	Defines the pathname to a work directory that this Context uses for temporary read and write access. The directory is made visible as a servlet context attribute of type java.io.File, with the standard key of java.servlet.context.tempdir. If this value is not specified, Tomcat uses the host's work directory CATALINA_HOME/work by default.
useNaming	Should be set to true (the default) if you wish to have Catalina enable JNDI.
cachingAllowed	If set to true, Tomcat will cache the static resources it serves (images, css and javascript file, for example).
antiJARLocking	Specifies whether Tomcat class loader should take extra care when reading resources from jar file, to avoid jar locking. Specifying this attribute to true will slow deployment of web applications to Tomcat. Default value is false. You can configure locking of any other resource file using antiResourcesLocking attribute.

■ **Note** You can find the complete reference of available context configuration attributes in the Apache Tomcat online documentation (http://tomcat.apache.org/tomcat-7.0-doc/config/context.html).

The <Context> element that defines the /examples application is included in the following code snippet:

```
<Context path="/examples" docBase="examples" reloadable="true">
```

The context definition defines a Web application under context path /examples that has all of its resources stored in the directory examples, relative to the appBase directory of the parent host (by default CATALINA_HOME/webapps/examples). This context also states that this application is reloaded when its files are updated.

The <Context> element is configured as a child of the <Host> element, and as a parent to the following elements:

- <Loader>: Used for configuration of web application class loader.

- <Realm>: Used to configure Tomcat's security realm, which is covered in Chapter 6.

- <Valve>: Used to configure Tomcat's valve, covered in Chapter 8.

- <Listener>: Used to configure Tomcat's listener, which is used to react on events occurring internally in the Tomcat engine.

- `<Manager>`: Used to configure session manager for the web application deployed in context container; we discuss sessions and session manager in Tomcat in Chapter 5.

- `<Parameter>`: Used to set parameters for ServletContext initialization.

- `<Environment>`: Used to configure values that will be available in the web application as environment entries.

- `<Resources>`: Used to configure JNDI resources for the web application deployed in this context; we cover JNDI resources configuration in Chapter 13.

- `<WatchedResource>`: Used to configure resources that will be monitored by auto deployer, and which will trigger web application redeployment if changed or updated.

Now that we covered the configuration of all containers available in Tomcat, let's take a look at the connector components, another key component of the Tomcat architecture.

Connectors

The connector components are responsible for accepting incoming requests in Tomcat, passing the request to the engine container defined for the given connector, accepting the resulting response from the engine container and passing the response to the calling client. The connector elements are configured in Tomcat's server.xml file using the `<Connector>` XML element. The `<Connector>` XML element is defined as a nested element within the `<Service>` element, at the same level as the engine container it communicates to.

The `<Connector>` element is defined by the org.apache.catalina.Connector interface. There are two main connector types available in Tomcat, based on the protocol they support:

- HTTP connector component, that supports HTTP protocol, which enables Catalina engine to run as a web server and servlet container, handling HTTP request from users via the browser.

- AJP connector component that supports the communication using AJP protocol, used for integrating Tomcat with Apache Web server, as described in Chapter 10.

Table A-8 describes the common attributes used to configure both types of connector component.

Table A-8. Common Configuration Attributes for the <Connector> XML Element That Can Be Used for Any Type of Connector Component

Attribute	Description
Port	Names the TCP/IP port number on which the connector listens for requests. The default value is 8080. This is the only required attribute for <Connector> element.
enableLookups	Determines whether DNS lookups are enabled. The default value for this attribute is true. When DNS lookups are enabled, an application calling request.getRemoteHost() is returned the domain name of the calling client. Enabling DNS lookups can adversely affect performance. Therefore, this value should most often be set to false.
redirectPort	Names the TCP/IP port number to which a request should be redirected, if it comes in on a non-SSL port and is subject to a security constraint with a transport guarantee that requires SSL.
proxyName	Specifies the server name to use if this instance of Tomcat is behind a firewall. This attribute is optional.
proxyPort	Specifies the HTTP port to use if this instance of Tomcat is behind a firewall. Also an optional attribute.
scheme	The name of the protocol scheme for the incoming requests. The default value is http. For SSL configuration this should be set to value https.
secure	Specifies the value returned by request.isSecure() method call. The default value is false, but should be set to true for secure SSL communication.
allowTrace	Specifies whether or not the TRACE HTTP method is allowed for incoming requests. Default value is false.
maxPostSize	The maximum size of the content submitted using POST HTTP method. If set to 0 or negative value, no limit will be set. By default maximum POST content size is set to 2MB.
parseBodyMethods	Specifies the list of HTTP methods that will be parsed to fetch request parameters, similarly to POST form submission handling. The advantage of this parameter is that it can be used for REST web applications, where PUT HTTP method is required. The default value is POST.
asyncTimeout	Timeout of asynchronous requests in milliseconds. The default value is 10,000.
uriEncoding	This attribute is used to configure the character encoding used to encode/decode URI values. By default it's set to ISO-8859-1.

Attribute	Description
useIPVHosts	If set to true, Tomcat will use the IP address of the network interface that received the request to determine the host container to redirect the request to. It's set to false by default.

The `<Connector>` element is configured as a child of the `<Service>` element, and cannot have any nested child elements configured.

The default server.xml configuration file defines two connectors, one HTTP connector for HTTP traffic and one AJP connector for communication using AJP protocol. Based on the connector type, you can set additional connector configuration attributes. In the next two sections, we will cover the configuration of HTTP and AJP connectors respectively.

The HTTP Connector

The HTTP connector handles all direct HTTP request received by Tomcat. In addition to standard connector attributes (described in Table A-8), you can configure additional attributes when configuring the HTTP connector. Table A-9 describes some of the possible attributes for the HTTP connector configuration. The full list of available attributes can be found in the online Tomcat configuration reference.

Table A-9. The Additional Attributes for the HTTP Connector Configuration

Attribute	Description
protocol	Sets the protocol to be used to transport incoming requests. Allowed protocol implementations are: org.apache.coyote.http11.Http11Protocol - blocking Java connector org.apache.coyote.http11.Http11NioProtocol - non-blocking Java connector org.apache.coyote.http11.Http11AprProtocol - the APR/native connector. The default value is HTTP/1.1, which uses Tomcat internal mechanism to pick either blocking Java connector or the APR connector.
address	Used for servers with more than one IP address. It specifies which address is used for listening on the specified port. If this attribute is not specified, this named port number is used on all IP addresses associated with this server.
compression	Specifies whether Tomcat should use compression when sending text-based content, saving bandwidth. Allowed values are off, which disables the compression; on, which enables compression for text-based content only; and force, which forces compression for all content. The default value is off.
compressableMimeType	Comma separated list of mime types that can be compressed if the compression attribute is set. The default value is text/html,text/xml,text/plain.
SSLEnabled	If set to true, the SSL traffic will be enabled on the connector. The default value is false.

Attribute	Description
connectionTimeout	Defines the time, in milliseconds, before a request terminates. The default value is 60,000 milliseconds. To disable connection timeouts, the connectionTimeout value should be set to -1.
maxThreads	Specifies the maximum number of threads that will be created to process requests on this connector. The default value is 200.
acceptCount	Specifies the number of requests that can be queued on the listening port. The default value is 10.

The following code snippet is an example <Connector> defining an HTTP connector:

```
<Connector port="8080" protocol="HTTP/1.1"
           connectionTimeout="20000"
           redirectPort="8443" />
```

Based on the protocol class specified in the protocol attribute, you can set additional configuration options specific to the protocol used. The list of all configuration options for all protocols is too big to be listed here, but you can find all available protocol configuration options on the Tomcat's online resources for the HTTP connector: http://tomcat.apache.org/tomcat-7.0-doc/config/http.html.

The AJP Connector

The AJP connector handles requests that have been forwarded by a web server that Tomcat integrates with, like the Apache Web server that sits in front of Tomcat. The AJP connector can be configured using the set of attributes described in Table A-10.

Table A-10. The Additional Attributes for the AJP Connector Configuration

Attribute	Description
Protocol	Sets the protocol to be used to transport incoming requests. Allowed protocol implementations are: org.apache.coyote.http11.AjpProtocol - blocking Java connector org.apache.coyote.http11.AjpNioProtocol - non-blocking Java connector org.apache.coyote.http11.AjpAprProtocol - the APR/native connector The default value is AJP/1.3, which uses Tomcat internal mechanism to pick either blocking Java connector or the APR connector.
Address	Used for servers with more than one IP address. It specifies which address is used for listening on the specified port. If this attribute is not specified, this named port number is used on all IP addresses associated with this server.
packetSize	Specifies the AJP packet size in bytes. The maximum value you can set this attribute to is 65536, and the minimum value is 8192. The default value is 8192.

Attribute	Description
requiredSecret	If specified, the AJP requests must contain the value of this attribute in order to be processed.
connectionTimeout	Defines the time, in milliseconds, before a request terminates. The default value is 60,000 milliseconds. To disable connection timeouts, the connectionTimeout value should be set to -1.
maxThreads	Specifies the maximum number of threads that will be created to process requests on this connector. The default value is 200.
acceptCount	Specifies the number of requests that can be queued on the listening port. The default value is 10.

The following code snippet illustrates the default AJP connector defined in the Tomcat's server.xml file:

```
<Connector port="8009" protocol="AJP/1.3" redirectPort="8443" />
```

Based on the protocol class specified in protocol attribute, you can set additional configuration options specific to the protocol used. The list of all configuration options for all protocols is too big to include here, but you can find all available protocol configuration options on the Tomcat's online resources for the AJP connector: http://tomcat.apache.org/tomcat-7.0-doc/config/ajp.html.

Summary

In this appendix, we explained the configuration of the Tomcat containers and connectors in the CATALINA_HOME/conf/server.xml file. We also demonstrated the default configuration of all components in the server.xml file distributed out of the box with Tomcat. We included the most common options that should get you up and running quickly when configuring Tomcat. However, due to the richness of Tomcat's configuration options, we couldn't list all available options in this appendix. For the full details about all configuration options for Tomcat components, take a look at Tomcat's online documentation (http://tomcat.apache.org/tomcat-7.0-doc/index.html).

APPENDIX B

The Web.xml File

In this appendix, we discuss the web application deployment descriptor, or `web.xml` file. The `web.xml` file is an XML file, defined by the servlet specification, with the purpose of acting as a configuration file for a web application. This file and its elements are completely independent of the Tomcat container. In this appendix, we will explain the Servlet 3.0 specific annotation based configuration that can be used instead of some `web.xml` configuration elements.

The Basic web.xml Configuration

The minimum requirements for web deployment descriptor is to have opening and closing <webapp> elements including Servlet API namespaces and schema definitions. Listing B-1 illustrates the minimal `web.xml` configuration file.

Listing B-1. Contents of the Minimal web.xml File

```
<?xml version="1.0" encoding="ISO-8859-1"?>
<web-app xmlns="http://java.sun.com/xml/ns/javaee"
        xmlns:xsi="http://www.w3.org/2001/XMLSchema-instance"
        xsi:schemaLocation="http://java.sun.com/xml/ns/javaee
        http://java.sun.com/xml/ns/javaee/web-app_3_0.xsd" version="3.0">

</web-app>
```

Every web application's web.xml configuration file will have at least few lines from listing B-1. The first line elements define the XML version and the document type definition (DTD) for the web.xml file, and you can see this element in most XML files, regardless of their purpose. The first element that is important to us is the <web-app> element, because this element is the container for all web application components. We will be examining the components that are the children of this element, but we won't examine every element of the deployment descriptor, which would be beyond the scope of this text. We'll describe only those elements that are most commonly used.

> ■ **Note** As from Java Servlet specification 2.4, the order of the children components of `<webapp>` element in `web.xml` file does not matter. Because Apache Tomcat 7 implements latest version of Servlet API (3.0), it applies to any web.xml configuration in latest Tomcat version. However, if you're using an earlier Servlet API version (2.4 or before), all of the definitions that we add to the `web.xml` file must be added in the specific order. For the correct order of elements in earlier Servlet API version, please consult the relevant Java Servlet specification, which you can find on Oracle Java website: `http://jcp.org/aboutJava/communityprocess/pfd/jsr315/index.html`.

Adding a Servlet Definition

The first Web component definition that we are going to add is a servlet. To do this, we use the `<servlet>` element and its sub-elements. The following code snippet contains a sample servlet definition:

```
<!-- Define a servlet -->
<servlet>
        <servlet-name>myServlet</servlet-name>
        <servlet-class>com.apress.MyServlet</servlet-class>
        <init-param>
                <param-name>paramName</param-name>
                <param-value>paramValue</param-value>
        </init-param>
        <load-on-startup>0</load-on-startup>
</servlet>
```

Descriptions of the `<servlet>` sub-elements can be found in Table B-1.

Table B-1. The <servlet> Sub-Elements

Sub-Element	Description
`<servlet-name>`	The string that is used to uniquely identify the servlet. It is used in the `<servlet-mapping>` sub-element to identify the servlet to be executed, when a defined URL pattern is requested, if there is a `<servlet-mapping>` sub-element.
`<servlet-class>`	Names the fully qualified servlet class to be executed.
`<init-param>`	Defines a name/value pair as an initialization parameter of the servlet. There can be any number of this optional sub-element. It also has two sub-elements of its own that define the name and value of the initialization parameter: • `<param-name>` element: Used to define the parameter name. • `<param-value>` element: Used to configure the value of the parameter passed to the servlet.

Sub-Element	Description
`<load-on-startup>`	Indicates that this servlet should be loaded when the web application starts. If the value of this element is a negative integer, or if the element is not present, the container is open to load the servlet whenever it chooses. If the value is a positive integer or 0, the container guarantees that servlets with lower integer values are loaded before servlets with higher integer values.
`<async-supported>`	Specifies whether the servlet supports asynchronous processing, new feature of Servlet API 3.0. Allowed values are true and false.

After examining the sub-element definitions, you can see that this servlet element defines a servlet named myServlet that is implemented in a class named com.apress.MyServlet. It has single initialization parameter named paramName, with a value paramValue. It also is one of the first preloaded servlets when the Web application starts.

Adding a Servlet Mapping

The next web component that we are going to add is a servlet mapping. A servlet mapping defines a mapping between a servlet and a URL pattern. To do this, we use the `<servlet-mapping>` element and its sub-elements. The following code snippet contains a sample servlet mapping definition:

```
<!-- The mapping for the Controller servlet -->
<servlet-mapping>
        <servlet-name>myServlet</servlet-name>
        <url-pattern>*.ap</url-pattern>
</servlet-mapping>
```

Descriptions of the `<servlet-mapping>` sub-elements can be found in Table B-2.

Table B-2. *The <servlet-mapping> Sub-Elements*

Sub-Element	Description
`<servlet-name>`	The string that is used to uniquely identify the servlet that is executed when the following defined `<url-pattern>` is requested.
`<url-pattern>`	Defines the URL pattern that must be matched to execute the servlet named in the `<servlet-name>` element.

This previous servlet mapping states that the servlet named myServlet is executed whenever a resource in this Web application, ending with .ap extension, is requested.

Configuring a Servlet Using Annotations

Servlet 3.0 introduced additional way to configure web application components, using annotations on the web application classes. In order to configure your servlet using annotations, you have to add the following XML element to web.xml file:

```
<metadata-complete>false</metadata-complete>
```

This element will tell servlet container that the configuration in web deployment descriptor isn't complete, and that it should scan all web application classes, looking for Servlet 3.0 annotations. In addition, you have to remove all <servlet> and <servlet-mapping> XML elements from your web.xml file, which are going to be replaced by annotation configured servlet.

To configure servlet and servlet mappings you will need only one annotation: @WebServlet. The following code snippet illustrates the configuration matching the XML configuration we used in earlier examples:

```
package com.apress;

import javax.servlet.annotation.WebInitParam;
import javax.servlet.annotation.WebServlet;
import javax.servlet.http.HttpServlet;

@WebServlet(
        name = "myServlet",
        urlPatterns = "*.ap",
        loadOnStartup = 1,
        initParams = {
            @WebInitParam(name = "paramName", value = "paramValue")
        },
        asyncSupported = false
)
public class MyServlet extends HttpServlet{
    //standard servlet implementation goes here
}
```

The servlet implementation class extends HttpServlet class, just like any typical servlet implementation. The implantation details include overriding doGet(..) or doPost() methods (or both), for handling GET and POST HTTP requests. The only addition, are the annotations on the class level, replacing the servlet configuration in web.xml file.

Adding a Servlet Filter

Servlet filters provide the necessary functionality to preprocess ServletRequest and ServletResponse objects as part of web application's lifecycle. To add a new servlet filter to a web application, you must add a <filter> element and a <filter-mapping> element to the web.xml file. The following code snippet contains a sample filter entry:

```
<!-- Define a Filter -->
<filter>
        <filter-name>SampleFilter</filter-name>
        <filter-class>com.apress.SampleFilter</filter-class>
        <init-param>
                <param-name>email</param-name>
                <param-value>admin@apress.com</param-value>
        </init-param>
</filter>
```

This filter definition defines a filter named SampleFilter that is implemented in a class named com.apress.SampleFilter. Descriptions of the <filter> element's sub-elements can be found in Table B-3.

Table B-3. *The Filter Configurable XML Sub-Elements*

Sub-Element	Description
<filter-name>	The string that is used to uniquely identify the servlet filter. It is used in the <filter-mapping> sub-element to identify the filter to be executed, when a defined URL pattern is requested.
<filter-class>	Names the fully qualified filter class to be executed when the string defined in the <filter-name> sub-element is referenced in the <filter-mapping> element.
<init-param>	Specifies the initialization parameters passed to filter implementation at creation time.

Configuring Filter Mapping

To deploy a filter, you must add a <filter-mapping> element. The <filter-mapping> describes the servlet filter to execute and the URL pattern that must be requested to execute the filter. The following code snippet contains a <filter-mapping> for the previous filter:

```
<!-- Define a  Mapping for the previous Filter -->
<filter-mapping>
    <filter-name>SampleFilter</filter-name>
    <url-pattern>*.jsp</url-pattern>
</filter-mapping>
```

Descriptions of the sub-elements of the <filter-mapping> are described in Table B-4.

Table B-4. The <filter-mapping> Sub-Elements

Sub-Elements	Description
<filter-name>	The string that names the servlet filter to execute when the defined URL pattern is requested.
<url-pattern>	Defines the URL pattern that must be requested to execute the named servlet filter.
<servlet-name>	If defined, this filter will preprocess all requests mapped to the specified servlet. The value of this element must reference the servlet name as defined in <servlet-name> element.
<dispatcher>	Specifies whether the filter should preprocess requests originating from within the web application itself (such as RequestDispacter.forward() and RequestDispatecher.include() requests). The allowed values are: • REQUEST: Filter will preprocess requests originating from the client only. • INCLUDE: Filter will preprocess internal include requests. • FORWARD: Filter will preprocess internal forward requests. • ERROR: Filter will preprocess requests to error handling components. Multiple values are allowed, and the default value is REQUEST.

■ **Note** Make sure that the <filter-name> sub-element in both the <filter> and <filter-mapping> elements match. This is the link between these two elements.

The result of these combined elements is a filter named SampleFilter that is executed whenever a JSP resource is requested in the application that owns this deployment descriptor.

Configuring Servlet Filter Using Annotations

Similarly to servlet configuration, you can configure your filters using annotations on the class that implements Filter interface. All filter settings are configured using @WebFilter annotations available as part of Servlet 3.0 API. Following snippet illustrates the sample annotation-based filter configuration.

```
package com.apress;

import javax.servlet.DispatcherType;
import javax.servlet.annotation.WebFilter;
import java.util.logging.Filter;
```

```
@WebFilter(
        filterName="SampleFilter",
        urlPatterns={"*.jsp", "*.do"},
        dispatcherTypes = {DispatcherType.REQUEST},
        servletNames = {"myServlet"}
)
public class SampleFilter implements Filter{
    //standard filter implementation goes here
}
```

For more details is servlet filters implementation, configuration and deployment in Tomcat, please refer to Chapter 8.

Configuring ServletContext Parameters

You can specify one or more parameters of the ServletContext in the web.xml file. Each of the parameters specified will be available to all servlet components defined in the same context (which includes every servlet, filter and any other component defined in the same web.xml file). You specify ServletContext parameters using <context-param> XML element, like in the following code snippet:

```
<context-param>
        <param-name>adminEmailAddress</param-name>
        <param-value>admin@apress.com</param-value>
</context-param>
```

The value of every specified parameter can be loaded in the servlet code, referenced by the parameter name:

```
String value = getServletContext().getInitParameter("adminEmailAddress ");
```

Configuring the Session

The next web component that we are going to add determines the life of each HttpSession in the current web application. The following code snippet contains a sample session configuration:

```
<!-- Set the default session timeout (in minutes) -->
<session-config>
    <session-timeout>30</session-timeout>
</session-config>
```

The <session-config> element contains only one sub-element, <session-timeout>, which defines the length of time that an HttpSession object can remain inactive before the container marks it as invalid. The value must be an integer measured in minutes.

To learn more about Tomcat's session configuration and handling, please read Chapter 5.

Adding a Welcome File List

We are now going to add a default list of files that will be loaded automatically when a web application is referenced without a filename. An example <welcome-file-list> is contained in the following code snippet:

```
<!-- Establish the default list of welcome files -->
<welcome-file-list>
    <welcome-file>login.jsp</welcome-file>
    <welcome-file>index.html</welcome-file>
</welcome-file-list>
```

The `<welcome-file-list>` contains an ordered list of `<welcome-files>` sub-elements that contain the filenames to present to the user. The files are served in order of appearance and existence. In this example, the Web application first tries to serve up the `login.jsp` file. If this file does not exist in the web application, the application tries to serve up the file `index.html`. If none of the files in the welcome list exists, an HTTP 404 Not Found error is returned.

Configuring Error Handlers

Tomcat, like any other servlet container, comes with the default error pages presented to the user when something goes wrong in the web application. You can customize these error pages in `web.xml` file using `<error-page>` configuration element. The following code snippet shows an example of error handler configuration:

```
<error-page>
    <error-code>404</error-code>
    <location>/not-found.jsp</location>
</error-page>
<error-page>
    <error-code>500</error-code>
    <location>/unexpected-error.html</location>
</error-page>
```

Each error handler is mapped to the specific HTTP status code, so that whenever servlet container returns the specified status code, the custom error page will be displayed to the user.

Configuring Mime Types

You can configure additional mime types handled by your web application using `<mime-mapping>` element. If your application uses non-standard URL extensions that do not match default mime mappings (for example serving pdf using .portable URL extension), the response mime type will be set to application-octet/stream by default. You can set the mime type for any custom URL extension in web.xml file, so that the content displays correctly in user browser (in the pdf example, the browser's pdf plug-in will open the content in the pdf-reader application). The following code snippet illustrates mime mapping configuration:

```
<mime-mapping>
        <extension>portable</extension>
        <mime-type>application/pdf</mime-type>
<mime-mapping>
```

Configuring Web Application Security

In this section we are going to take a look at the web.xml configuration elements used for web application security settings.

Adding a Security Constraint

We are going to add a security constraint to protect a resource in our web application. The following code snippet contains a sample <security-constraint> element:

```
<!-- Define a  Security Constraint on this Application -->
<security-constraint>
    <web-resource-collection>
    <web-resource-name>Apress Application</web-resource-name>
    <url-pattern>/*</url-pattern>
    </web-resource-collection>
    <auth-constraint>
    <role-name>apressuser</role-name>
    </auth-constraint>
</security-constraint>
```

Descriptions of the <security-constraint> sub-elements can be found in Table B-5.

Table B-5. *The <security-constraint> Sub-Elements*

Sub-Element	Description
<web-resource-collection>	Used to identify a subset of the resources and HTTP methods on those resources within a web application to which a security constraint applies. The <web-resource-collection> sub-element contains two sub-elements of its own that are defined in Table B-6.
<auth-constraint>	Defines the user roles that should be permitted access to this resource collection. It contains a single sub-element, <role-name>, which defines the actual role name that has access to the defined constraint. If this value is set to an *, all roles have access to the constraint.

The <web-resource-collection> element specifies the configuration of secured web resources. Table B-6 lists the XML sub-elements used to configure <web-resource-collection>.

Table B-6. *The <web-resource-collection> Sub-Elements*

Sub-Element	Description
`<web-resource-name>`	Defines the name of this Web resource collection.
`<url-pattern>`	Defines the URL pattern that will be protected by the resource.

This security constraint protects the entire Apress Application web application, allowing only users with a defined `<role-name>` of `apressuser`.

Adding a Login Config

To make a security constraint effective, you must define a method in which a user can log in, so that his role can be checked. To do this, you must add a login configuration component to the Web application. An example of this is contained in the following code snippet:

```
<!-- Define the Login Configuration for this Application -->
<login-config>
    <auth-method>BASIC</auth-method>
    <realm-name>Apress Application</realm-name>
</login-config>
```

Descriptions of the <login-config> sub-elements can be found in Table B-7.

Table B-7. *The <login-config> Sub-Elements*

Sub-Element	Description
`<auth-method>`	Used to configure the method by which the user is authenticated for this Web application. The possible values are BASIC, DIGEST, FORM, and CLIENT-CERT. If this value is set to FORM, the <form-login-config> sub-element must be defined.
`<form-login-config>`	Specifies the login and error page that should be used in FORM-based authentication. The sub-elements of the <form-login-config> are defined in Table B-8.
`<realm-name>`	Defines the name of the resource that this login configuration applies. This value must match a <web-resource-name> that was defined in a security constraint.

If you specify FORM based authentication in the <login-config> section, you have to specify the form login page and login error page that will be displayed to the user. Table B-8 describes the XML elements used to configure these details.

Table B-8. *The <form-login-config> Sub-Elements*

Sub-Element	Description
<form-login-page>	Defines the location and name of the page that will serve as the login page when using FORM-based authentication.
<form-error-page>	Defines the location and name of the page that will serve as the error page when a FORM-based login fails.

The results of this <login-config> sub-element definition states that the <web-resource-collection>, with a Web resource named Apress Application, uses a login method of BASIC authentication.

Tomcat security and login configuration are covered in more detail in Chapters 6 and 7.

Summary

In this appendix we presented the most commonly used settings used to configure servlets and its components in the web.xml file. We also illustrated the annotation-based servlet configuration introduced as part of Servlet API 3.0. The described configuration options will enable you to configure servlets for a typical web application. However, not all Servlet API configuration options could fit in this Appendix. For complete reference of configurable options take a look at Java Servlet specification (http://jcp.org/aboutJava/communityprocess/pfd/jsr315/index.html).

Index

Made in the USA
Lexington, KY
11 April 2012